P9-DXE-312

THE DAY I WAS PROUDEST
TO BE AN AMERICAN

The Day I Was Proudest
To Be an American

DONALD ROBINSON

DOUBLEDAY & COMPANY, INC.

Garden City, New York

TO *Luis Muñoz Marín*
GOVERNOR OF PUERTO RICO
WHO HAS MADE DEMOCRACY A GLOWING
REALITY FOR HIS PEOPLE AND ALL THE
REST OF US AMERICANS

Contents

APPOINTMENT WITH AMERICA   17
DONALD ROBINSON

THE LAND

ONLY IN AMERICA   29
LLEWELLYN MILLER, *Magazine Writer*

PEOPLE IN AMERICA

THE GOLDEN PALACE   37
EDWARD CORSI, *Former U. S. Commissioner of
Immigration*

EAST SIDE STORY   41
KATHRYN MURRAY, *TV Performer*

MONDAY IN THE BERKSHIRES   45
HANS MAEDER, *Director, the Stockbridge School*

HOUSE CALL   48
DR. MILAN D. BAKER, *Medical Director, Culver
Military Academy*

THE FOREIGNERS' SECTION   52
H. F. JOHNSON, *President, S. C. Johnson & Son*

THE PRIVATE AND THE COLONEL   56
GEORGE MEANY, *President, A.F. of L.-C.I.O.*

WHEN YOU GO ON RELIEF   58
    JOHN DEMARTINO, *New York Barber*

TOUGH GUYS   61
    FRANK HOWLEY, *Vice-Chancellor, New York University*

STREET FIGHT IN COLOGNE   64
    CARL R. HELLSTROM, *President, Smith & Wesson*

WELCOME PARTY   68
    PFC SEYMOUR SHIPLACOFF, *U. S. Army*

MARSHAL ZHUKOV RECEIVES   71
    LIEUTENANT GENERAL JAMES M. GAVIN,
    U. S. Army

CONTROVERSIAL MATERIAL   74
    PATRICK MURPHY MALIN, *Executive Director,*
    American Civil Liberties Union

THE PARADE UP MARKET STREET   78
    ROGER LAPHAM, *Former Mayor of San Francisco*

THE LEADERS OF AMERICA

A CONFERENCE WITH EISENHOWER   83
    JAMES P. MITCHELL, *Secretary of Labor*

TRUMAN AND THE H-BOMB   86
    CHET HOLIFIELD, *Congressman from California*

F.D.R. SPEAKS FOR FREEDOM   90
    EDWARD TELLER, *Nuclear Physicist*

EXECUTIVE ORDER 94

WILLIAM H. DAVIS, *Former Chairman, War Labor Board*

PLANE FLIGHT FROM BOSTON 97

KATE SMITH, *TV and Radio Performer*

MAIDEN SPEECH IN CONGRESS 99

CLIFFORD P. CASE, *U. S. Senator from New Jersey*

HARDSHIP CASE 102

IRVING M. IVES, *U. S. Senator from New York*

POLITICS, FLORIDA STYLE 106

ELMO ROPER, *Public Opinion Analyst*

THE REAL LEADERS 109

RICHARD L. NEUBERGER, *U. S. Senator from Oregon*

AMERICANS AT WAR

SALUTE TO AN ENSIGN 115

ADMIRAL ARLEIGH A. BURKE, *Chief of Naval Operations*

THE "BATS" OFF GILBERT ISLANDS 118

ADMIRAL ARTHUR W. RADFORD, *Former Chairman, Joint Chiefs of Staff*

HOMAGE TO A DEAD HERO 122

CAPTAIN BENJAMIN F. WILSON, *Winner of the Medal of Honor*

CRASH LANDING 125

COLONEL CHESLEY G. PETERSON, *U. S. Air Force*

SOMETHING FOR THE BOYS   130
ROSALIND RUSSELL, *Stage and Screen Star*

THIS WAS THE ARMY   136
IRVING BERLIN, *America's Song Writer*

TOP SECRET FROM WASHINGTON   138
DOUGLAS MACARTHUR II, *U. S. Ambassador to Japan*

LOOKING BACK   141
GENERAL OMAR N. BRADLEY, *Former Chairman,
Joint Chiefs of Staff*

SAVED—1,000,000 CASUALTIES   145
GENERAL CURTIS E. LEMAY, *Vice Chief of Staff,
U. S. Air Force*

"TELL IT TO SWEENEY"   148
LIEUTENANT COLONEL DAVID F. MACGHEE,
Former Prisoner of War in Korea

EASTER IN KOREA   153
MAJOR GENERAL CHARLES I. CARPENTER,
Chief of Chaplains, U. S. Air Force

PEARL HARBOR, FIFTEEN YEARS AFTER   156
WILBER M. BRUCKER, *Secretary of the Army*

AMERICANS AT WORK

BRIDGE OVER THE GOLDEN GATE   161
ERNEST G. SWIGERT, *Past President, National
Association of Manufacturers*

CONTENTS

STOCK REPORT 165
G. KEITH FUNSTON, *President, New York Stock Exchange*

STARTING WITH A YEAST CAKE 168
WALTER HARD, *Vermont Chronicler*

JUSTICE ON THE ASSEMBLY LINE 172
A. J. HAYES, *President, International Association of Machinists*

A LETTER BY THE UNION 176
J. C. RICH, *Editor, The Hat Worker*

POLICE STATION 179
EVA MARIE SAINT, *Screen and TV Actress*

OPERATION BOOTSTRAP 183
LUIS MUNOZ MARIN, *Governor of Puerto Rico*

AMERICANS AT SCHOOL

CLASSROOM CRISIS 191
ISIDORE STARR, *New York Schoolteacher*

THE JUVENILE DELINQUENTS 193
LOUIS N. DEL VECCHIO, *New York Schoolteacher*

OLD SCHOOL TIES 196
HOWARD E. WILSON, *Dean, School of Education, University of California at Los Angeles*

THE CHURCH IN AMERICA

THE BISHOP IN DETROIT   201
>REINHOLD NIEBUHR, *Vice President, Union Theological Seminary*

BIBLE IN THE DESERT   203
>NELSON GLUECK, *President, Hebrew Union College—Jewish Institute of Religion*

MIDNIGHT IS THE ZERO HOUR   206
>ED MARCINIAK, *Editor,* Work

BAD NEWS   209
>ARLIN H. ADAMS, *Wisconsin Minister*

MIRACLE IN SOUTH DAKOTA   212
>ROBERT W. SHIELDS, *Minister-Editor-Writer*

AMERICA'S HEALTH

FAMILY DOCTOR   219
>DR. DWIGHT H. MURRAY, *Past President, American Medical Association*

VICTORY OVER POLIO   223
>BASIL O'CONNOR, *President, the National Foundation for Infantile Paralysis*

HEART ATTACK   227
>JOSEPH USHKOW, *President, Endo Laboratories*

AMERICA AND ITS MINORITIES

TRAIN RIDE TO ARKANSAS   233
MORDECAI W. JOHNSON, *President of Howard
University*

THE KIDS TAKE A STAND   236
RICHARD B. KENNAN, *Secretary, National Commission
for the Defense of Democracy Through Education*

SHOULDER TO SHOULDER   238
LESTER B. GRANGER, *Executive Director, National
Urban League*

A MATTER OF MANNERS   241
DOROTHY CANFIELD FISHER, *Novelist*

VOYAGE TO PUERTO RICO   246
FERNANDO SIERRA BERDECIA, *Secretary of Labor,
Commonweatlh of Puerto Rico*

ADVICE FROM JUSTICE BRANDEIS   251
MORRIS L. ERNST, *Attorney*

AMERICANS ABROAD

VIENNA 1955   257
JOHN FOSTER DULLES, *Secretary of State*

THE POWER TO FORGIVE   260
EZRA TAFT BENSON, *Secretary of Agriculture*

BERLIN BLOCKADE   262
ROBERT D. MURPHY, *Deputy Undersecretary of State*

MY FAVORITE ROLE   266

> IRENE DUNNE, *U. S. Alternate Representative to the
> United Nations*

SERGEANT SCOGGINS IS HOST   269

> WILLIAM I. NICHOLS, *Editor,* This Week

IN THE JUNGLES OF INDIA   275

> DICKEY CHAPELLE, *Photographer and Foreign
> Correspondent*

NIGHT OUT IN AMSTERDAM   279

> LEONARD PARIS, *St. Louis Editor*

REVOLUTION IN HUNGARY   282

> LEO CHERNE, *Chairman, International Rescue Committee*

THE MAN IN THE STREET   287

> HENRY M. JACKSON, *U. S. Senator from Washington*

THE DAY I WAS PROUDEST
TO BE AN AMERICAN

APPOINTMENT WITH AMERICA

DONALD ROBINSON

FROM earliest childhood we hear it. They drum it into our ears at home, at school, at church. Through life the refrain continues, sometimes loud, sometimes soft. We get it in the press, over the air, on the job. The words may vary but the theme is always the same: Love your country. Be proud of it.

Along the line, I ask myself, "Why? Why should I be proud of the country in which I happened by genetic chance to be born? Don't the lexicographers define pride as an 'unreasonable conceit of superiority' ? "

So often, I realize, people take pride in national values that are inane, distorted, hurtful. I recall the insular Frenchman with whom I talked at the Sorbonne. "Why should our French children study Shakespeare?" he said. "We have Racine." And the rich banker I met in Rome. "Travel abroad, *signore?* Nonsense. Nowhere else is there anything worth seeing."

I am reminded of the New England farmer bragging about the Green Mountains to a young exchange student from India. "I'll bet you ain't got nothin' in your place that shapes up to mountains like them," he said.

The Indian boy glanced at the two-thousand- and three-thousand-foot peaks, and remarked, quite gently, "Well, we do have the Himalayas."

I remember the unshakable conviction of Gamal Abdel Nasser, the Egyptian dictator, that his nation had true democracy.

"What about freedom of the press?" I asked while I was interviewing him in Cairo.

"The newspapers here are free to print anything at any time they desire," he stated.

"Can they criticize you?"

He was dumfounded at the notion. "Criticize me? Certainly not."

I hark back to former-day Prussians and the ingrained vanity they had about their military prowess. I think of the chauvinistic blatherings of modern-day Russians with their pretensions to having originated virtually every new idea of the century. And their Sputnik-stimulated claims to absolute international supremacy.

I ponder over Samuel Johnson's pithy "Patriotism is the last refuge of a scoundrel." Over Stephen Decatur's heedless "My country, right or wrong." Over H. G. Wells's stern warning about "Crazy combative patriotism that plainly threatens to destroy civilization."

Yet I have to admit to myself that there is a sharp distinction between patriotism and patriolatry. That there is another sort of pride of country than that which I've been scorning—a kind based on a second, happier definition of the word "pride." When we regard it as meaning, "A sense of one's own worth and abhorrence of what is beneath or unworthy of oneself," pride of country takes on a richer tint. It becomes a hale, uplifting emotion, good for each individual and better for his country.

At last it seems plainly cut. To have pride in the fine facets of your country's character, the generous, the liberal, the democratic and to abjure those things which are ignoble, is praiseworthy in terms of mankind's historic striving for national and international decency.

It is when your pride is in the false, the vicious, the evil that the results can be odious.

Edmund Burke once said, "To make us love our country, our country must be lovely." With this I agree. I pause, though, to consider what a country is.

It is land and water. It is men, women, and children with a feeling of social homogeneity and an awareness of their mutual interests. It is the institutions, customs, and traditions the people have developed. It is all of these factors plus something else. A sense of the future. A nation may not have a yesterday, but it must expect a tomorrow.

Countries can have personalities, I know. (An eminent professor at the University of Illinois even maintains that nations can be psychoanalyzed and their responses to diverse situations predicted.) I know, too, that national personality is a composition of a country's geography, institutions, government and the predominant traits of its citizens, all interwoven so closely that there is no separating them. This means to me that actions by governments, as a rule, reflect the will of their people. That in evaluating a country you cannot honestly distinguish too much between its government and its populace. They are usually one.

Exceptions to this rule can be cited, of course, like Hungary. However, they are few.

A bitter judgement on people, this, when we review the barbarisms of the past and the not-so-far-in-the-past—when we note the French atrocities in Algeria; Soviet Russia and its slave-labor camps; the Germans and their Buchenwalds; the Genghis Khans, the Attilas; and, not to be forgotten, us Americans vis-à-vis the Indians.

I console myself with the thought that countries can change their personalities for the better. The Sweden of 1958 is no more the saber-rattling, militaristic Sweden it was under Charles XII. The Turkey of today is not the same Turkey it was before Atatürk. Our own United States is a far different nation from what it was at the shift of the century, when "Manifest Destiny" was the jingoistic slogan.

Again Burke's admonition that a country must be lovely to earn the love of its citizens comes to me. It makes me wonder what are the elements of America that genuinely merit our love and our pride. I mull here over Adlai Stevenson's stirring expression of faith in the American liberties.

He put it thus: "When an American says that he loves his country, he means not only that he loves the New England hills, the prairies glistening in the sun, the wide and rising plains, the great mountains, and the sea. He means that he loves an inner air, an inner light in which freedom lives and in which a man can draw the breath of self-respect."

But I recognize that this is merely part of the answer. Our liberties are precious. Without them probably nothing else would count. Still, there must be other qualities in America of which to be proud.

So I decide to make a search for the best in America. I resolve to seek out the most admirable traits in us Americans as people, and to determine the aspects of our society, in peace and war, that do us most credit.

How do I go about it? I set out to meet a cross section of Americans, people of varied colors, creeds, occupations and opinions, persons of fame and of anonymity, of much authority and of none, of wealth and of poverty, of wide education and of little.

I request them all to describe the incident that most graphically illustrated for them this country's caliber, the one occurrence that made each of them feel proudest to be an American.

This approach I use because I believe one dramatic incident can equal a thousand perorations in distilling the qualities of a person or a nation.

It is no easy goal I choose. I see that soon. Many people are constitutionally incapable of thinking anecdotally. No matter how they try, they cannot cast their experiences in a dramatic mold.

I ask them, "Tell me the day you were proudest to be an American."

They hem, they haw, and eventually they say in an apologetic tone, "I'm proud every day to be an American."

My batting average is excellent, I discover, if I can secure one impressive story from every twenty people I contact. The hunt is worth its rigors, though. The right stories can be so moving.

It works out that about half the stories are written by the persons involved. The remainder I write, after talking with the people and listening at length to their accounts. Insofar as I can, I use their own words. In a few cases I am requested to tell stories in the third person. I do.

Some may stigmatize me as a flag-waving Pollyanna for focusing on the good side of America. They may say I am trying to veil our failings. It is not so.

I am sickeningly awake to the Little Rocks and the Birminghams. I am aware that our northern cities crowd Negroes into ghettos and treat them ill in dozens of ways. I am alive to the discrimination against Puerto Ricans. I know that Jews are shut out of many jobs and organizations, that Catholics suffer social and political abuse.

I see the poverty, the housing unfit for human habitation, the disease. I see erosion of the land and pollution of the rivers. I see decrepit school buildings with overcrowded classrooms and under-paid teachers. I see essential research laboratories stifled for lack of funds and scientists. I see delinquent children, knives and zip guns in hand. I see corruption.

I see undemocratic forces, in Washington and out, persecuting the innocent. I see pressures at work to make us a nation of social, economic, and political conformists. I see Congress forging bars of legal iron to keep immigrants from our shores and to make it de-meaning for foreign tourists to visit us. I see us losing ground, mili-tarily and diplomatically, to the Soviet Union.

These are things which I acknowledge, and sadly deplore. Nevertheless, in my search, I find other things to be as true.

For every Little Rock with its bigotry, demagoguery, and disorder, the South has scores of school districts where integration has been peaceably, amicably achieved. Pleasanton, Texas, for example. This south Texas town approved integration on October 26, 1957, by a vote of 323 to 88. Members of the student council met the new Negro pupils at the school doors and made them welcome.

"We wanted to show the world it could be done in a Christian-like manner," said D. C. Baldree, the high-school principal.

I have before me a clipping from the New York *Times* of March 9, 1956, stating that "A resolution welcoming Negroes to the University of Texas was adopted by the Student Assembly last night." And a clipping from the *Times* of October 2, 1956, reporting that "The University of Oklahoma Independent Students Association last night elected a Negro law student as its representative on the university's Student Senate." It is the first time in the history of the school that a Negro has been selected for such a post. I read Bradbury Smith's splendid new book, *Why We Behave Like Americans* and I come to such provocative items as these: "There are more Negroes (128,000) in colleges in the United States than all the Germans in German universities. There are more automobile-owners among American Negroes than among all 216,000,000 Russians and all the 193,000,000 Negroes in Africa." "Since 1940 Negro wages have risen 400 per cent as against 250 per cent for whites."

I hear the same sort of encouraging reports about Puerto Ricans, Jews, and the other minorities. The bad spots may be glaring, but the good are increasing.

It is true in other spheres. In 1945 Henry Wallace's prediction that 60,000,000 Americans would have jobs after the war was derided as a wild pipe dream. Today more than 66,000,000 are gainfully employed and the number of families whose annual incomes exceed $5,000 is mounting by 1,100,000 a year. In 1960 the statisticians say it will be 20,000,000, 44 per cent of our families. Wages may still be low for some, but it is significant that the average man in the United States need labor only 30 minutes to earn the price of a pound of butter. In Switzerland, to pick a European country at random, he would have to put in 117 minutes; in the U.S.S.R. 270 minutes. A pound of tea costs an American 49 minutes work; a Swiss 188; a Russian 960. Tea is the Russian national drink.

Slum clearance goes apace. More than 500,000 splendid public-housing units have been built for low-income families. Not as many as one would want, perhaps. Enough, though, to matter. An Egyptian diplomat, Dr. Mohammed El Zayyat, made me conscious of how much.

"Show me the worst slums in New York City," he requested.

I drove him through the smelly, squalid streets of Harlem. Shamefaced, I said, "Horrible, isn't it."

"No," El Zayyat commented, "it's wonderful."

Where I had been fixing on the cankered hovels, he had been eying the 143 modern fourteen- and sixteen-story apartment houses that the public-housing authorities have put up for the poor, affording Harlem new hope in addition to an exciting new sky line.

"It is fantastic that you've been able to do so much," El Zayyat said.

America's death rate is steadily declining, from 17.78 per thousand in 1900 to 7.7 per thousand in 1955; life expectancy is rising, from 47.3 years in 1900 to 69.5. The educational picture has its shining side, too. Our high-school crop was 94,883 in 1900. In 1955 it was 1,275,000. Our universities diplomatized 27,410 in 1900; in 1955, 285,138. And our teachers are gradually winning raises in pay and prestige.

Talk about corruption in unions. It is rooted regrettably deep. However, the leaders of organized labor no longer ignore it as once was their wont. Now, they are warring against it. Talk about juvenile delinquency. Surveys show that most parents are alert to its implications now. Talk about McCarthyism. It has gone out of style. For the moment, certainly. Talk about the American "iron curtain" against foreign visitors. Finally it has been relaxed, and the demands on Congress to ease racist restrictions on immigration are crescendoing. Talk about the alarming lag in the development of intercontinental ballistic missiles and of means for traversing outer space. A public outcry has forced a speed-up, verifying again that the people's will can be irresistible in our American democracy.

We can even talk now about American culture. "In the four quarters of the globe," Sydney Smith wrote in 1820, "who reads an American book, or goes to an American play, or looks at an American picture or statue?" He couldn't be as caustic today. The names of William Faulkner, Ernest Hemingway, Robert Frost, Eugene O'Neill, and Arthur Miller would refute him. So would the names

of the American painters Grant Wood and John Marin, the sculptor
Jo Davidson, the architect Frank Lloyd Wright, the composers Aaron
Copland and Gian-Carlo Menotti. To be sure, the menu served up
on television and at the movie houses is mostly mush. Yet, on occasion,
TV sponsors and Hollywood producers do give us art, and if Broadway is 90-per-cent tinsel, the new off-Broadway theaters, clustered
down in Greenwich Village, aren't. They are presenting drama at
its livest. As for our magazines, many of them are doing a thoughtful,
incisive job of relating their millions of readers to the world they
dwell in. It may be relevant to note here that, despite TV, Americans
are reading a lot of books. They bought 525,400,000 in 1956. Plus a
couple of million textbooks.

Naturally, as I go about my search for good in America, I peer
into my own background for incidents that have made me proud
to be an American. I think of the kindliness that I have encountered
in supposedly dour, aloof Vermont; of the autumn morning my wife
and I moved into our small farmhouse atop Red Mountain near
Arlington. We were sitting in the living room, surrounded by heaps
of trunks and cartons, when we heard a knock on the door. It was
Jim Canfield, our eighty-one-year-old neighbor at the foot of the
mountain.

"You city slickers are so stupid that you probably don't even know
it's going to be cold tonight," he said. "I've brought you a load of
firewood."

I remember Dorothy Canfield Fisher, the renowned novelist, and
her husband John, both in their late seventies, who jeeped miles up
New England's ruttiest road to pin a note on our door, saying "Welcome," before we'd been introduced.

I remember Phil Mears, the proprietor of the local garage, offering
me a tender steak from a deer he'd shot. "How much do I owe you,
Phil?" I inquired.

"Hell, you don't owe me nothin'," he declared. "We're neighbors,
ain't we?"

There comes to mind an evening in New York City when I listened
to justice speak. Irving Slonim, an assistant district attorney, was
telling how he'd spent weeks ferreting out evidence to acquit the
defendant in a criminal case he was prosecuting.

"But wasn't that the duty of the defense counsel?" someone asked.

"Justice is everybody's duty," Slonim said.

I remember San Francisco and the scientists at the U. S. Naval Radiological Defense Laboratory who deliberately exposed their bodies to lethal radioactive materials in their investigations of radiation disease. I recall a group of teen-agers I interviewed in Madison, Wisconsin. While everyone was bemoaning the spread of juvenile delinquency these boys and girls organized a volunteer army of high-school students who moved through the city, block by block, cleaning up every piece of trash in the streets, the yards, the playgrounds, and the parks. In some of the shabbier sections of town they painted the house fences. The kids contributed the paint themselves.

More recollections return. A night in Washington when Senator Leverett Saltonstall of Massachusetts was leaving the Senate Office Building, hours late for dinner, dead tired after a day of incessant hearings, conferences, roll-call votes.

"Had a rough day of it, Senator?" a guard said.

"Sort of," Saltonstall sighed. "But I'm not complaining. That's what I hired out for."

I recall the time Governor Luis Muñoz Marín of Puerto Rico proved to me how little racial prejudice exists in his jewel of an island. I'd informed him that I'd noticed the ugly epithet for Jew—K-I-K-E—painted in large white letters on the sidewalk of the most elegant boulevard in San Juan.

"I don't believe you," Muñoz exclaimed.

"It's true," I insisted.

Shocked, he telephoned his chief of police and ordered an immediate inquiry.

Several days after my return to New York I received a photostatic copy of the official police report. It stated that the police had had samples of the paint analyzed in their crime laboratory. No clue was found as to its origin. They had questioned hundreds of passers-by. No one saw the lettering done. They had checked the people residing in the vicinity. None had the name "Kike." They had gone over their lists of subversive organizations. None was called "Kike."

As Muñoz pointed out in a letter to me, the Puerto Rican police investigators didn't even know what the nasty word "Kike" meant.

I relive a ten-thousand-mile swing I made through Europe and the Middle East to write about the American aid program in action. I see again the industrial plants, railroads, port facilities built with Marshall Plan funds in France, Germany, and other war-devastated countries. I see dead economies that have been revived; hungry, jobless people who have been fed and given work. I see peasants in Greece who have been taught to get more out of their land; fellahin in Egypt who have been shown how to combat blindness in their children.

I hear again the words of beautiful Queen Frederika of Greece. I was having cocktails with her and King Paul in the cosy study of the royal palace at Athens.

"Just suppose I'd gone to some Greek peasants and asked them for permission to give their tax money to an unknown, far-off place called Delaware or Nebraska. They would have laughed at me and told me I was crazy. But you Americans didn't laugh when your government asked for authority to help far-off places like Greece and Pakistan. You said, 'Go ahead and help them.' "

I hear the words of Germany's aged Chancellor Konrad Adenauer resounding through his low-lighted office in Bonn.

"America has given us Germans faith in ourselves, in democracy, and in the future."

At least these two Europeans see America as it actually is.

Thinking back, I arrive at a day I was particularly grateful to be an American. It was January 26, 1952.

This was "Black Saturday," the day anti-Western mobs went berserk in Cairo, killing, burning, looting. They turned Cairo into a city of smoldering ruins—and hundreds of charred, mutilated corpses. They caught one young British doctor I knew, jerked his arms out of their sockets, punched in his face until there was no face left, and threw what remained of his body in a fire.

My wife and I were in famous old Shepheard's Hotel when the mob put it to the torch. Trapped, we had to take refuge in a small garden with some other Westerners. The garden was surrounded on three sides by the blazing hotel, and the flames kept stretching out closer and closer toward us. On the fourth side, separated from us by an iron fence, was a milling throng of a thousand howling, foaming-at-the-mouth Egyptians brandishing knives and guns. They were trying to pull down the fence and get at us.

In the United States the police can be depended upon to restore order when a riot erupts. It was different in Cairo. The policemen there had joined the rioters. Firemen did come to battle the fire. They could do nothing. The mob slashed the hoses.

Only one thing saved our lives. The U. S. Embassy tracked down the whereabouts of every American in Cairo, and got help to those who were in danger. In our case, Ambassador Jefferson Caffery telephoned the military governor of the city.

"There are some Americans at Shepheard's," he said, "and my government will take a very dim view of it if they're hurt."

The governor took the hint and sent some soldiers to escort us out through the mob.

We gave blessings that afternoon for the protection the U. S. Government provides its citizens abroad.

My search for the best in America does not end. It never can. Failings we have. Who can deny them? But with our potential for good, we should be able to overcome them. The outlook for tomorrow, if there be no war, is Fair.

A century and a quarter ago Alexis de Tocqueville wrote, "America is a land of wonders, in which everything is in constant motion and every change seems an improvement. The idea of novelty is there indissolubly connected with the idea of amelioration. No natural boundary seems to be set to the efforts of man; and in his eyes what is not yet done is only what he has not yet attempted to do."

I say to him, "Amen."

Words of thanks now to Burke Wilkinson, Special Assistant to the Secretary of State, for his keen, sympathetic co-operation in this project, and to Lieutenant Colonel James G. Chesnutt of the U. S. Army and Colonel F. Clarke Newlon of the U. S. Air Force for theirs. The Services should have more public-information officers like these two, with their devout regard for the people's right to truth. Thanks also to Oscar Schisgall for his grand, talented helpfulness, to Frank K. Kelly of the Fund for the Republic, to Henry Lamar, of the National Association of Manufacturers, and to Pat Dirringer for her taste as well as her typing. Above all, thanks to Kitty Robinson, who makes the making of any book an absorbing adventure.

New York, May 1958

THE LAND

ONLY IN AMERICA

Magazine Writer

You start on the Eastern seaboard, and you go north or south or west. You will discover many Americas. In each the look of the land and the way of the people will be different.

Llewellyn Miller has seen America from ocean to ocean, border to border. She is one of the country's most brilliant magazine writers, whose articles have appeared in virtually every leading periodical. Her travel reports are famous. So are her many journalistic coups, including an interview with Lucky Luciano, the exiled gangster, in his Naples hide-out. Born in Kentucky, Miss Miller broke into the newspaper business as a caricaturist, served for several years as drama critic for the Los Angeles Record, edited a string of movie magazines. Then she switched to magazine and book writing. She has twice been president of the Hollywood Women's Press Club, and for four years an officer of the Society of Magazine Writers.

A WOMAN driving alone is a fool to pick up a stranger. At worst, there is the possibility of robbery, blackmail, or grimmer trouble. At the least, boredom from hours of a hitchhiker's chatter is a near certainty. But it was too late to withdraw by the time I remembered the warnings.

I first saw the wanderer early one morning in a snack bar at Bryce Canyon, Utah. She was a small, spare lady of middle years, dressed in good tweeds. She sat beside me at the counter, ordered coffee, and matter-of-factly took a roll out of her capacious handbag.

"From ze dinner—a shame to waste," she said, with a smile from the brightest blue eyes I have ever seen.

We fell into talk. She was Dutch. Her children were grown. She was free to go where she liked within the limits of the small amount of money the Netherlands permits its citizens when they travel. In her case, this was one thousand guilders, about $260.

Through the severest personal denials she was trying to make the $260 last for a swing around the whole United States.

"I sleep on ze night bus or in hotel for never more zan one dollar ze night. And one dollar ze day for food. No more," she told me. "Is worth sacrifice to see your beautiful Amerika."

She was with a big sight-seeing group so our paths parted. I caught up with her an hour later at one of the lookout points above Bryce Canyon. She was standing alone, gazing raptly into the chasm.

"Magnificent," she gasped. "Just magnificent. Now you see why I not care how bare my room? Anywhere is good hotels. Only in Amerika is sights like zis."

Chance brought us together again at the snack bar later. I had just telephoned for a reservation at the Grand Canyon. Nothing was left but a cabin with two bedrooms, and I'd taken it. As I quit the phone booth I saw my Dutch friend was in difficulties. She had discovered that her bus was not going to the Grand Canyon; it was heading directly on to Zion Canyon.

"I am so disappoint," she was saying. "To come so far and not see ze Grand Canyon. Is no way I can go? I shall always have sorrow to miss."

I had sorrow too. It seemed a dreadful injustice that this appreciative visitor should be denied the view that is one of the marvels of the world.

"I'm driving there this afternoon," I heard myself saying. "Would you like to come with me? I'll be going to Zion Canyon tomorrow and I can get you back to your group there."

Her face struggled with several expressions: surprise, hope, questions. No doubt she had also been warned of strangers. Then, as impulsively as I'd spoken, she decided.

"I pay you to go. Is worth anyzing not to miss."

"No, no," I said. "I'm going anyway. The trip will cost you nothing." I went further than I had intended. "I have to pay for two bedrooms. Like your roll—a shame to waste. You'll be my guest."

It embarrassed her to accept, but in the end she came, and I was glad she did.

Never will I forget her reaction to the Grand Canyon. Her eyes filled with slow tears as she looked across the awesome sixteen-mile gap and down on the endless peaks of the mountain range that rises a full mile from the floor of the gorge. For a solid hour she stood there wordless with wonder as the sunset flared and faded, from vermilion and rust to misty blue and green and purple.

"I am reverent like in church," she whispered at last. "No one can describe. One must see to believe. Nowhere else anyzing like zis. Nowhere but in Amerika."

Our journey together stretched from one day to four. Finally we separated hundreds of miles westward at Las Vegas. And when she waved good-by I had much to think about.

"Nowhere but in America." The phrase echoed in my mind the day through.

I thought of lush Minnesota with its ten thousand sparkling lakes. The yellow, endless plains of southern Texas. The windy uplands of the Ozarks. League after league of thick spruce and pine and fir bordering the great Columbia. Aspens crowning Michigan's Upper Peninsula. Live oaks dripping Spanish moss in Georgia. Stately maples bursting into all the colors of fire when autumn touches New England.

I thought of Florida with cypress trees tiptoeing on arching roots into crystalline lakes where water skiers in bathing suits whiz in January while in Vermont other skiers, bundled in wool, streak on fifteen-foot snows down Mount Stowe's horrifying championship runs.

I thought of the Sequoia National Forest where flourish the oldest living things on earth—the giant evergreens that were already two thousand years old when Christ was born. "Nowhere but in America."

My thoughts turned to the great wall of the Rockies. Not the highest mountains on earth—but surely such savage peaks and gulches have never been conquered elsewhere by men and women in covered wagons. I thought of the white vaults of Carlsbad Caverns, largest known cave in the world, hung with stalactites lengthening for sixty million years. Of the fish grown eyeless in the lightless deeps of Kentucky's Mammoth Cave. Of Niagara gushing its staggering flood. Of Old Faithful spouting its geyser of steam and spray every sixty-six minutes.

Only in America . . .

I thought of alligators grinning evilly under the wild orchids in the Everglades. Of Big Horn sheep that bounce around Colorado's crags. Of slab-faced moose wandering down from Canada for juniper berries. Of the jolly black bears that waddle out on the roads of Yellowstone National Park to beg for cookies. Of the buffalo, who nearly died out but are now coming back in such numbers that buffalo-burgers are standard fare in the cafeteria under Mount Rushmore's gigantic faces. I thought of the little town of prairie dogs near Devil's Tower National Monument in Wyoming—almost the last town the prairie dogs have, though their cities once covered entire states.

I thought of the Empire State Building, tallest anywhere, and the other shining towers of New York where, Radio Station WNYC reminds us, "Over eight million people live together in peace and harmony and enjoy the benefits of democracy." I thought of the glass-sheathed United Nations Building standing high over the East River, and for what it stands.

I thought of the royal span of the Golden Gate Bridge and the sea lions barking in the fog off sophisticated San Francisco. I thought of Detroit, where goggling tourists can watch a car start as four wheels and drive off the assembly line under its own power eighty minutes later. I thought of the glittering cliff of apartment houses banking Chicago's Lakeshore Drive, and of the placid Taos Pueblo, an apartment house old before Columbus set sail. I thought of the mystery of the ghost town, Mesa Verde in Colorado, whose thousands of inhabitants left their belongings in their cliff dwellings about the year 1200 as if to return the next day—and never came back.

Only in America . . .

I thought of Milwaukee, where much of the speech is overlaid with German. Of New Mexico, where people whose ancestors marched in with Coronado still speak only Spanish. Of the lilt of Finnish and Norwegian and Danish in the north woods settlements. Of the special telephone exchange in San Francisco where operators give and take numbers in Chinese.

I thought of Hollywood Bowl, where movie stars in mink and school children in dungarees listen together to symphonies under the stars. I thought of the Cathedral of the Pines in New Hampshire where twenty thousand people of all faiths have gathered to worship under the murmuring trees that nature placed as regularly as the columns of a church. I thought of the modern Catholic cathedral shaped like a fish in Kansas City, and the Swedenborgian Wayfarer's Chapel, made all of glass, on the shores of the Pacific. I thought of the Yankee Stadium.

I thought of machines—the threshers and harvesters and plows as big as prehistoric monsters. The refrigerators, washers, electric sewing machines, and stoves. The radios—more than one for every person in the country. The telephones and blenders and hot-water heaters we take for granted. I thought of the cowboy streaking past the Petrified Forest in a ten-gallon hat, high-heeled boots and tight levis on a motorcycle. I thought of other cowboys herding cattle in their own planes.

I thought of Los Alamos.

I thought of American foods: succulent lobsters from cold Maine waters; abalone from California; clam chowder in Boston and conch chowder in Florida; barbecued salmon in Washington State and clambakes on Cape Cod; tamales in El Paso; wild rice harvested by Indians in Wisconsin; catfish and razorback hog meat in Arkansas; sweet corn, popcorn, hominy, grits, corn pone, spoon bread, Indian pudding, bean-hole beans, Boston brown bread, tortillas, hot cakes, waffles, maple syrup, jambalaya, fresh sugar cane along the bayous of Louisiana, cranberries from the frost bogs of Massachusetts, hot dogs at night baseball games. "Courbyon" in New Orleans, collard greens in pot likker in Georgia, peach leather and benne-seed wafers in Charleston, smoked muskellunge from the lakes below Duluth, watermelon, peanuts, candied yams, coon, possum, squirrel, turkey, Virginia tobacco, Kentucky Burgoo, juleps, rose geranium liqueur, bourbon in flasks for the fall carnival of football, Coca-Cola, ice-cream cones, chewing gum.

Only here. Only here.

I thought of drive-in movies, county fairs, church suppers, block parties, Sunday-school picnics, hay rides, chuck-wagon cookouts. Of drugstores where you can buy dinner and of supermarkets where you can buy drugs. Of the Sears Roebuck catalogue.

I thought of hillbilly songs, spirituals, Uncle Remus stories, and the legend of Paul Bunyan and his blue ox, Babe. I thought of comic books.

I thought of the battlefield at Concord where Minutemen fell in their farmers' clothes; and of the battlefield at Gettysburg where we were annealed as one nation, indivisible. I thought of the changing of the guard at the Tomb of the Unknown Soldier on the quiet hill above the nation's majestic capital.

Nowhere, nowhere but in America.

And I thought of my Dutch friend's remark as we skimmed across the border between Utah and Nevada. "Such a big country. And so rich in different zings. But best of all, it is so free. No passports. No *cartes d'identité*. You go thousands of miles and no one asks who or why. Everyzing is twice as beautiful when you are as free as here."

PEOPLE IN AMERICA

THE GOLDEN PALACE

EDWARD CORSI

Former United States Commissioner of Immigration

---

*It has always been so. The newcomer to America finds that
most of our people have open doors and open hearts. And that
this is a country rich in opportunity.*

*Edward Corsi's career bears witness to the truth of this state-
ment. Born in Italy in 1896, Corsi came to the United States as
a boy, worked his way through St. Francis Xavier College and
Fordham Law School, and went on to make a splendid name for
himself in social work, politics, and liberal causes. In addition
to three years as U. S. Commissioner of Immigration, he has
been director of the New York City Emergency Home Relief
Bureau, Industrial Commissioner of New York State, Republican candidate for U. S. Senator, Special Assistant to the Secretary of State for migration and refugee problems, and, most
recently, director of the La Guardia Memorial House in New
York. He told me this story.*

MORE than 1,300,000 immigrants came to the United States in
1907. Some 300,000 were from Italy. I was one of them.

We landed at Ellis Island, a grim, barred immigration station out
in the middle of New York Harbor. The shoving, the pushing, the
milling of the multitudes that every incoming ship dumped here
were simply appalling. The shrieking and the weeping of the women
and the children were even worse. It was a bedlam.

For three never-ending days my family and I were detained. We
sat and sat and sat. Endlessly we stared at the Manhattan sky line,
so near and yet so far. Each immigrant family had to have fifty
dollars to gain admission to the United States, and we didn't have it.

We weren't released until an uncle appeared in our behalf and
proved that he had the fifty dollars.

That was my introduction to America. I was ten years old.

A few years later, I was introduced to another kind of America. It
was Christmas Eve, a big night for Italian immigrants in New York.
I was almost beside myself with excitement. I could hardly wait to

get through work and home to the fiesta. Then the head of the firm where I had a job as a messenger boy called me in.

Mrs. Vincent Astor, the wife of the multimillionaire, had purchased an extremely expensive Christmas gift for her husband, and it hadn't been delivered. She wanted it picked up at once and brought to her house in Rhinebeck, ninety miles from New York. I had to go. There would be no fiesta for me.

"You be careful," the boss said as he gave me the package. "Don't you let this out of your hands for one minute. It's worth a lot of money, more'n you'll ever see."

Clutching the package with a tentacle-like grip, I got on the train at Grand Central Terminal. I was frightened; it was my first train ride. Besides, I was scared of "stick-up men." I kept looking over my shoulder to see if I were being followed.

To Rhinebeck was a long, lonely ride. By the time the train reached there it was one o'clock in the morning. It felt a million miles away from home to me.

Sleepily I stepped off the train. It was snowing so heavily that I could scarcely see ahead of me. There was no one to greet me, of course; no one knew when I was coming.

A couple of sleighs were at the station to meet passengers. Inside of seconds they were gone. And, before I could speak to him, the stationmaster had locked the doors and left, too. I was all alone in the night, with no idea where to find the Astor estate.

Slowly I started to walk through the snow. In my mind I had an idea that the Astors dwelled in a huge golden palace, and I figured that I would see it shining through the darkness.

Up the deserted white road I walked. And walked. I must have trudged a mile or more when I saw it: a great castle, standing out against the snow. Exhaustedly I ran toward it.

It wasn't a castle at all. It was a clump of tall trees.

On I walked. Finally I came to a farmhouse. Banging on the door, I managed to awaken someone. He told me that I was on the right road.

I kept on for miles. At last I got there, cold, sodden wet, and so miserable I wanted to cry.

There were lights on. Mrs. Astor was still up, waiting anxiously for the arrival of her package. She came to the door herself, a handsome young woman in her twenties.

"Why, you poor kid," she exclaimed.

She didn't stop to look at the package. She swept me inside, stripped off my soaked coat, handed me the softest towel imaginable to dry myself with, and wrapped me in a warm fleecy bathrobe. She had a servant fix me some hot food. After that, she gave me a ten-dollar gold piece and put me to sleep in a luxurious guest room.

"Sleep well," she said.

I hid the ten-dollar gold piece under my pillow. I was afraid somebody might steal it.

In the morning Mrs. Astor took me with her on a tour of the whole estate while she distributed Christmas gifts to all the servants. Later she had her own chauffeur drive me to the station.

I had a lot to think about on my way back to New York. And for the next sixteen years.

A great deal happened in those sixteen years. I graduated from college, obtained my citizenship, became active in social work among the very same sort of immigrants that I used to live with. In 1931, following shocking revelations of racketeering in the Immigration Service, President Herbert Hoover asked me to take over the administration of Ellis Island, to clean it up, and to run it not as a stockyard but as a friendly center for the reception of human beings. He named me United States Commissioner of Immigration and placed the gateway to America in my custody.

It was a proud day for me when I first reported for duty. I got a salute from the same Italian interpreter who, twenty-four years before, had translated for the Corsi family.

But it was not the day I was proudest to be an American. That was still to come.

In the summer of 1933 President Franklin D. Roosevelt, who'd continued me in my post, appointed a commission to study immigration problems. On that commission was Mrs. Vincent Astor.

One day Mrs. Astor telephoned me to ask if she could come down and inspect Ellis Island. Delightedly I said, "Yes." When she arrived I personally showed her around the island and explained our operations. Then I invited her to lunch. Soon I was sitting in my private dining room with her—Mrs. Vincent Astor—as my guest.

That was the day—the moment—when I was proudest to be an American. This country of ours had given me, the little immigrant boy, an opportunity to get an education, to do the work I preferred, and to forge ahead in it. It had trusted me with high office. As nothing else, that day showed that in America men are treated as well as created equal.

You probably wish to know whether Mrs. Astor recognized me. No, she didn't. She seemed very interested in me and in my background. She wanted to hear my entire life story, but she didn't realize that we'd met.

All through lunch I asked myself, "Should I tell her about that snowy Christmas morning in Rhinebeck?"

I decided not to.

In subsequent months Mrs. Astor visited Ellis Island often. On each occasion I wondered whether I should tell her. I didn't.

This will be the first time Mrs. Astor—the present Mrs. Lytle Hull—hears of it.

EAST SIDE STORY

KATHRYN MURRAY
TV Performer

*How different it can be in America than in the "old country"!
Kathryn Murray has a tale to tell on this score.*
*A television personality in her own right, Mrs. Murray is
perhaps best known as wife-partner to Arthur Murray, the famous dancing teacher. She helps him run his 450 fabulous
studios around the country, at which more than 3,500,000
people have learned to dance.*
*Mrs. Murray's TV reputation has come from eight years as
mistress of ceremonies for "The Arthur Murray Party" program,
during which she has played hostess to many of the biggest
TV, screen, and stage stars. New Jersey-born in 1906, this
petite, vivacious brunette has been voted one of America's ten
best-dressed women. She wrote this.*

I HAD a serious operation on my spine some years ago, and I had
to spend several long, monotonous months in the hospital afterward, convalescing. It was sheer misery. I had to lie absolutely flat
on my back; I couldn't even have a pillow under my head for reading.

Each dreary day seemed forever.

One afternoon an elderly relative by marriage came to call. I
knew very little about her. For one thing, her formidable foreign
accent was a barrier between us. For another, she'd been very re-
mote with me. Aloof, almost. She didn't have much to say now either.
I tried to draw her out, but my questions fell flat beneath her mono-
syllabic answers. I kept prodding, though. I asked her about her
youth, her marriage, her early life in the United States, anything
to get her talking.

Finally she began.

Sara was born in a village that is now part of Poland, in a region
notorious for its vile anti-Semitism. Always the dread of a bloody
pogrom was present in her home. Twice in her childhood, her house
was burned to the ground by Jew-hating peasants—searing horrors
still etched deep in her mind. She had a physical remembrance,

too—a foot deformed by frostbite while she and her rabbi father were hiding for their lives in a haystack.

This much told, Sara lapsed into reverie, her head nodding in silent wailing.

I whispered, "But you grew up. You married. Things got better. Tell me about it."

It was an arranged marriage, to a young man from a neighboring village. He was very poor and she had to work with him in the fields in order to scratch a living from their bare little farm.

Eventually a baby was born to them. It started Sara dreaming. Someday her daughter Rachel would live in a place where a Jew could breathe without fear. They would save to go to America.

Alas for dreams. Late one night, tiny Rachel awakened with a burning fever. The frantic parents heated the croup kettle. It did no good. They had to have help. But where? There was a government hospital twenty miles away. But could the baby stand the trip in the freezing cold? They harnessed the old plow horse to the cart.

When they reached the hospital the next morning Sara was numb with the cold, fatigue, and worry. In she tottered and held out the baby in her arms.

The attendant ignored the child. He droned endless questions: Name, address, occupation, religion. Then he asked for payment in advance.

The parents didn't have any money. Not a kopeck.

"No money, no hospital," the attendant said.

"But our child is dying."

"What difference does it make if a Jew-child dies!" the attendant said.

A dead baby rode home in the wagon with Sara that day.

The grief-stricken parents now lived only for the day they could go to America. At last they got here. The husband found a night job in a bakery, and Sara settled down to a tenement existence on the lower East Side of New York. Soon a midwife was needed for a new baby, Rebecca.

Cruelly, terribly, history repeated itself. Little Rebecca developed a racking cough. By evening she had all the symptoms of pneumonia. Sara, alone in the tenement flat with the baby, broke down.

Her anguished cries brought a neighbor, who said, "You must take your baby to the hospital at once."

To the hospital? A Jew without money? Sara clutched the baby fiercely to herself. If the child must die, she moaned, it would be at home in her arms—not at the closed doors of a hospital.

"You're in America now. They take care of you here," the neighbor argued.

Sara wouldn't heed her. The neighbor practically had to drag her down the five tenement flights and through the streets to the new Gouverneur Hospital.

A nurse took one glance at the gasping baby wrapped in a shawl. Within moments the baby was in a clean, white crib with a doctor at her side.

The baby lived, and Sara went to the synagogue to give thanks to God, and to America.

Three more children came. Boys. It was not easy supporting them and Sara had to go out to work, in the same bakery as her husband. Many a night she would bring the newest baby along with her and bed it on a blanket in a corner while she labored.

Telling me about it, this tall, gaunt woman made it sound so real that I could see her kneading the mounds of dough, thrusting the heavy shovelfuls of loaves into the oven.

The children grew older. In Rebecca a dream unfolded. She wanted to become a doctor. Such a dream would have been unheard-of for a girl in the old country. Still, Sara told herself, other East Side children were achieving college degrees. Why not her daughter?

It would cost a lot of money. The tuition for the New York Medical College was a hundred and fifty dollars a year, and there were books to buy. No matter. In America anything was possible.

The parents skimped even more, and Rebecca entered medical school. Suddenly catastrophe came. The husband was taken very ill. So ill that he couldn't work.

Sara was desperate. How could she earn money to pay for medicines, food, and rent, let alone tuition for Rebecca. And for the boys. They had to have an education too.

Hour after hour Sara paced the floor, trying to think of something she could do. One sleepless night an idea came to her. She would go into business for herself. She knew of a wholesale bakery on 101st Street which threw away its rejects—the loaves of bread that were broken or misshapen. If she could buy them at a low price, she could run a bargain outlet shop.

The wholesaler agreed (after all, what had he to lose?) and Sara was the happiest woman on the East Side.

Then her castle of cards collapsed. There was only one vacant store in the whole neighborhood, and the real estate agent wouldn't rent it to her unless she gave two months' rent in advance. This she couldn't do. She hadn't the money to pay a week in advance.

Poor Sara's dream was shattered.

The children sought to console her. "Don't worry about it, Mama," Rebecca said. "So I'll drop out of medical school. I didn't want to be a doctor anyway."

But Sara was inconsolable. She wept that night through.

Sara wasn't beaten, though. In America anything is possible, she repeated over and over again, and she decided to go to see the owner of the building himself. Maybe he would be more lenient.

Listening to her, I could visualize the shabbily dressed, limping woman, with her heavy accent, as she went uptown to the office of the owner of the building. I could imagine how frightened she was. He was a busy executive. Would he even see her?

He gave her five minutes. No more.

"Please," she begged him, "trust me for the rent."

He was all business. "Why should I trust you?" he said.

Sara had solely one answer. "So my children, they should be able to go to school."

"What's that got to do with me?"

She looked at him. "Mister, you're an American, no? You want all children, they should have an education, no? That's how Americans are. So give me a chance to give my children an education."

"Lady," the landlord said, "don't worry about paying the rent in advance. The store is yours."

A week later the store was open. For Sara it meant working sixteen and eighteen hours a day, seven days a week. But she didn't mind. Not Sara.

I sighed as she finished her story. "What a hard life you've had—even here in America," I said.

She turned toward me and her sad, sunken eyes brightened. "Hard? Work isn't hard—not when you have hope.

"You should just think of the opportunities my children have had in America. My daughter a doctor. One son a lawyer; one a businessman, and my other son, well, he's not done so bad either!"

We smiled at each other. No, her other son hadn't done so badly. She meant my husband, Arthur Murray.

MONDAY IN THE BERKSHIRES

HANS MAEDER
Director, The Stockbridge School

---

*A new American, who has had to struggle to get here, can
often see qualities in us we're hardly aware of. Like neighborliness. We take it for granted, yet to others it is one of our unique
characteristics.*

*Hear Hans Maeder on this score. Few men have seen as
much good and bad as this forty-nine-year-old, German-born
educator. He was a Nazi as a boy, a member of the Hitler
Youth. But an old teacher taught him to think for himself
and he became a confirmed anti-Nazi, fighting the storm troopers in the streets of Hamburg. When Hitler came to power he
escaped to Denmark and organized an anti-fascist underground
there. The Gestapo denounced him to the Danish police and
he was deported to Switzerland. There he organized another
underground and was deported again. A man without a country,
he went to Kenya, working as a planter and teaching native
children on the side how to read and write. He had one hope:
somehow to get to America and found a school where young
people could learn to live at peace in a free, tolerant world.*

*From Kenya he made his way to China, where he was bombed
by the Japanese. On to the Philippines. Next to Honolulu. He
was there on Pearl Harbor Day. Despite his long record of anti-
nazism, he was interned as an enemy alien along with some
Gestapo agents who tried to hang him. In 1942 he won his
release, headed for New York, and obtained a job helping under-
privileged youth. After the war he secured his American citizenship and a teaching post in a fashionable school. Soon he was
the director. But always he dreamed of a school of his own.
Finally he got it. In 1949 he established the Stockbridge School,
dedicated to "Education for World Understanding." Then disaster.*

This is the story he told me of what occurred:

IT WAS Monday in the snowy Berkshires. The faculty and students
were at lunch, lazing over dessert before the start of a busy afternoon. Everyone was relaxed and cheerful—until the cry, "Fire!"

Moments later our chief building was an ugly, spitting mass of flame. There was no fighting it. In fifty minutes nothing was left except a pile of ashes.

No one was hurt, thank heavens, but it looked like the end of the Stockbridge School.

I'd worked so hard to make the school a reality. Years of planning had gone into it, and years more of trying to get the right people to sponsor the project. After that had come the biggest hurdle: money. In November 1947 I'd heard that the one-million-dollar Mark Hanna estate, near Stockbridge, Massachusetts, was for sale for $90,000. Twelve hundred glorious acres with a huge manor house, the biggest stables in New England and other fine buildings. It was a marvelous buy. Unfortunately my wife and I had exactly $293 between us. But I argued the price down to $60,000, took an option, and promptly sold off 400 acres for $48,000. I was thereby able to get the rest of the land and all the buildings for $12,000 borrowed dollars.

There were merely sixteen students when we opened and not even enough money for books. Bit by bit we grew. By 1953 we had seventy boys and girls, some from as far off as Formosa, Thailand, and the Yemen. And superb equipment. That very fall we'd put in a new science laboratory and an excellent gymnasium.

Now most of our school was burned to nothing. The boys' dormitory with all their belongings, our gym, our science lab, our theater, our workshop were in ruins. Worse yet, almost every classroom was destroyed. Not even a pencil remained.

I wasn't so sad as I was tired. Tired deep down inside me. Twenty-five years of effort had gone up in smoke, and I just didn't have the strength to keep on trying.

"It was too good to be true," I muttered. "I guess we'd better call it quits."

Downcast, I turned away from the rubble to make arrangements for sending the students home and disbanding the school.

As I walked along I saw one of our neighbors, James Downs, coming toward me.

"Professor," he said, "what can we do for you?"

I didn't know what he meant. Nobody had ever before offered to do anything for me. In most parts of the world your neighbors don't come to your aid when you're in trouble. A man is supposed to suffer calamities by himself.

All I could say to him was, "I don't know what you can do. Or anybody. Let me think about it and call you."

Downs was the first of many. A steady procession of cars arrived —neighbors bringing blankets, sweaters, food. The telephone began to ring steadily—people offering to lodge our boys until we could find new quarters for them.

The local plumber came by. On his truck were six beds and mattresses.

"I reckon your boys can use 'em better than we can," he declared. "I have a couple of dressers in the attic that you can have, too."

The local department store telephoned. "Do your boys need clothing?"

It even sent over a load of iceskates when it became known that the boys had lost theirs.

A Stockbridge church sent a check. The children in its Sunday school had contributed $5.57 for us.

I could scarcely believe it. Though some of our New England neighbors had regarded Hans Maeder suspiciously as a foreigner in their midst, now they were all standing by me.

Their openheartedness was what I needed. I telephoned Jim Downs.

"I know what you can do for me," I said. "I want you to round up some pencils and paper. We're going to have school as usual tomorrow."

Today the Stockbridge School is bigger than ever. We've erected not one but three new buildings and we're planning more. But what I'm most proud of is the discovery I made on the day of the fire: Americans have a heart.

HOUSE CALL

DR. MILAN D. BAKER
Medical Director, Culver Military Academy

Dr. Milan D. Baker has something to say on the subject of neighborliness, too.

From his early childhood in Nebraska, Dr. Baker had his heart set on following in his doctor father's footsteps. He studied medicine at the University of Nebraska, interned in Philadelphia, and hung out his shingle in Battle Creek, Nebraska. When poor health laid him low in 1938 he gave up his practice to accept a position as medical director of Culver Military Academy, one of the country's outstanding preparatory schools. He planned to stay a year, but liked working with the Culver cadets so much that he remained permanently. Dr. Baker is now forty-nine, but he still recalls his early "G.P." days in Nebraska with nostalgia. Here is an account he wrote of them.

WINTER in Nebraska on a day after a blizzard. The thermometer was down to sixteen below zero. If you were foolhardy enough to go out, the icy winds slashed at your face like a razor-edged scalpel. . . .

The telephone rang. "Doctor, I've got an awfully sick boy. I can't get him to you. Can you get to us?"

It was F. L. Sebastian, a farmer who lived eleven miles out of Battle Creek, the little town where I was practicing. His son was running a fever of 105.

I doubted if I could make it to the Sebastian farm. Most of the roads were blocked solid with snow. But a 105 fever was nothing to fool with.

"O.K.," I said. "I'll try."

At the local café I found three townsmen, Bud Story, Walter Rouse, and Bud Bridges, sitting around a warm stove.

"Sebastian's kid is real sick," I broke in on them. "Will one of you guys ride along with me and help shovel me out if I get stuck?"

All three said they'd come.

The direct route south, which ran over the hills, was absolutely impassable. It was six feet deep in snow. We had to swing west through the flatlands, turn south and east, doing three sides of a square. It was twenty-five miles extra driving, but it was our only chance.

For the first few miles the going wasn't too bad. Then the wind changed and the snow began to gather in ridge-like drifts, three to four feet high, cutting across the road like obstacles in a steeplechase.

"Looks mighty bad, Doc," one of the fellows said. "Mebbe we'd better head back while we can."

I thought of the Sebastian boy and his 105 fever. "Let's try it a little farther," I said.

Sure enough, we got stuck. No matter how we shoveled, the car wouldn't budge. Neither forward nor backward. And it was still nine miles to the Sebastian home.

Abandoning the car, we hiked to a farmhouse about a half mile down the road. "Will you lend me a horse?" I asked the farmer.

"Sure, Doc," he said.

Now the torture really started. Leaving my shovelmen warm in the farmhouse kitchen, I mounted the horse and set out.

I had never been what might be called a horseman. Furthermore, I'd not been in a saddle for years. Each jog of the horse's hoofs felt like a hammer blow in every part of my body. And, Lord, was it cold. My face, my legs, my arms turned numb. Then my body. I almost fell off the horse.

A voice aroused me from my frozen lethargy. A man, hunched in a big sheepskin coat, was leaning against a mailbox. It was a mile or so before the Sebastians'.

"You Dr. Baker?"

"Yes."

"Sebastian told me you were coming. I'm Joe Ambrose. Doc, I got a very sick girl at my house. I wish you'd see what you can do for her."

"How far do you live from here?"

"About a mile that way." He pointed down a road that led off in another direction.

An examination of his little girl, Elsie, showed that she was suffering from quinsy. I had to lance the abscess.

Back on the horse again I painfully climbed. It was getting dark, and even colder. The thermometer at the Ambroses' door was down to twenty below zero.

Somehow I made it to the Sebastians. It was lucky I did. The father hadn't exaggerated. Seventeen-year-old Curtis was critically ill. He had a severe streptococcus infection of the throat, sinuses, and ears. Both of the ears were draining pus and his temperature was now over 105.

All evening long I worked on the lad, trying to arrest the infection and bring the fever down. It didn't help much. By midnight his condition was touch and go.

There was just one thing to do. If the boy was to pull through, we had to move him to a hospital. And soon.

But the nearest hospital was in Norfolk, nine miles on the other side of Battle Creek. And the road to Battle Creek, as I knew only too well, was blocked.

It looked as if we were licked. As if young Curtis Sebastian might have to die.

I picked up the phone. "Get me Art Rodekohr, the County Commissioner of Roads," I asked the operator.

Quickly I told Art of our predicament. "It's a matter of life and death," I said. "Can you get the road into Battle Creek cleared for us by morning?"

"Clear eleven miles of that snow by morning?"

"Yes. By morning. Or it'll be too late."

"I'll do my damnedest," Art said, "but I can't get it done that quick. No one could."

"Try," I begged.

Shortly before daybreak we decided to take our chances on getting through to Norfolk. We had to. Curt was pretty low. Carefully we bundled him up and put him in the Sebastian car. Then we headed slowly down the lane and out onto the main road.

It had been cleared as far as we could see. And farther. All the way to Battle Creek.

We had no trouble driving Curt to the Norfolk hospital. He got better there fast.

That afternoon I hunted up Art Rodekohr to thank him for clearing the road.

"Don't thank me," he said. "I didn't have anything to do with it."

"What do you mean?"

"Well," he explained, "when you called me last night everybody on the party line was listening in. They passed the word and a hundred and fifty of Sebastian's neighbors turned out in the dark with their teams and scrapers. By the time my crew and I could get to the job, the road was clear."

THE FOREIGNERS' SECTION

H. F. JOHNSON
President, S. C. Johnson & Son

Years back, a foreign visitor was a rara avis *in the United States. Now, times have changed. With the various exchange programs for students, government officials, industrialists, and trade unionists, throngs of foreigners come to America every day.*

How do they find us on our own home grounds? Herbert F. Johnson can report on this from an excellent vantage point. From 1954 to 1955 he served as a top official of the Foreign Operations Administration in Washington, and had an opportunity of meeting the various foreigners the FOA brought here. Johnson, who was born in Wisconsin fifty-nine years ago and educated at Cornell, heads S. C. Johnson & Son, the world's largest wax manufacturer, with its main headquarters (a striking place designed by Frank Lloyd Wright) in Racine, Wisconsin, as well as many other plants in foreign countries. The third Johnson to run this family-owned enterprise, he is one of America's new breed of international-minded businessmen. He wrote this report.

I SPENT a year looking at the United States through the eyes of foreigners. It was an enlightening experience.

Don't believe it when someone tells you that familiarity with Americans breeds contempt. Quite the contrary, it is unfamiliarity that leads to suspicion and distrust. Expose a foreign citizen to a few months of informal contact with us on our home ground and he will return to his country a confirmed booster of the United States.

He may be amused by some of our folkways. He may think us a bit odd ("Delightfully screwy, especially in Texas," according to a Greek railroad man). He may be disappointed in a number of our foibles. But he likes us.

I know.

As an official of the Foreign Operations Administration in Washington, I had a chance to talk with hundreds of foreigners, men and women of all nationalities, occupations, and stations of life, who were brought to this country under FOA auspices to study American industrial practices.

I learned a lot from them—about us.

Our friendliness is the first thing they noticed. Time after time, I was told almost the identical story: "I was standing on the corner, wondering which direction the bus ran, and three different people approached me politely to ask if they could be of any help."

It is true that in about half the cases they added, "Of course, I received a different set of directions from each person." But as a Japanese shoe manufacturer declared, "After all, that is only an expression of your famous individualism."

"I came here believing Americans were hostile to foreigners," the wife of an Indian industrialist told me, "so, in the beginning, when they would go to such pains to help me find my way I thought that perhaps they were preparing to snatch my purse. Gradually, though, it dawned on me that if indeed Americans are suspicious of foreigners, then they are remarkably inept at identifying one—even one wearing a sari and with a caste mark on her forehead."

Our helpfulness was next on the list. Here was how Mrs. Masood Husain, the wife of a Pakistani waterway engineer, described her "wonderful" first day at the U. S. Army's Waterways Experimental Station in Vicksburg, Mississippi.

"We had just unpacked for our four-week stay, and I was in a state of hypnosis and bewilderment at what to do next. Where to eat? Where to shop? What to do with three suitcases of unwashed laundry?

"Suddenly there was a knock at the door and in walked two officers' wives. Within the next three hours I'd been taught how to get in and out of a supermarket, how to get milk delivered (Isn't it amazing? You just open your door and there it is!), where the best laundry in town was, and, best of all, how to operate that fabulous contrivance, the electric stove."

The lack of ceremony on the part of Americans came as a shock to some. However, after the initial surprise wore off, they were all delighted with our dearth of class consciousness. Saeng Chulcharitta, a railroad man from Bangkok, couldn't get over a dinner at the home of a Mr. Christianson, an executive of the Chicago, Milwaukee and St. Paul Railroad. Mrs. Christianson had prepared and served the dinner, and Mr. Christianson had personally mixed the drinks.

"Imagine top-ranking railroad officer and spouse acting as servants to visitors from Asia!"

While Ramachandra Deo, an Indian mining engineer, was standing in line to meet the Governor of Idaho he frantically debated with himself as to how deep he should bow and whether to address him as "Your Excellency" or "Your Highness." Fortunately he managed to overhear the greeting of the man ahead of him, so he swallowed hard, thrust out his hand, and said, "Hi, Governor."

To me it sounded like a simple thing, but it remained one of Mr. Deo's most vivid memories of this nation.

The easygoing relationship between American employers and employees was especially astonishing to these people.

An Egyptian factory manager touring a Ford assembly plant in New Jersey was absolutely dumfounded when the union representatives in his escort group joked gaily with the top management man.

"They even called him by his first name," he recalled. "In our land a man in his position is always addressed as 'Mr.' He does not joke with subordinates. In America, it seems to me that the only use you have for a last name is to differentiate one Charlie from the other."

Our friendliness, our warmth, our informality—such are the dominant sensations that these foreign visitors, almost to a man, took back with them. And it made me proud to hear them talk about it.

But my greatest pride, as an American, came the day I sat down to lunch with an Iranian road engineer and heard him tell of his encounter with the Tennessee Legislature. Better than any other, his story gave a picture of what our country represents to the foreign visitors among us.

Passing through Nashville, Tennessee, this engineer had a few hours to spare. He decided he would spend them watching a state government in action and he went over to the capitol building. Approaching the lady receptionist, he asked her to direct him to the section for foreigners.

The receptionist was wonderful. She didn't say there was no such thing as a section for foreigners. Instead, she took the engineer right into the house chamber and introduced him to the Speaker. The Speaker was just as good. He seated the engineer right on the floor of the house itself in the chair of an absent representative.

"At this treatment, I glowed all over," the engineer told me.

And he had more to glow about. He heard his name spoken over the public-address system. Before he knew it, a round of applause had broken out and one of the lawmakers was escorting him down the aisle. He found himself standing upon the rostrum, looking down on the assembled legislators. He'd been called up to make a speech.

"I was so astounded that I could hardly believe it," he said to me. "But I did the best I could to express to them what I felt. I told them of my country, and of what it meant to me and to my people to receive the kind of help that you people in the United States have been giving us—the highways, the irrigation dams, the bridges that are to us like pearls from heaven."

There was silence when he finished. Then there was a long roll of applause and his hand was being shaken by dozens of people all at once.

Later, as he was hurrying from the statehouse to catch his train, still in a kind of daze, the receptionist came up to him. With a twinkle in her eye, she asked him whether they had put him in the foreigners' section "with the bars on the window."

"Madame," he said to her, "they put me in the only place you Americans ever put foreigners. They seated me on the throne."

Listening to him tell the story, I liked us Americans.

THE PRIVATE AND THE COLONEL

GEORGE MEANY

*President, American Federation of Labor and
Congress of Industrial Organizations*

---

*Rank does have its privileges in certain areas of American
life, in the Armed Forces, for instance. But it also has its
distinct limitations. As George Meany points out, this wouldn't
be America otherwise.*

*Meany is president of the world's largest, and most demo-
cratic labor movement, the thirteen-and-a-half-million-member
American Federation of Labor and Congress of Industrial
Organizations. A New Yorker, born in 1894, he started as a
plumber when he was sixteen, became active in the A.F. of L.
Plumbers Union, and in 1934 was elected president of the
New York State Federation of Labor. Five years later he was
named secretary-treasurer of the entire A.F. of L., thirteen
years after that, president. It was chiefly due to his tireless
efforts that the A.F. of L. and C.I.O. merged in 1955, and he
was the unanimous choice as head of the united organization.
Since then, his courage and statesmanship have made the A.F.
of L.-C.I.O. a vast force for political and economic progress. He
recounted this story to me.*

T HE incident took merely a split second but there were one hundred and seventy-five years of the best kind of American democracy wrapped up in it.

It was on a crowded air liner en route from New Orleans to Washington, D.C. We'd stopped at Atlanta, and I'd gotten off for a smoke.
When the public-address system blared out our number I hurried
to get back aboard.

As I was making my way up the aisle of the plane I noticed a
little Army private in front of me. He was young and eager, obviously
heading home on his first leave. Suddenly he stopped short. His
shoulders sagged, and I could hear him gulp. A colonel was sitting
in his seat!

Then the little private straightened up, stepped forward, and
tapped the colonel on the arm.

"Sorry, sir," he said. "This seat is taken."

The colonel rose. And apologized. And gave the private back his seat.

In that moment I caught the spirit that makes America what it is. It could only happen here in the United States. Thank heaven, it can.

WHEN YOU GO ON RELIEF

JOHN DEMARTINO

New York Barber

This is a country in which poor men can hold their heads as high as rich men, even when fate seems to be going against them. John DeMartino knows this. He lived it.

In the opinion of the cognoscenti, *DeMartino is the best barber in New York City. He is a member of that vanishing genre—the artisan who takes enormous pride in the work of his hands. Sixty-one now, he was born in Salerno, Italy, and learned barbering as a child from his uncle. He came to the United States in 1910, did a stint in the U. S. Navy during World War I (earning his citizenship thereby), and has been wielding his shears ever since. He is the star attraction of Martini's Barber Shop on West Seventy-second Street in New York. Here is the story he told me of a moment life looked dark.*

You can tell a lot about a country from the way it treats a man when he is down on his luck. Some countries let him starve. In others they help a fellow, but rub his nose in the dirt while they are doing it. I do not know which is tougher.

Once in my life I was down on my luck. It taught me plenty about this country.

It was back in January 1939 that things went bad for me. I'd been doing fine up to then. I was not getting to be a millionaire, of course. If I remember right, I was earning forty-five dollars a week, and that is not much when you've a wife and two young kids to support. Just about enough for food and the rent on a three-room apartment, four flights up, in the Bronx. Still, we had enough spaghetti to eat, enough red wine to drink, and we didn't owe a dime to anyone. I am the sort of guy who would rather die than borrow money.

All of a sudden I caught a cold. Naturally I couldn't take a day off to nurse it. A barber makes his living out of commissions and tips. If you don't work, you don't eat.

Before I knew what hit me I was running a terrible fever. One hundred and four, I think it was. Lucy, my wife, called a doctor. Pneumonia, he said.

The doctor gave me that new drug, sulpha. It didn't help. The next day I was worse. Pleurisy had set in.

They took me to the hospital—it was St. Clare's—in an ambulance, and I was there for two and a half weeks. I almost died. You won't believe it, but my hair turned absolutely white in that time.

At last they let me out. I was so weak that I could hardly walk up the stairs to our little apartment. This worried me very much.

"When do I go back to work?" I asked the doctor.

"You don't," he said. "You've got to take at least two months off to build up your health."

Two months! I nearly fell through the floor. Good God, how were my children to eat? There was not five dollars left in the house.

"What are we going to do?" I asked Lucy after the doctor went.

She sat down on the bed beside me. "I know how you feel, John, but there is no other way out. We must go on the relief."

My stomach turned over. "On relief? Never!" I shouted. "All my life I have lived without charity. I am not going to start now."

"But what else is there?"

"I will go back to work," I said. "Tomorrow."

"You cannot do it, John. You have not got the strength. You will die."

"Then I will die," I said. "It is better than asking for relief. I've heard other barbers tell how it was with them in the old countries. They make you crawl like a worm before they give you a dollar."

"Darling, darling," Lucy said. "Be sensible. You can't even walk to the subway now, let alone stand on your feet twelve hours a day, cutting hair. You will fall down on your face. They will take you back to the hospital, and this time you will not come home to me."

She was right. Inside me, I knew it. "O.K.," I said. "Go. Go to the relief, if you must."

But, even as I said it, I made up my mind on this one point. If those relief people tried to make me crawl like a worm, I would throw them out of my house. Even if it meant that we all had to starve. There is something more important than food. A man must be able to hold up his head.

I could not sleep nights until the city relief investigator came. I was too nervous.

Finally the investigator knocked at the door, a tall, thin, Swedish fellow in his forties. He had a big brief case with him, full of blanks to be made out, questions to be answered, all sorts of papers. I never saw so many.

I decided to set him straight from the start. "Listen here," I said, "I am a hard-working man, and I have worked hard all my life. I have never taken charity before and I am only doing it for a little while now. Just until I get on my feet. So don't you try to shove me around."

He looked at me, surprised. "Are you an American citizen, Mr. DeMartino?" he said.

"Yes," I answered him.

"Good," he declared. "Then you should know this. There's nothing on earth to be ashamed of because you're applying for relief. You have a perfect right as an American citizen in this city to call on the government for help when you're in need of it. That's what we have a government for."

"Are you kidding?" I said.

"No, I'm not kidding."

"You mean you do not think I am a beggar?"

"No, I don't think you're a beggar. I think you're just a guy who needs a little help to tide him over a rough spot, and we're going to see that you get it."

"Thank you, mister," I said. "Thank you."

I could not say more to him. There was too large a gulp in the middle of my throat. A gulp because he was such a decent guy. And because this was such a decent country—a country where they treat you well whether your luck is up or down.

Unfortunately I could not return to the barbershop in two months. It was closer to four before the doctor would let me go. I did not have to worry, though. The relief gave us money to live on.

It is a funny thing about that relief money. As soon as I started working again, I told the relief office about it. By mistake, they mailed us another check anyway.

We could have used the money; I was only working two days a week. But I took the check back. It made me feel better in my mind.

TOUGH GUYS

FRANK HOWLEY
Vice Chancellor of New York University

Rooting for the underdog is an ingrained trait with most Americans. You see it in sports, politics, and international affairs. Going to the assistance of the underdog if he is being treated unfairly is another American characteristic. A good one, too.

Frank Howley, now vice-chancellor of New York University, was involved officially in an instance of this and he has written about it. A fifty-five-year-old New Jerseyite, Howley was educated at N.Y.U. and the Sorbonne, went into business, and got to head his own advertising agency. Entering the Army in 1940 as a captain, he rose to be a brigadier general with the all-important assignment of U. S. Military Governor of Berlin from 1945 to 1949. After he retired from the Army he traveled, lectured, and wrote five books. In 1952 he was appointed to his present post at N.Y.U., the biggest institution of higher learning in the United States.

IT WAS July 1945 when the conquering armies of the United States, Great Britain, France, and Russia were occupying the city of Berlin.

The combat soldiers of each army usually kept to their own assigned parts of town, but scraps among them were not unique, usually over those things for which fighting men fight—wine, women, song, or just for the hell of fighting.

One day two of my G.I.s reported to me in exceptionally bad condition, with black eyes, split lips, and that sort of thing. I said to them, "Well, I can see what you two characters have been up to. You didn't get enough fighting during the war, you have to go out and get into scrapes when the war is over."

The answer was, "Yes, sir, we wus fightin'."

"Who were you fighting with?" I demanded.

"Some Russians, sir," was the answer.

"Well," I said, "you're wrong on at least two counts. In the first place, you're wrong to get into fights. In the second place, you've been fighting with the Russians, who were our allies during the war. And it's obvious you got licked. That's wrong, too. Now get out of here and down to the dispensary to get sewed up. Then report to the captain, because you two are going to do some extra guard duty until you cool off your fighting spirits."

"Yes, sir," they said, and went on their way to the dispensary.

They were hardly out of my office when there was a great commotion in the hall. In came the top general of the French, Major General Geoffrey de Beauchesne. He was accompanied by a couple of colonels and a few aides. They were dressed up in their finest calling clothes, with gold braid and all that sort of thing.

"My dear Colonel Howley," said General de Beauchesne, "I have something of the utmost sentimental importance to our two armies to report to you. It happened yesterday and is the sort of thing which builds the endless affection between our two great peoples.

"You know," he said, "we lost a whole generation in the First World War at Verdun. And in order to rebuild the armies of France we now have to draft seventeen-year-old boys. Some of them are not too strong physically because they were raised during the occupation when food was not all it should be. One of these soldiers, a young boy who says he is seventeen, but I think he is perhaps sixteen, was walking on the edge of the French sector when about a dozen giant Russian soldiers seized him and beat him up. They played cat and mouse with him, pushing him around, slapping him, taking his cap and knapsack away, and in general disgracing him in his own eyes and shaming him before the German spectators. The boy was crying, and was really at the end of his endurance, when two of your American G.I.s came by.

"The two American soldiers took the French soldier away from the rowdy Russians and said something nice to him, but he did not understand. They also said something to the Russians, not sounding very nice, which the Russians also did not understand. They did understand, however, that they—all twelve of them—had to give back to the boy his equipment, including his hat, and stop beating him. This they would not do. Instead they resumed their beating of the little French soldier.

"Your two G.I.s pitched into the fight and it was then three against twelve, instead of one against twelve.

"Of course, after some time the three were well beaten up, but the Russians were not without scratches and blows either. And after a while they'd had enough and returned to the French soldier his beret, his knapsack, and his equipment, and went on their way.

"My French soldier reported to his captain and his captain brought him to me. He no longer feels disgraced, and he naturally thinks the two American soldiers are great friends to have done this for him.

"All of us French wish to thank you and the American people for producing such loyal, courageous young men."

"*Vive l'Amérique et vive la France*," said the general.

Out the Frenchmen marched, with a clicking of heels. The air was full of the spirit of the "Marseillaise."

When they had gone I picked up the telephone and called the dispensary. "Let me talk to those fellows that just got beat up," I said.

One of them came on the phone. "Yes, sir."

I said to him, "Are you one of the two guys who got in the fight with those Russians who were pushing that French kid around?"

"Yes, sir," was the reply.

"Why did you do it?" I asked him.

"Well, sir," he said, "Joe and me couldn't stand there and see anybody being pushed around like that."

"All right," I said, "never mind about walking that guard duty."

"Yes, sir," he said, and hung up.

Americans like that who would rather take a licking than stand idly by while little people are pushed around can make you proud you are an American. Can give you a lump in the throat.

STREET FIGHT IN COLOGNE

CARL R. HELLSTROM
President, Smith & Wesson

Carl R. Hellstrom, the dynamic president of Smith & Wesson, also has a story to tell about the readiness of Americans to go to the aid of the underdog. He saw a case of it in Germany, too, and recounted it to me.

Hellstrom is the sixty-three-year-old production genius who revitalized Smith & Wesson, the venerable Springfield, Massachusetts, firm in 1941 after it was on the verge of collapse and turned it into the world's leading revolver manufacturer. Born in Stockholm of aristocratic Swedish stock, he reached the United States when he was twenty-one. At twenty-three he was assistant superintendent of all Allied shell production in America. By thirty he was a leading figure in American industry with a half-dozen key inventions to his credit. He became a citizen of the United States in 1919. There is no more sincere American.

STREET fights are not a hobby of mine. In fact, I don't like them. Still, I'll always enjoy the memory of a bloody, knockdown fight that I got into once during a trip to Europe. It was in a good cause, and it was a means of introducing me to a great guy.

This was in the fall of 1926. The American Legion had run a veterans' excursion to Paris and, after it ended, a few of us spilled over into Germany. Just to see the sights.

One evening I found myself in Cologne with a few hours to kill between trains. I had nothing else to do so I went for a walk. I wound up in a large public square that turned out to be a hangout for gangs of young German toughs.

Those toughs were nasty. Very nasty. While I was ambling around I saw a bunch of them picking on an old Jewish pushcart peddler who was struggling to get a load of fruit up a steep grade into the square. His pretty daughter and her young sweetheart were helping him.

The toughs crowded in on the three of them, blocked their path, and started to annoy the girl. When her boy friend protested they tipped over the cart and began to beat him up. It made me sick.

A tall, lean guy was standing alongside me. I had never seen him before. In a slow, Texas drawl he said, "You look like an able-bodied Yank, how about teaching those ——s a lesson!"

I thought it was a fine idea, and I said so.

Together, we tore into the toughs. It was touch and go at first, they were too many for us. They had me backed against a wall and were throwing punches—hard punches—in my face.

Out of the fog I heard a new voice. "Can you use another hand, boss?"

Two American Negroes, who'd been across the street watching, had come to our aid.

The four of us were enough for the dirty punks. More than enough. We soon had the situation in hand and after that we gave those birds a taste of what they'd been dishing out. We really poured it into them until the police came and broke it up.

We had no trouble clearing ourselves with the police. All we had to do was tell them the truth. They threw those young toughs in jail and let us go. But we were a sad-looking lot. Our faces were bleeding and bashed in; our clothes were in shreds. One of the Negroes had to have four stitches taken in his head.

The Texas friend felt bad about it all. "It's all my fault," he kept saying. "I gotcha into the fight."

He insisted on paying the doctor's bill himself. And he made our two Negro friends take money for new suits. The poor guys were flat broke.

You'd think he would have been satisfied with this. He wasn't. He started worrying about the peddler. It bothered him that the old man's cart had been wrecked and all his fruit trampled underfoot in the mud.

"That poor devil probably lost everything he had in the world," he fretted.

He went over to the peddler, who was sitting dejectedly in a corner of the police station, and handed him a roll of bills. There must have been two hundred dollars' worth of marks in it.

"Here, Pop," he said, "go buy yourself a new cart."

I tried to make him let me pay half of everything. He wouldn't listen.

"Forget it," he said. "This is my party."

"O.K.," I finally agreed. "But are you sure you've got the dough?"

"Sure," he said. "I've got plenty."

He told us he was in the oil business in Texas and doing fine.

With that, the four of us went out to celebrate together until train time.

That should have been the finish of the story. But it wasn't. It had a wonderful epilogue.

I was caught with my family in Europe at the outbreak of World War II in September 1939. Luckily I managed to get us passage on a liner to the United States. The day after we sailed, a terrifying report came over the radio. The British ship *Athenia* had just been torpedoed by a Nazi U-boat only a few miles away.

There was almost a panic on our ship, and a great demand arose that we turn back at once. The Americans aboard wanted to go on, though, and they called a public meeting in the saloon.

Before the meeting opened, I went below to get a toy for my four-year-old son, Douglas. It was in our automobile, stowed deep in the ship. As I approached the car I saw a tall man sitting on the running board. In a Texas drawl he asked if he were in my way. The man's face was familiar, and that drawl—I'd heard it before. I took a second look. Things clicked. It was my friend of years back from Cologne.

He spotted me immediately. "Put it there, pal," he whooped.

I did, and we had a grand reunion right on the running board, reliving the "Battle of Cologne."

One point baffled me. "What are you doing down here in the bottom of the ship?" I asked.

"I belong here."

"What! *You* going third class?"

"Sure. I don't have any money. Never have had any."

I couldn't believe it. Here I'd been thinking all this time that he was a Texas oil millionaire.

I told him so.

He roared; that laughter of his nearly exploded the ship. "Me, a millionaire? Hell, no, I'm just an ordinary rigger."

I remembered the doctor's bill he'd paid that day in Cologne. And the money he'd slipped the two Negroes. And the two hundred dollars he'd given the peddler.

"Not so ordinary," I thought. "Not so ordinary, at all, at all!"

I invited him to come up and meet my family. He wouldn't. He said third-class passengers weren't allowed in first class and he was afraid he might embarrass me. I practically had to drag him above.

That's when the best of all took place.

Upon arriving on the top deck, we met U. S. Senator Alexander Wiley of Wisconsin, leading my small son by the hand. The senator wanted to know whether I was going to the meeting. He stated in no uncertain terms that all good Americans would be there.

Something in his tone bothered my boy. He fixed his eyes uncertainly on me and said, "You are a good American, aren't you, Daddy?"

My Texas friend smiled down on him. "You bet your life he is, sonny."

To have a guy like that say this to my kid! Well, it was a big day for me. It still is.

WELCOME PARTY

PFC SEYMOUR SHIPLACOFF

United States Army

Billions of Marshall Plan dollars have been poured out of the United States Treasury to help foreign countries recover from the devastation of World War II. The Marshall Plan was not the only foreign-aid program emanating from these shores, though. Millions of private citizens did their bit in their own way.

Seymour Shiplacoff chanced on one of these private aid programs in operation, and he has written about it. A thirty-year old New Yorker, Shiplacoff attended Brooklyn College for a spell, quit to go to work, then enlisted for a four-year stretch in the Air Force. After his discharge he studied printing at the University of Missouri and obtained a newspaper job. The military life beckoned again, and he enlisted in the Army in 1955. He's hoping to make a career of it now. Which doesn't keep him from writing poetry on the side.

M Y train pulled into Phoenix, Arizona, at eleven o'clock on May 7, 1951. Lugging my duffle bag with one hand and a musette bag with the other, I strode into Union Station. On a huge blackboard, a sign was chalked: "Men Reporting to Williams Air Force Base, Call——" I went into a phone booth and dialed the number. I was informed that a car would pick me up by 4 P.M. So I sat down to wait.

The station was crowded with little clusters of men, women, and children. Surprisingly, they all seemed to know each other. They acted like some sort of a welcoming committee, and I wondered whom they were expecting.

Attracted by my uniform, several of the youngsters flocked around me and I tried to entertain them with tales about airplanes and war stories I made up for the occasion. They ate it up.

One of the mothers saw what was going on. She came over and asked if the children were annoying me.

"Certainly not, ma'am," I answered. "But, if you don't mind, what's the reception committee for?"

"We are welcoming some people from Europe," she declared.

"You've got everything here but a brass band," I said. "Some 'big wheels' coming, huh?"

She grinned. "Maybe not 'wheels' in your sense of the word, but they're important to us."

She explained that a group of neighbors in Phoenix had been supporting a family of displaced persons in Europe. After years of effort they'd gotten them admitted to the United States and raised enough money to provide a home for them. Now the D.P.s were coming.

In the midst of her explanation the public-address system blared the arrival of a train from New Orleans. The noisy waiting room quieted to a whisper and I saw a sight I had never seen before. A man, a woman, and a small boy, with identification tags pinned to their clothing, stood hesitantly in the doorway. The man wore a dark blue suit, old and patched. His shoes had seen their best days on more than one person. The woman had on a heavy coat and a kerchief on her head. The little boy was in short pants and a shirt whose cut was not American. The complexions of all three were sallow, their faces thin and haggard. The man's wrists extended beyond the sleeves of his jacket and the bones of his hand seemed to be trying to twist themselves out of a thin layer of skin. The boy had a number branded on the inside of his right arm near the elbow.

They glanced about the station, at the people who were waiting to take them to their new home. Suddenly they saw me and my uniform. A fearful expression leaped into their eyes. The little boy, terrified, hid behind his mother.

The woman who had spoken to me went forward and talked with them. Followed by the rest of her group, she ushered them toward the exit and some automobiles outside. The D.P.s didn't take their eyes off me as they passed, looking for a weapon, afraid of arrest. They had been forced to run so much in their lives and they hadn't the strength to run any more.

The station emptied and I stood alone. I was dumfounded. I couldn't get out of my mind the picture of these pitiful people, frightened, not knowing what was to become of them. Then I thought of the strangers who were willing to help them after their own country had turned on them. It gave me a funny feeling inside. It even brought tears to my eyes. Here I was, wearing the uniform of a country in which people were willing to spend their money, their hearts, and love on persons less fortunate than they were. This was my America and it filled me with an overwhelming pride.

While I stood there, staring out at the railroad tracks, a young man about my age approached me. He and his family had been part of the welcoming committee.

"Mom says she wants you to spend the weekend with us, O.K.?"

"It's a deal," I said.

"There's a dance Saturday night. I'll fix you up with a date." He gave me an address and left.

He did fix me up that Saturday night. I married the girl he introduced me to.

MARSHAL ZHUKOV RECEIVES

LIEUTENANT GENERAL JAMES M. GAVIN

Former Chief of Research and Development, U. S. Army

It is an interesting footnote to the history of the Cold War that one of the first post-World War II disputes between the United States and Soviet Russia grew out of a simple question of fair play. It marked the first occasion on which an American Army officer "told off" a high Russian general. And for good cause.

The man who did the "telling off" is a consistent fighter for his principles. So much so that he quit the U. S. Army, early in 1958, in protest against cuts in military appropriations. The cuts imperiled the national defense, he felt.

He is fifty-one-year-old, New York-born, Lieutenant General James M. Gavin, and until his retirement he was the Army's Chief of Research and Development. Reputedly he was the "guttiest" soldier in the Army as well as one of its brainiest and most broad-visioned. An intrepid paratrooper, he made combat jumps into Sicily, Italy, France, Holland, and Germany. When he was merely thirty-seven years old and the youngest major general in the Army, he was given command of the crack 82nd Airborne Division and he led it from the Normandy beachhead to the Elbe. After V-E Day, he was designated United States representative on the Berlin Kommandatura, the four-power body set up by the victorious Allies to govern the German capital. Here he had his introduction to Soviet-style thinking. This is his account of the incident, as he told it to me.

TROUBLE with the Soviet Union came quickly in Berlin. We Americans didn't think it right to push other people around just because we were bigger than they were. The Russians did.

Early in the summer of 1945 the four members of the Berlin Kommandatura—the Russian Major General Garbatkov, the British Major General Nears, the French Major General de Beauchesne, and I—met to draw up plans for a great parade to celebrate the victory over Nazi Germany. The initial problem we had to settle was which of the four armies was to lead the march. Today this may seem a trivial point, but at the time it had large political significance.

Elsewhere in the world the Russians were intoning sweet words about international co-operation and the rights of small nations. Not in Berlin. General Garbatkov, a big, bull-like man, dripping medals to his waist, leaned across the table to me and said, "We Russians or you Americans will head the parade. No one else."

"But what about the British and the French?" I protested.

"They don't count," he barked.

It didn't matter that the British and French representatives were listening. Their feelings were of no consequence to him. So far as he was concerned, only the two big powers, Russia and the United States, had to be considered. We were the strongest, therefore we could dictate to the others.

The very idea irritated me. In fact, it made me "sore as a boil." Damn it all, I thought, we hadn't fought the war for this—to act like Napoleon and Tsar Alexander I meeting on a raft at Tilsit and dividing the world between them.

"Nothing doing," I said. "We've got to do this the fair way. Let's march in alphabetical order."

"No, no," Garbatkov shouted.

"All right," I said. "Why don't we all draw lots to see who marches first."

Garbatkov's face turned a violent red. "I won't have it," he yelled. "It's got to be the Red Army or the Americans. No one else."

There was no budging him. And there was no budging me either.

Finally Garbatkov played his trump card. As though the mere mention of it would frighten me, he said, "We must go and see the marshal."

He meant Marshal Georgi K. Zhukov, the renowned Russian general who had commanded the Red armies which captured Berlin and who'd been appointed Military Governor of the Soviet Zone of Occupied Germany.

Out the four of us trooped, got into our respective cars, and drove to Marshal Zhukov's imposing headquarters in Potsdam. We were taken directly to him. This time, the vodka and caviar that the Russians usually plied us with were missing. The marshal sat us down about a bare coffee table and started in.

"What's the trouble?" he said.

Garbatkov told him.

Zhukov scarcely waited for him to finish. Completely ignoring the British and French representatives, he turned toward me and said:

"Garbatkov is right. This is something for the Russians and the Americans to decide between us."

I objected.

"We Americans don't do things that way."

Zhukov sat up stiffly. His eyes narrowed. "Young man, you're forgetting something," he said. "You're forgetting who captured Berlin. The Red Army captured it, and we did it all by ourselves, without any assistance from anyone."

That burned the dickens out of me. I knew how much the Russians had done to help defeat Hitler. How they'd struggled all those bloody miles from Stalingrad to Berlin. But I also knew what the Western Allies had done. How we'd battled the Nazis in Africa, Sicily, Italy, France, Belgium, Holland, and Germany. I remembered how hard my own beloved 82nd Division had fought against the Nazis. It alone had suffered almost ten thousand casualties.

I thought of all the British, French, and American dead and I couldn't contain myself. I stared straight at Marshal Zhukov and I said, "When you talk about who did the most to lick the Germans, I look in back of me and I see a long line of white crosses, down through Italy and into Africa. Don't tell me that you alone captured Berlin."

It was one of the few really successful moments of the war for me, a moment when I was able to act on pure principle. I was fighting for something Americans truly believe in—fair play.

I must say that Marshal Zhukov took my remarks with good grace. They appeared to impress him a good deal. He muttered something about "discussing the matter with higher authority," and let it go at that.

What happened with the parade?

You can be sure of this. All four nations participated in determining the line of march. As I recall it, the Americans marched first, the British second, the French next, and the Russians, they marched last.

CONTROVERSIAL MATERIAL

PATRICK MURPHY MALIN
Executive Director, American Civil Liberties Union

---

*Even in a democracy it can be hazardous to defend the demo-
cratic way of doing things. Undemocratic pressures are always
dangerously present. The question is: Will someone stand up
against them? That is how you assay a democracy's worth.*

*Patrick Murphy Malin has been fighting democracy's battles
for decades—successfully. Descendant of a Quaker family that
landed in America in 1680, he was born in Missouri in 1903,
educated at Pennsylvania and Columbia Universities, and
taught economics at Swarthmore College for thirteen years. Between 1940 and 1947 he was in Europe, helping displaced persons, as vice-director of the Intergovernmental Committee on
Refugees. The D.P.s didn't know him by name; they referred to
him as "the pipe smoker from heaven." In 1950 Malin was designated executive director of the American Civil Liberties
Union, an organization whose mission it is to resist any and all
violations of civil liberties in the United States. With Malin at its
helm, the A.C.L.U. has been doing a magnificent job of it. He
wrote this story.*

SOMETIMES I despair for the good sense of some of the American people. Here we have the finest, freest form of government
on earth, yet too many of us let misguided or vicious people gnaw
away at our civil rights without so much as raising a finger in protest.
It makes me wonder whether we appreciate the worth of democracy;
whether we realize that liberty is an indivisible totality; whether we
are aware that a man who is half free is half a slave.

Invariably, though, someone, someplace, renews my faith by
standing up for democracy regardless of the risk. By declaring his
own personal war against those who would erode liberty.

It renews my faith because . . .

So long as there are men in the United States who are willing to
fight for freedom, our democracy will live on. Freedom cannot die
here so long as there is one American alive who cherishes its flavor
and is ready to do battle to preserve it.

Such a man is a Los Angeles engineer named Fred Buch.

Unlike many of us, Buch chose to be an American of his own volition. As a boy of sixteen in his native Austria, he studied our Constitution and promptly decided to emigrate to the United States. The way he put it was this:

"People are basically good all over the world, but only America created a Bill of Rights which protects the individual from narrowness and despotism."

In 1923 Buch applied for admission to the United States. He expected to get it in a few months. It took sixteen years. Congress had passed a law restricting immigration to a paltry trickle, and he had to wait. He went from country to country—Egypt, Turkey, France—hoping always that one day his U.S. visa would come.

The outbreak of World War II caught Buch in France. Although he had long fought against nazism, he was thrown into a prison camp as an enemy alien. Eventually the French Government agreed to release him if he could find some other country to go to. At that precise moment his U.S. visa finally arrived. But it was a week too late. The French ports were already occupied by the Germans. Buch had to remain in the prison camp—with the Nazis coming close.

He escaped from the camp three steps ahead of the Gestapo. Miraculously, he located his wife and their two infant children, crossed the Spanish border with them on foot, and reached Lisbon. There he learned that his U.S. visa had expired. America was kind, though. It extended the visa, for him and for many others—as I know from personal experience in working on the refugee problem from 1936 to 1947. Late in 1940 Buch and his family got to the country of their choice. The land of the Bill of Rights.

The Buchs found happiness here. He obtained work, set up a nice home, and, as quickly as possible, became a citizen.

Just one thing bothered him. The discovery that Americans tended to take their democracy for granted. They didn't recognize, he felt, that "Liberty is not necessarily a permanent possession. That human rights can be lost as well as gained."

It was different with him. The freedoms guaranteed by the Bill of Rights meant a lot. Each year he and his family actually celebrated the first day of national Bill of Rights Week as a holiday. He made it a point to put up copies of the Constitution and the Bill of Rights wherever he was working.

That's what caused the trouble.

December 1953 saw Buch working as a civil engineer in the Los Angeles office of the California State Division of Architecture. When Bill of Rights Week came around, he quietly pinned copies of the Constitution and the Bill of Rights to the office bulletin board.

They didn't stay there. A higher-up in the office pulled both documents down, and an official order was issued to every employee forbidding the posting of "controversial material" on the office bulletin board.

Buch was appalled. He couldn't believe that the Constitution and the Bill of Rights, the two documents he worshiped, might be regarded as controversial by any American citizen 164 years after their adoption as the guiding principles of this republic. However, the week was at an end, and he decided to wait until the following year to establish once and for all the rightful place of these documents in the public offices of California.

In December 1954 President Eisenhower again proclaimed Bill of Rights Week. Again Buch quietly pinned up copies of the Constitution and the Bill of Rights.

A superior of Buch's spied them there. Furiously he tore them down, ripped them up and tossed them into a wastebasket.

Buch took the matter up with the head of the whole office. It got him nowhere. Neither the Constitution nor the Bill of Rights could be displayed, the head ruled. In his opinion they both were definitely "controversial."

As I said, Buch is the kind of American who will fight for democracy. He appealed the decision to the Governor of California, Goodwin J. Knight.

The Governor was as outraged as Buch. On December 15 he wired back, "Posting of Federal Constitution and Bill of Rights on State office bulletin boards would certainly be in order . . . as a source of inspiration of State employees."

One would think this would have settled the question. It didn't. When Buch showed the Governor's telegram to his chief, he refused to do anything about it.

There is no more space for the Bill of Rights in this office, Buch was bluntly told, than there is for "foreigners who have no understanding of the American way of life."

He was even charged with being a Communist—for no other reason than upholding the Bill of Rights—and threatened with the loss of his Civil Service job.

Fred Buch had a career and a family to think of. He could have given up his crusade and jeopardized his livelihood no more. But the Bill of Rights counted too much to him for that. He carried on his fight.

The Southern California Branch of the American Civil Liberties Union joined in with him, and the case was brought directly to the attention of Anson Boyd, chief of the whole State Division of Architecture.

On December 23, 1954, an order went out from Boyd to the Los Angeles office. It was an order that thrilled Buch and all of us in the A.C.L.U. It directed that the United States Constitution and the Bill of Rights be prominently displayed in the Los Angeles office of the Division of Architecture—not only during Bill of Rights Week but throughout the entire year.

There, framed in glass, it hangs today.

THE PARADE UP MARKET STREET

ROGER LAPHAM

Former Mayor of San Francisco

Be it in one man or a nation, what you hope for most is an understanding heart. San Francisco's former Mayor Roger Lapham is here to say that Americans, as a group, are so blessed.

Lapham is himself a man with a deeply understanding heart. Between 1944 and 1948 he gave San Francisco one of its finest, most sympathetic administrations. Born in New York in 1883, he went into the shipping business soon after he graduated from Harvard. Starting as an agent, he became traffic manager, treasurer, president and chairman of the board of the big American-Hawaiian Steamship Company, in San Francisco. He was a key, calm figure on the waterfront and it was largely through his efforts that the turbulent labor relations in San Francisco's maritime industry were stabilized. In 1941 President Roosevelt appointed him to the National Defense Mediation Board, later to the potent War Labor Board whence he was drafted to run for the mayoralty of the Bay City. In 1948 President Truman chose him for the ticklish job of directing Marshall Plan aid to China, two years later for a similar post in Greece. In both he excelled.

THE Chinese civil war was drawing toward its tragic climax when I got to China in June 1948. Refugees were pouring in on Tsingtao by the hundreds of thousands. I can still see their gaunt, hungry faces. Especially the children's. Theirs were the saddest.

I'd gone out to China to supervise Marshall Plan aid, but there was not much that could be done any more for the Chinese. The situation was too far gone. It was economic chaos, with conditions dreadful in the refugee camps.

We Americans didn't sit back, though. Somehow we managed to distribute at least a bowlful of rice each day to every man, woman and child in each refugee camp.

Never will I forget the look in the eyes of those starving people as they were handed their bowls of rice.

"We owe you our lives," they were wordlessly saying.

Greece was in serious straights, too, when I arrived in Athens in 1950 to head the Marshall Plan Mission there. The destruction wrought by the civil war was enormous. Thousands of homes had been razed to rubble by the Communist guerillas.

We set out to help rebuild those homes.

Never will I forget the gratitude of the Greek people. Peasant women in the small mountain villages clustered around me and kissed my hand. Their cheeks were literally running with tears of thankfulness.

In Greece and China, both, our aid missions were staffed by a group of splendid Americans: top specialists in public health, agriculture, transportation, electric power, labor relations, and a dozen other vital fields. They were a dedicated lot of men. Obstacles meant nothing to them. They devoted their full energies to doing all that was possible, and a lot that seemed impossible, to ameliorate the conditions about them.

A member of the British Embassy in Athens once said to me, "You Americans intrigue us. We've learned from years of experience that some things just can't be done. But, in your innocence, you fellows plunge ahead and do them."

These Marshall Plan men could honestly be described as modern Crusaders. A Greek cabinet minister said as much to me. "The United States," he remarked, "has done a great deal for us. Your aid has rebuilt our roads, erected power plants, factories, and hospitals. It has given us enormous material benefits. But what has impressed me the most is the willingness of the members of your mission to work all hours of the day and night, without any thought to their own interests or comfort.

"The example they have set for us will be remembered long after your material aid has been forgotten."

To work with such men was an inspiration.

Yet, strangely enough, none of these things, or men, gave me my proudest day as an American. That came in my own country. There I saw how understanding and how sympathetic everyday Americans can be.

It was while I was serving as mayor of San Francisco. As part of my official duties, I had to lead a big parade up Market Street to celebrate our California State holiday—Admission Day. General Jonathan Wainwright, the commander of our troops on Corregidor, was to ride with me in an open car as the guest of honor. He'd just been flown in from Tokyo after three years in a Japanese prison camp.

The date was September 9, 1945, less than a month after the surrender of Japan.

I met General Wainwright fifteen minutes before the parade was to start, and talked with him alone. He was pitifully thin and drawn, and, he confessed, in horrible pain from an abscessed tooth which had swollen one side of his face.

He seemed very nervous, and I asked him why.

"All those people out to see me," he said. "Why? What do they want?"

He said it again and again. "All those people out to see me. Why?"

Then he added, "God help me, I'm the general who surrendered the greatest body of U. S. troops in history."

Now I understood. General Wainwright expected to be hissed.

It made me wonder myself what the reaction of the crowds would be. Would they realize that this soldier had to obey the toughest orders any American general has ever received—to surrender? That he'd carried this burden in loneliness for years?

The people of San Francisco realized it. They jammed the streets and cheered the emaciated general to the echo. When we reached the reviewing stand his eyes were filled with tears. So were mine.

THE LEADERS OF AMERICA

A CONFERENCE WITH EISENHOWER

JAMES P. MITCHELL
Secretary of Labor

Here is an untold story about President Dwight D. Eisenhower, by a member of his official family. It affords a rare insight into the man in the White House. And, incidentally, into the thinking of his Secretary of Labor.

Because he'd been a business executive, unionists were bitingly critical when James P. Mitchell was appointed Secretary of Labor in October 1953. Today he is hailed, through the labor movement and beyond, as the best Secretary of Labor the United States has ever had, an unflinching, effective champion of liberalism. The fifty-eight-year-old New Jerseyite drove a truck and ran a store before he got into personnel work with the Western Electric Company. During the war he headed the Army's labor-relations division and was a prime factor in keeping munitions production moving. He also was largely instrumental in keeping the Army from riding roughshod over the workers. After V-J Day he became personnel director of R. H. Macy & Co. in New York, then vice-president in charge of labor relations for Bloomingdale Bros. In April 1953 President Eisenhower designated him as Assistant Secretary of the Army for manpower. Five months later he promoted him to be Secretary of Labor. This is the story Secretary Mitchell told me about a call he made on the President.

No man in the world carries more terrible responsibilities than the President of the United States. You see it when you sit with him at cabinet meetings. Every week crucial questions are brought to him that mean the difference between war or peace, freedom or slavery, wages or bread lines, for hundreds of millions of people. He must decide.

For that reason, most members of the Cabinet hate to bother the President on any matter unless it is of immense, immediate urgency. He has so much on his mind.

I worried about this as I was flying to Denver on a September day in 1955. I had requested an appointment with President Eisenhower at the Summer White House and it had been granted. But now I wondered. Was my problem big enough? At a time of great international tension would Mr. Eisenhower even be interested?

So far as I was concerned the problem was vital. I felt that the happiness and productivity of large numbers of people were at stake. Would the President think so?

"What brings you out here, Jim?" the President said when I was led into his office.

"Old people," I declared.

"What about them?" he asked.

I told him that hundreds of thousands of men and women were being denied jobs simply because they'd passed the age of forty-five. These older people were fully able to work. Often they could handle a job better than younger persons. But some employers were reluctant to hire them. I'd been getting letters like this one: "I'm strong, I'm healthy, and I'm experienced but I can't get a job because I'm over forty-five."

And like this, from a woman of fifty-three: "Employment managers won't talk to me. I'm too young to draw a pension, and evidently too old to work. What am I supposed to do? Starve?"

And this, from a man of sixty-one: "The government ought to organize a firing squad to get rid of all of us 'old' folks."

The President could hardly contain himself. "If this keeps up, Jim," he exploded, "we're going to have a revolution of old men and I'm going to be in it."

I pointed out to the President that the situation could get worse. Much worse. That our population was growing steadily older. That where the average life span was forty-seven at the beginning of the century, it was sixty-nine today. That by 1975 half of the adults in this country would be forty-five and older. That there could be widespread unemployment and distress.

"We've got to do something about this right now," the President exclaimed. "We can't afford to squander our manpower just because of senseless prejudice."

In powerful terms he directed me to throw the entire force of the United States Government behind a drive to awaken employers to the worth of older workers.

People are the most important thing in a democracy, he said.

My appointment was to have been for fifteen minutes. It stretched to an hour and a half. It didn't matter to the President that other callers were waiting. The welfare of America's older people meant most.

Flying back to Washington, I thought again and again of what the President had said to me.

I liked hearing that in a democracy people are the most important thing.

TRUMAN AND THE H-BOMB

CHET HOLIFIELD

Congressman from California

This is the real story of why the United States has thermo-nuclear weapons in its arsenals today.

Representative Chet Holifield, who wrote it, is one of the leading authorities in Congress on atomic energy, and by far its greatest and most conscientious expert on civil defense. Fifty-three years old now, Holifield was born in Kentucky and brought up in Arkansas. He hadn't enough money to finish high school so he went to work in a tailor shop. That led him to start his own firm for manufacturing and selling men's clothes. It has been very successful.

A New Deal Democrat, Holifield was elected to Congress from California in 1942, and he has since been consistently returned. His record has been one of steady liberalism. During recent years he has made nationwide headlines by his investigations into the dangers of radioactive fallout and the lack of civil defense countermeasures.

MEN in public office are sometimes faced with momentous decisions on the basis of incomplete evidence. It can be a torturous dilemma for them. If they wait for more information, it may jeopardize the safety of the nation.

A few years ago I had a hand in such a decision. It was a soul-racking experience.

In July 1946 I was one of the two members of the House of Representatives designated by Speaker Sam Rayburn to serve on the President's Atomic Bomb Evaluation Commission. In that capacity I witnessed the atomic-bomb tests at Bikini. Shortly afterward I was appointed to the Joint Committee on Atomic Energy that had been set up by Congress to keep a watchful eye on the operations of the Atomic Energy Commission.

Few committees have ever had such critical matters to weigh. There were vital defense policies to be fixed, bitter scientific controversies to be adjudicated, serious moral issues to be resolved.

The atomic bomb that fell on Hiroshima had ushered in a new and terrible phase of warfare. True, the United States had a monopoly on the A-bomb, but no one knew how long it would last. We were, therefore, confronted with a crucial question.

Should the United States try to develop a still deadlier weapon than the A-bomb?

The distinguished nuclear physicist Dr. Edward Teller and a few other scientists maintained to the committee that it could be done. They claimed that fusion of the light elements of hydrogen would cause an explosion ten thousand times greater than that produced by the splitting of the atom. They said it could give us a weapon so powerful that the bombs which destroyed Hiroshima and Nagasaki would seem like peashooters by comparison.

Fervently Teller and his group urged that the government try to develop such a weapon. If we didn't do it first, they warned, the Russians might.

Teller's group was in a minority, though. Most leading scientists were violently opposed to his thinking. Attempting to build an H-bomb, they argued, would be throwing hundreds of millions of taxpayers' dollars down the drain.

As if this weren't enough, it was held by many in high places in the government that it would be an indecent, dreadful act to build so horrible a weapon.

Then the U.S.S.R. shattered our complacent notions of an American monopoly of the atomic bomb. In September 1949 it exploded an atomic bomb of its own. I can tell you that the news came as a real shock both to our scientists and our military leaders. They never thought the Russians could overcome our atomic lead in so short a period.

Would the Soviet Union now go on and try to build the H-bomb? That was the one thought in the mind of every man on our committee.

The same thought was in Dr. Teller's mind. Urgently he renewed his pleas that an all-out drive be undertaken to determine the feasibility of the hydrogen weapon.

But the Atomic Energy Commission still said no. A majority of its five members was dead set against it. So was a majority of its top-level Scientific Advisory Panel.

They had new arguments. They said that we couldn't afford the precious uranium that would be required for an effort to trigger a hydrogen bomb. In case of war we might need that uranium badly for regular A-bombs.

Whom to believe? What to do when the future of the country might be hanging in the balance?

The late Senator Brian McMahon, then chairman of the Joint Committee on Atomic Energy, was a man of intense patriotism and conscience. He decided that the hydrogen enigma had to be probed further. On his own volition he appointed a special subcommittee of five senators and representatives to visit the nation's atomic plants and interview key scientists. The mission of the subcommittee was to evaluate the possibility of developing a hydrogen weapon.

It was a hard, baffling assignment that this committee, of which I was named chairman, had. Everywhere we went we heard conflicting testimony. No one—except Dr. Teller and his group—had any sure hopes of success.

Late in December 1950 we reported our findings back to the full committee. Our conclusion: the national security demanded a crash program of scientific exploration into the hydrogen-weapon field.

Many long nights of soul-searching went into that decision. We clearly recognized the risks. We knew that almost insuperable problems had to be solved before an H-bomb could be perfected. We were fully aware of the great moral quandaries posed by a search for the near-ultimate in destructive power.

Yet we were convinced that the effort had to be made. If Dr. Teller's ideas could be translated into reality, the new weapon would re-establish American supremacy in the arms race with Communist Russia. And evil as the weapon might be, we couldn't permit the Reds to get it first. Unlike us, they would have no compunctions about using it.

If the Teller ideas didn't work out, at least the haunting fear of Soviet discoveries in this area could be ruled out and our scientific resources could be turned to other channels.

The full committee endorsed our report, and we took it to the White House. The final decision wasn't ours, of course. It was up to President Harry S. Truman. His was the end responsibility for the defenses of the United States. It was he whom history would judge.

The situation that man was in! There, on the one side, was the Atomic Energy Commission with its big-name scientists adamant against the H-bomb. A billion-dollar bet, they called it, with the odds completely in the wrong direction. There, on the other side, were we, persuaded that an H-bomb was possible but having to admit that the evidence was far from certain. In the background was a loud public outcry against the whole project on moral grounds.

Carefully, quietly, the President heard us out. "I'll let you know my decision in a few days," he said.

They were tense days, very tense days, as we waited for the White House word.

Early in the New Year it came. Senator McMahon got hold of me. "The President just phoned," he excitedly reported. "He's decided to take a chance and go ahead."

I didn't know whether to cheer or to weep.

A day arrived in November 1952 when our hopes as well as our fears were realized. A hydrogen bomb *was* possible. Full-scale tests in the Marshall Islands of a device that pointed the way to the hydrogen bomb were successfully completed.

I received the news with mixed emotions. It was a source of satisfaction that our huge gamble of scientific effort and scarce nuclear materials, not to mention hundreds of millions of tax dollars, had paid off. It was tragic to think that the destructive force of weapons had reached a stage where a single bomb could release more explosive energy than all the bombs dropped in World War II put together; where one bomb could virtually wipe out a city of a million people in a matter of moments; where clouds of radiation would be released that would linger in the atmosphere for twenty years and rain a new kind of death upon all exposed to it.

But it was fortunate that we had it. In August 1953, somewhere behind the Ural Mountains, the Soviets exploded a hydrogen device too—merely nine months behind us.

Despite the misgivings I had when I heard the A.E.C.'s report of the Soviet explosion, I was most proud and thankful that day: for the wisdom of Senator McMahon; for the genius and the persistence of Dr. Teller; for the courage and foresight of the members of the Joint Committee on Atomic Energy on which I was privileged to serve; for the dedicated effort of all the scientists, engineers, and administrators who labored night and day to achieve success; and, over all, for the calm determination and right decision of President Truman, who set into motion the whole vast project.

Had America failed to explore the hydrogen-weapon potential, the Soviets would have bested us. We and the whole world might be on our knees before them today.

F.D.R. SPEAKS FOR FREEDOM

EDWARD TELLER
Nuclear Physicist

To be great, a leader must have wisdom. He must have vision. He must be understanding. Franklin D. Roosevelt was well endowed with these qualities.

Edward Teller, who ranks among the greatest scientists in today's world, has written of Roosevelt's impact upon him. It was an impact that changed history. For Dr. Teller is the man who invented the device which made possible America's hydrogen bomb. Rightly, he is known as "the father of the H-bomb."

From boyhood, this fifty-year-old, Hungarian-born nuclear physicist has been hailed as a bona fide genius. He took his Ph.D. at the University of Leipzig, studied further at Göttingen, came to the United States in 1935 as a physics professor at George Washington University. During World War II he was a key man in the making of the A-bomb at Los Alamos. After World War II he led the campaign to get the United States to build an H-bomb. Now he is director of the Radiation Laboratory of the University of California at Livermore and, deservedly, the most influential scientist in the country.

MAY 10, 1940. That was the black Friday on which the armies of Nazi Germany invaded Holland, Belgium, and Luxembourg. In violation of all international law and morality, Adolf Hitler sent his panzers into the Lowlands, and dispatched his Stukas to bomb their people.

First it had been Austria. Next it had been Czechoslovakia, Poland, Denmark, and Norway. Now, it was the turn of the Dutch, Belgians, and Luxembourgers.

Hour by hour I followed the bulletins that came over the radio. They made me think about the many intelligent, well-meaning people around the United States who still failed to recognize the brutal, expanding power of the Nazi empire. They worried me greatly. Would this country ever awaken to the imminent danger to all free countries?

And I thought of my own peculiar problem as a physicist. I was aware of the possibility of developing an atomic bomb. In fact, I hadn't the slightest doubt that such a weapon could be produced and that the effects would be devastating beyond belief.

Was it right for me to contribute with my work to the ability of man to hurt his fellow men so dreadfully?

At the time, I was in Washington, D.C., teaching physics at the George Washington University. Until the report came that the Nazis were on the march again, I'd planned to spend the evening at home. I had a ticket to hear President Roosevelt address the Eighth Pan-American Scientific Congress, but I wasn't intending to go. I was too busy. Besides, I didn't care much for official functions.

I changed my mind and went. If the President said anything about this latest act of Nazi aggression, I wanted to be there, listening.

I'll always be grateful I went. President Roosevelt did speak out on this score. For the first time he stated with total clarity the position of the United States Government. It was that the Nazi dictatorship menaced the freedom of the entire world.

I still remember his words. They were directed straight at the isolationists whose myopia had alarmed me so.

"A continuance of these processes of arms," he warned, "presents a definite challenge to the continuance of the type of civilization to which all of us . . . have been accustomed.

"We, and most of the people in the world, still believe in a civilization of construction and not of destruction. We, and most of the people in the world, still believe that men and women have an inherent right to hew out the patterns of their individual lives, just so long as they as individuals do not harm their fellow beings. We call this ideal by many terms which are synonymous—we call it individual liberty, we call it civil liberty and, I think, best of all, we call it democracy."

"Here in America," he said, "we permit ourselves by common consent to search for truth, to teach the truth as we see it—and by learning a little here and a little there, and by teaching a little here and a little there, to allow the normal processes of truth to keep growing for the well-being of our fellow men."

It was horribly different in Nazi Germany. "Teachers and scholars are not permitted to search for truth, lest the truth, when made known, might not suit the designs of their masters. Too often they are not allowed to teach the truth as they see it, because truth might make men free.

". . . Can we continue our peaceful construction if all the other continents embrace by preference or compulsion a wholly different principle of life?" he asked.

Then he issued a call to arms. ". . . I am a pacifist. You, my fellow citizens of twenty-one American republics, are pacifists too.

"But I believe that by overwhelming majorities in all the Americas, you and I, in the long run if it be necessary, will act together to protect and defend by every means at our command, our science, our culture, our American freedom and our civilization."

There was more that had to be said, and President Roosevelt said it that evening. He knew he was addressing a Scientific Congress.

"You who are scientists," he said, "may have been told that you are in part responsible for the debacle of today because of the processes of invention for the annihilation of time and of space. . . ."

I had the weirdest feeling as he said this. It was as though the President were talking to me personally. As though he realized my doubts about the atom bomb. I knew he had read a secret letter written to him by Albert Einstein pointing out the enormous, deadly power to be had in an atomic bomb.

". . . I can assure you," he went on, "that it is not the scientists who are responsible, because the objectives which you held have looked toward closer and more peaceful relations between all nations.

"What has come about has been caused solely by those who would use, and are using, the processes that you have made along lines of peace in an entirely different cause . . .

"The great achievements of science and even of art can be used in one way or another, to destroy as well as to create; they are only instruments by which men try to do the things they most want to do. If death is desired, science can do that. If a full, rich, and useful life is sought, science can do that also. Happily for us that question has been solved—for in the New World we live for each other. . . ."

The speech lasted a mere twenty minutes. Yet it managed to change my outlook in an important and permanent fashion. When I left the hall I had a sense of determination and a clear understanding of what I wanted to do. I could in all conscience work on atomic power, trusting that, in American hands, it would be employed both to defend democracy and to enrich it.

I am not conscious of being particularly proud of anything, and on the night of President Roosevelt's address I was not yet an American citizen. I didn't receive my citizenship until a year later.

But on that evening of May 10, 1940, my course was set. I learned that I had come to a country which stood for the freedom of its citizens and for the indivisible freedom of people everywhere.

EXECUTIVE ORDER

WILLIAM H. DAVIS
Former Chairman, War Labor Board

Here is another untold presidential story, this one about Franklin D. Roosevelt, who rescued the United States from its worst depression and led it victoriously through its most terrible war.

Willaim H. Davis was President Roosevelt's chief advisor on labor matters during the war. As chairman of the National War Labor Board, he was responsible for adjudicating labor-management disputes. The fact that there were so comparatively few wartime strikes, and those which did occur were resolved so speedily can be attributed in considerable part to his diplomacy and Yankee common sense. A down-Easter, born in Maine in 1879, Davis—when he is not off settling a strike—is the country's outstanding patent lawyer. He got his legal training at George Washington Law School, worked as a patent examiner for a year, and entered private practice in 1903. He was Deputy Administrator and National Compliance Director of the N.R.A., later chairman of the New York State Mediation Board. In 1941 President Roosevelt named him vice-chairman of the National Defense Mediation Board, soon made him chairman. After Pearl Harbor he gave him the chairmanship of its successor, the War Labor Board. In 1945 Davis was promoted again, to be director of the Office of Economic Stabilization. He told me this story.

LORD ACTON, the great English historian, once wrote a letter to his friend, Bishop Creighton, in which he observed that "Power tends to corrupt and absolute power corrupts absolutely." It is difficult to disagree with him when you look back at the men who have ruled the nations of the world these past few thousand years.

However, there is something about the presidency of the United States which seems to imbue its holders with a sense of democratic proportions. The traditions of the office are such that the men who hold it appear, almost invariably, to become more democratic rather than less.

It is true even in periods of national emergency. We may lend our Presidents immense powers, but it doesn't seem to go to their heads. Few dictators, for example, have exercised the powers of a wartime Abraham Lincoln, Woodrow Wilson, or Franklin D. Roosevelt, yet all three maintained their democratic perspective. No one of them ever advanced any doctrine of presidential infallibility.

Look at F.D.R. A billion people throughout the world acknowledged him as their leader during World War II. But, for all his prestige and influence, he had no delusions of grandeur. He always kept in mind the old American axiom that it is the people, not their leaders, who have the final word.

It showed up on one occasion in front of me, and it impressed me a lot. I don't know when I enjoyed a White House conference so much. Whether former Supreme Court Justice James F. Byrnes had as satisfactory a time, I'm not prepared to say.

This was in the middle years of the war. The one important thing was to turn out the guns, tanks, and planes our Army and Navy had to have to defeat the Axis. Organized labor had, therefore, voluntarily agreed not to strike "for the duration," and management had promised to refrain from lockouts. Our job at the War Labor Board was to help them settle their disputes amicably.

. Since unionists and industrialists are only human, some strikes did occur. It is probably good that they did. In a democracy the right to strike is a precious one which must be invoked from time to time, regardless of cost, or it may die of atrophy.

In this case the United Mine Workers and the operators of the nation's soft-coal mines got into a rugged battle over a new contract. The situation grew bitter, and John L. Lewis, the president of the miners, called his 450,000 members out on strike.

The only means of preventing a crippling shutdown was for the government to take over the soft-coal mines and operate them until the dispute could be resolved. President Roosevelt agreed, so we drafted an Executive Order for his signature, putting Secretary of the Interior Ickes in charge of the mines, and calling on the miners to work for the government.

I went over to the White House with Jim Byrnes to submit the Executive Order to Mr. Roosevelt. At the President's request, Jim had resigned from the Supreme Court to become Director of Economic Stabilization.

Smoking a cigarette through his long holder, the President read through the Executive Order. He took his pen in hand to sign it.

Then he looked up and said, "I wonder if these miners will go back to work when I ask them to."

Jim, who really is a sentimentalist, said, "Why, of course, Mr. President. How can you think otherwise?"

He made quite a speech. "Why, who could doubt it? The President of the United States?"

Mr. Roosevelt, who knew somewhat more about labor relations than Jim Byrnes did, glanced at me and said, "What do you think, Will?"

Being a Yankee, I replied, "Well, I don't know, Mr. President. What do you think?"

"Well," he declared, "I'll tell you. These miners are very thoughtful people. They get down underground there, and they are alone a great deal, and they do a lot of thinking. You know, John thought that they would follow him to the polls in '40, but they didn't, they followed me."

At that point, Byrnes threw out his chest. He was remembering how the miners had voted for Roosevelt in 1940 despite John Lewis' support of Wendell Willkie.

Mr. Roosevelt went on. "But it doesn't follow that they will follow me into the mines. You know, they are pretty smart, and they may think I know more about politics than John does, but they know darned well that John knows more about mines than I do."

With that, he gave us his big, infectious grin, a grin that said wordlessly, "Don't worry. I know my place."

Did he sign the order? Of course. It had to be done. Did the miners go back to work? In their own good time. Not that I, or the President, blamed them too much.

PLANE FLIGHT FROM BOSTON

KATE SMITH

TV and Radio Performer

Important men can be big in many ways. Kate Smith watched one prove it.

Miss Smith is the singer who made Irving Berlin's "God Bless America" virtually a national anthem. A fifty-seven-year-old Virginian, she has been an idol of the air waves for almost three decades. Her first public appearance was at the age of four in a church choir. Since then she has starred on more than 10,000 radio shows, made over 1000 television appearances, and recorded more than 2200 songs. During World War II she sold $500,000,000 worth of war bonds, traveling 52,000 miles in the process at her own expense. When the King and Queen of England visited the United States in 1939 President Roosevelt invited Miss Smith to sing for them at the White House. He introduced her to them in these words. "This is America . . . this is Kate Smith." Here is a story she gave me about another distinguished American.

ONE evening, in the last grim months of World War II, Ted Collins —he's my manager—and I were on a plane bound for New York. We'd been up to Boston, helping out at a war-bond drive.

A chunky young man in civilian clothes was on the plane with us. We noticed him at once. He had such a happy grin. Besides, he had no hands. Just hooks.

When the "No Smoking" sign went off he reached for a package of cigarettes in his breast pocket. He couldn't quite manage it, though. Not with those mechanical "hands."

Across the aisle was a small, white-haired man in his late seventies. He saw the young man fumbling for the cigarettes. Quietly he went over, took the package out of the young man's pocket, removed a cigarette, placed it in his mouth, and lit it.

Beyond a few words of thanks, nothing was said. Obviously the young man didn't know who the elderly man was.

We did.

He was Henry Stimson, the Secretary of War.

It didn't surprise us, though. In America you expect important people to have a heart.

Incidentally, we got to know the young man's name. He was Harold Russell, a paratrooper whose hands were blown off in the war. He was soon to achieve fame and two Academy awards enacting the crippled veteran in the film, *The Best Years of Our Lives*. And later he became National Commander of Amvets. But then he was still an unknown.

MAIDEN SPEECH IN CONGRESS

CLIFFORD P. CASE

United States Senator from New Jersey

Times come in the Congress of the United States when parti-
san politics are forgotten. Senator Clifford P. Case learned that
soon after his arrival "on the hill."

Case, a fifty-four-year-old New Jersey lawyer, is an "Eisen-
hower Republican," noted for his espousal of honest liberalism.
He entered politics in 1937, served in the Rahway, New Jersey,
Common Council for four years, then was elected to the State
Legislature. In 1944 he campaigned successfully for Congress
and, in office, won a fine reputation as an advocate of civil-rights
legislation and an opponent of anti-labor laws. He resigned in
1953 to become president of the Fund for the Republic, but re-
entered the political arena the following year to run for the
Senate on a brave anti-McCarthyism platform. His record as a
senator has been courageous and constructive. He told me this
story.

I T is a tradition in the United States Congress that freshmen congressmen say little. They are supposed to spend their first term
listening. A wise idea this is, for legislating is an art that requires
a thorough apprenticeship.

Still, it sometimes occurs that a new representative cannot stay
silent, though it may mean disregarding congressional custom. An
issue may arise whereon he has to stand up and be counted—aloud.

This happened to Clifford P. Case early in his first term in the
House of Representatives. He learned a great deal that day about
the innate democratic decency of the men and women who make
America's laws.

An anti-poll-tax measure was before the House and Congressman
John E. Rankin of Mississippi got up to speak on it. To Case's amazement, Rankin launched into a wild, vituperative attack on Jews and
Negroes in which he impugned their intelligence, their courage, and
their patriotism.

"Kikes and niggers," he called them.

He went so far as to question the loyalty of Supreme Court Justice
Felix Frankfurter. "The Jewish Justice," he sneered.

To hear such things in the legislative halls of a nation which was
founded on the concept that "all men are created equal" was more
than Case could tolerate. It made him sick to his stomach.

He thought about it a lot that night. He had to go up to New
Jersey for a conference, and throughout the entire trip he couldn't
get Rankin's ranting out of his mind.

The other congressmen who'd been present in the House had
chosen, wisely perhaps, to ignore Rankin. Not Case. Freshman or
not, he decided he had to protest.

On the way back to Washington the next morning he jotted down
a couple of notes on an envelope. When the House reconvened he
acted fast. It is possible under the rules for a congressman to talk
five minutes on an amendment to a pending measure. He moved,
therefore, to strike out a few words of the bill before the House.
The stratagem worked. He got the floor.

A maiden speech in the Congress of the United States is an awesome affair to the man making it. Case's hands were perspiring, his
knees shaking.

"Mr. Chairman," he said, "I am native-born, white, a gentile—a
Protestant. That I am these things entitles me to no special status
or distinction. Indeed, I had no choice as to any of them, except
the last. But because I am these things, and thus a member of the
comfortable majority in this country, I find myself under compelling
obligation to express my disagreement with certain remarks made
yesterday in this chamber by the Gentleman from Mississippi."

Point by point, then, Case answered Rankin's baseless charges
against the Jews and the Negroes.

"No group in this country," he stressed, "has a monopoly on patriotism. Men of all races, colors, and creeds, whether native or foreign-
born have equally sacrificed their lives or given the best years of
their youth in the war. The casualty lists show that."

Case then spoke about Justice Frankfurter. "He is utterly devoted
to our American democratic system and the great principles of liberty,
equality, and justice under law upon which it rests. His devotion,
I suggest, is but the deeper because he springs from a race which
has known little but persecution since its history has been recorded."

"Mr. Chairman," Case closed, "I did not rise in defense of Justice
Frankfurter or of the courage and patriotism of minority groups in

this country. They need no defense by me. I rose because I could not by remaining silent permit any inference that I acquiesced in the sentiments to which I have taken exception. And, more important by far, because of my deep conviction that whenever we of the majority in this country permit such sentiments to go unchallenged, not only are we guilty of a wrong to the minority groups concerned, but we risk the greater danger of brutalizing ourselves."

Apprehensively Case returned to his seat. He'd used strong words. Would his fellow legislators resent them? Would they stand with him, an unknown freshman? Or would they back the veteran Congressman Rankin?

He soon found out.

Congressman after congressman made it a point to come over. There were dozens of them.

"We want you to know we agree with you, not Rankin," they said.

These congressmen were not only members of his Republican Party. They were Democrats, too.

"In something like this, it doesn't matter whether we're Republicans or Democrats," one declared. "We all hate bias."

Case was a happy man when he went home that evening. He knew it for himself. The Congress was in good hands.

And Mr. Rankin? He soon left Congress. Mississippi voters took care of that.

HARDSHIP CASE

IRVING M. IVES

United States Senator from New York

Officials charged with the administration of justice can be vengeful and cruel under the law. Or they can be clement. In America the tradition is toward mercifulness.

United States Senator Irving M. Ives observed this tradition put to the test, and he has written an account of it. Ives is senior senator from New York and a leader among the nation's liberal Republicans. Born in New York in 1896, he was graduated Phi Beta Kappa from Hamilton College (despite time out for rough infantry fighting in France in World War I). After ten years in banking, he switched to politics. For sixteen years he was a member of the New York State Assembly, where he sponsored the first legislation to be enacted by any state prohibiting discrimination in employment because of race, creed, color, national origin, or ancestry. In 1946 he was elected to the U. S. Senate, and returned to it in 1952 with the largest plurality ever received by a candidate for public office in New York State. In the Senate he has been a strong supporter of civil rights, public housing, and immigration reform.

Each week thousands of letters on political issues cascade into a United States Senator's office. Some loudly demand that the senator vote for a piece of pending legislation. Others insist that he vote against it. Some are complimentary, some are vituperative. A wise senator reads all his mail religiously. He has to if he is to stay abreast of the views of his constituents.

Then comes the non-political mail. The letters from people seeking jobs, asking assistance in their dealings with the federal government, pleading for help in their personal lives. Thousands of these pour in, and the wise senator pays close attention to them, too. That's his job as the people's representative in Washington.

I learned of the case I'm going to tell you about through a letter—one of the most moving letters that has ever reached my office. It was written by a married woman in a small rural town near Albany, New York.

"For our children's sake," she wrote, "I beg you, I beg you, I beg you, please do something to help my husband."

There could be no question that her husband needed help. He was a deserter from the U. S. Army.

But did he deserve help from a United States Senator? Does any man who deserts the Army in time of war merit anyone's help?

I looked into the case.

I discovered that the husband was a pleasant, friendly fellow in his early thirties. Not the most intelligent chap in the world, perhaps, but he had his good instincts. Since his real name cannot be used here, I'll refer to him as Edward Gordon.

He was a country boy, I found, with little in the way of education. He quit school after the seventh grade. His widowed mother was a bedridden invalid, and he had to support her. It would have been the poor farm for her, otherwise.

He could only get the kind of jobs open to a boy of his age, carrying newspapers, delivering groceries, and things like that. Still, he and his mother got by. They rented out a room to a lodger and managed to eke out a living. For a while.

In the spring of 1943 the ax fell. Eddie was drafted.

A simple lad, Eddie was unaware of the provisions of the draft law. He had no idea that he could apply for deferment on the grounds of extraordinary hardship. He merely knew that the Army had called.

It worried him sick. Who would take care of his mother?

Luck was with him. So he thought, anyway. He had a reassuring last-minute conversation with the lodger, and the man agreed to tend to the mother in return for free rent.

Eddie, as I said, was not the brightest boy. When he took the Army General Classification Test he was marked at the lowest level of intelligence acceptable. He was a conscientious youth, though. He worked hard at being a good soldier, and his officers liked him.

That autumn he was given his first long furlough. He went home.

It was awful. His mother was in appalling circumstances. The lodger had neglected her completely. Lying in bed, she was desperately ill, uncared for, and in want.

Hysterically, she clung to him. "Eddie, Eddie," she sobbed, "promise you'll never leave me again."

Eddie had no idea of what he ought to do. Almost mechanically he started for camp at the end of his furlough. He got as far as the railroad station.

How could he leave? he asked himself. How could he let his mother die for lack of attention?

He rushed back home.

The next day he wrote a buddy at camp and asked that his belongings be sent to him. It is an amazing fact that nobody at camp interfered with shipping these things to him. Nobody thought it odd. Nobody in the Army came after him.

In the months that followed, Eddie made no effort to hide from the Army. He stayed in the same town, dwelled in the same house, carried on as he had before. He behaved as if he were doing the right thing—the only possible thing.

No one questioned him about it. No one bothered him at all. For years.

The boy supported his mother faithfully up to her death. And he was as good to his wife, after he married, as he'd been to his mother. They lived a quiet, happy life. They didn't have much money, but they had two fine children, blond and blue-eyed like him, whom he adored.

Eddie forgot all about the Army—until a day in 1955. Then two quiet-spoken men in civilian clothes walked into his home. FBI agents.

"You're under arrest," they said.

They took him away to an army stockade, stunned and confused. His family was left behind, miserable—and with no means of support.

Four months later he faced a general court-martial. It found him guilty as charged and it sentenced him to fifteen years' imprisonment at hard labor.

That was when his wife, Beatrice, wrote me. She was desperate. I could see the smudges her tears had left on the cheap scratch paper.

"As God is my judge," she wrote, "Eddie didn't know he was doing wrong when he done what he did. He never would have done it if he knew it was wrong. Not him.

"My Eddie is a good man. I swear it to you. All his life he's tried to do the right thing. Always. There ain't no better, sweeter husband and father. Anywhere. I love him very much and he loves me. Please, please, don't let them take him from us. My kids are crying for their daddy. Me, I'm crying, too."

What was I to do about it?

The Army, and all forms of government, must have certain rules and regulations, and there must be punishment for those who disregard such rules. Our entire democracy would fall apart if this weren't so.

Yet, were these rules made to punish a man like this? After all, he never should have been drafted in the first place. Suppose it were put to a vote. How would the people of the United States vote on the question: should Eddie Gordon be sent to prison for fifteen years or should he be returned to his wife and children?

For hours I thought about it. Finally I made up my mind. I picked up the phone and called a high official of the Department of the Army.

I told him the facts as I knew them. Then I pleaded for mercy for Eddie Gordon.

"I realize Gordon's guilty of a serious crime," I declared, "but fifteen years is an awfully long time."

The army official said he would look into the case at once. There was a phone call from him that afternoon.

"I was too late, Senator," he said. "Gordon's case has already been reviewed. A decision was reached on it yesterday."

"And——?" I anxiously asked.

"The Judge Advocate General recommended that, in view of the extenuating circumstances, Gordon's sentence be reduced to four months. Since he's already served that, he's on his way home right now."

Now this I know as I contemplate the case: ours is not a vindictive nation. We do not seek the destruction of those who make missteps; we seek their redemption. When a case arises in which justice lies in kindliness rather than severity, we Americans are not afraid to be kind. Our government exists to promote the welfare of its citizens, not to dominate them.

POLITICS, FLORIDA STYLE

ELMO ROPER
Public-Opinion Analyst

Although some politicians regard integrity as an expensive luxury, it is indulged in more widely than you'd expect.

Elmo Roper had his eye on an example of this, and he told me about it. A fifty-eight-year-old Nebraskan, Roper has been polling public opinion with startling accuracy for twenty-five years. Educated at the University of Nebraska and the University of Edinburgh, he passed twelve years in the jewelry field and then went into marketing research. Later he broadened his polls to cover the public's views on politics, labor problems, and foreign affairs. Today the Roper poll is an institution. During the war Roper served as a deputy director of the Office of Strategic Services and as a consultant to the Armed Forces. He writes extensively for magazines, does a widely read newspaper column, and is active in many democracy-minded organizations like the Fund for the Republic.

THE more I survey public opinion in these United States, the more convinced I become that—given the facts—the American people can be depended upon to make the right choices. On issues and on men.

Take the case of John B. Orr, the representative from Dade County in the Florida State Legislature. Not so long ago the political dopesters thought this thirty-seven-year-old war veteran was through in Southern politics.

"He won't get enough votes at the next election," they said, "to serve as pallbearers at his political funeral."

They claimed that he'd deliberately committed political suicide, but they were wrong.

A native of Florida, Jack Orr is a practicing attorney in Miami. In 1954 he was elected to a first term in the Legislature and very quickly won the regard of his fellow representatives by his keen, conscienceful views on social questions, as well as by his courteous, soft-spoken manner. A fighter he was, but never a rabble-rouser. Observers predicted a fine future for him in politics.

Then the desegregation battle came to a boil.

Florida was not as bitter as some of the other Southern states when the U. S. Supreme Court first handed down its epochal decision in 1954 against separate schools for Negro and white children. Local officials spoke of "going along" with the high court ruling. They conceded that, in the long run, integration was inevitable.

Unfortunately this reasonableness didn't last. The prejudice that spewed up in Alabama, Mississippi, and Georgia seeped down into Florida as in those states the die-hard extremists stepped into a leadership vacuum. Before long, "segregation" became a rallying cry, and "integration" a dirty word.

Feelings ran so high that a special session of the Legislature was convened in Tallahassee in July 1956 just to circumvent the Supreme Court decision and preserve segregation in the state's schools.

This put Representative Orr right on the spot. Like most liberal thinkers, he was opposed to segregation. Still, to vote his convictions publicly was to invite disaster at the polls.

One by one, the votes were recorded in the Florida House of Representatives on the resolution to maintain segregation in defiance of the Supreme Court. Man after man said "Aye." When it came Orr's turn to vote, he said, "Nay."

The final tally was eighty-nine for segregation to one against.

From all over the state denunciatory telegrams and letters poured in on Orr. A woman wrote him that desegregation is anti-Christ. Another sneered, "Almighty God is laughing at these silly people who try to upset natural laws for human beings." He was informed that the "good, old Southern Negroes" want segregation.

His telephone rang with abuse. "Traitor!" some called him. And "Public Enemy Number One."

"We hope the Ku Klux Klan will take care of your situation," a person said.

One anonymous caller threatened, "You and your family leave town within two hours, or . . ."

Heartsick, Orr resolved to take his case to the people. With elections only three months off, he decided to do something no other office seeker in Florida had dared—to talk out boldly on the segregation issue.

He went from group to group, talking candidly, understandably, and without heat to anyone who would listen. He told them what he had said in the Legislature itself.

"I believe segregation is morally wrong. . . . The existence of second-class citizens is repugnant to our great democratic principles. . . . Each time that we do not practice what our officials preach, the Communists score a propaganda victory. . . . For us to set an example of hypocrisy and deceit—of disregard for our laws—will surely do more harm to our children than will result from their being seated in a classroom next to one whose skin is of a different hue. . . ."

The political experts begged him not to talk so openly. He wouldn't heed them.

"I believe," he told people, "that . . . had we devoted as much energy, time, and talent to discovering means to live within the law instead of in defiance of it, we could have found a way. . . .

"Perhaps the most dangerous by-product of our activity . . . is the attitude of disrespect for our laws and the principles of common decency that is developing. To defy the highest court in our land is unthinkable to me. . . .

"I hope that God gives us the wisdom and strength to conquer prejudice and bigotry and to renew our faith in our Constitution."

The political experts said, "This is the end of Jack Orr in politics."

However, they didn't realize the innate decency and intelligence of the citizens of Dade County. On November 6, 1956, these citizens of Dade County streamed to the polls and re-elected Jack Orr by a 27,000-vote majority.

It was the biggest news of the year to me when I heard of it. It demonstrated once again that in the United States a politician does not have to remain silent on an issue of civil rights despite overwhelming opposition; that he can break with prevailing public opinion and still earn the respect and votes of his constituents; that he can hold true to his beliefs regardless of the political risks. In this time of social and political crisis it was convincing proof that the American people do hold freedom of speech and discussion dear; that they do want honesty and sincerity in their elected representatives.

It renewed my hope for democracy.

THE REAL LEADERS

RICHARD L. NEUBERGER
United States Senator from Oregon

The real leaders of the United States are, of course, the voters. They have the ultimate say at the polls. There are those who claim that this is a poor system. That our voters think only of themselves, not of their country or the world beyond. United States Senator Richard L. Neuberger has seen differently.

The junior senator from Oregon is a battling, liberal Democrat. Born in Portland forty-five years ago, he became a newspaperman after he graduated from the University of Oregon. Later he got to be one of the country's best, most prolific magazine writers. From his student days on, he was active in state and national politics, and in 1940 he ran successfully for the Oregon House of Representatives. Then came election and re-election to the State Senate (while his wife, Maurine, was winning election to the lower house of the Legislature). In 1954 he did the "politically impossible." He won election to the U. S. Senate, the first Democrat chosen for that post in Oregon in forty years. As a senator, he has been a crusader for civil rights, public power, and, foremost, international co-operation. Here is his own report on John Doe, Voter.

ON all four major Senate roll calls involving tariff and import duties during the 1955 session of Congress I had supported the recommendations of the President of the United States, Dwight D. Eisenhower. This meant voting to extend the reciprocal-trade treaties, drafted to stimulate commerce between our own country and friendly nations. Now I was going home to Oregon to report. If every bit of visible evidence could be believed, I was in for a bristling reception.

The mail cascading into my Senate office had run five to one against the trade bill. Delegations from Oregon had importuned me to cast a *nay* vote; none had appeared on the other side. Hundreds of members of trade unions insisted in letters and telegrams that continuation of reciprocal trade would cost them their jobs. Even though the trade bill was sponsored by a popular Republican President, the Republican-dominated Legislature of Oregon overwhelmingly passed a resolution urging its defeat.

I would be less than honest if I boasted of having cast my vote in favor of the trade treaties without some feelings of political trepidation. After all, how defiantly could a new senator challenge prevailing sentiment in his home state?

I suppose a major factor in my decision was a phone call to my wife in far-off Salem, the capital of Oregon, where she was serving in the Legislature. We had discussed the Legislature's resolution denouncing the trade program. She had been one of the few members to speak against it on the floor.

"People are really stirred up," Maurine told me. "Cherry growers think their markets are going to be flooded with Italian cherries. Plywood manufacturers are afraid of Canadian plywood. Fishermen claim they can't compete with tuna from Japan."

"But under the old high tariffs industry and agriculture just dried up," I reminded her.

"Of course," she answered.

"Well, what do we do?" I asked.

My wife's reply was reassuring. "Vote your conscience," she said. And I did.

But what could I say to the constituents who had made me Oregon's first Democratic senator in forty years?

What was there to say except the truth? I had to tell Oregon fishermen, orchardists, and lumbermen that, in the interests of the free world and the preservation of international friendship, they might have to tolerate some foreign competition with their own products. But did this not mock at every notion about the selfishness of the average American voter? What would he care about strengthening our allies if it was at the possible expense of his own pocketbook?

I began to tour the state. Deliberately I visited the areas where people were most disturbed over my vote on the trade treaties. If I avoided these areas, rumors would merely increase and multiply. I talked as earnestly as I could with fruit growers, lumberjacks, and businessmen on Main Street in nearby towns. I conceded that extension of reciprocal trade might result in lowering import duties on certain goods which they considered as rivals for their markets. Yet, I asked, what alternative faced the United States if it was to be tied by bonds of commerce with the rest of the free nations?

One episode of this journey around the state where I was born and raised I shall never forget.

It occurred in the council room of the Lincoln County courthouse in the seacoast community of Newport, where I was meeting with a band of men who made their living from the ocean. They were fishermen. Many of them had boats not yet paid for. All had families to support. They advised me in stern and belligerent tones that they could not set down their tuna, salmon, and crab on the wharves as cheaply as such catches could be imported from Japan—unless duties on Japanese fish products were sent soaring. Yet I had worked to keep off the tariff on fresh Japanese tuna! What kind of an Oregon senator was I?

I glanced around at the hostile faces, which were weathered by the spray and the sun and the sleet. I talked for my political life, literally.

I told them things they'd never been told before. I said that we had four choices as far as Japan was concerned: (1) We could let Japan trade with us. (2) We could sustain Japan with doles out of the U. S. Treasury. (3) We could let Japan starve on its cramped little islands. (4) We could look the other way while Japan traded with Red China, thus allowing Japanese industrial skill to be consolidated with the immense resources of the Chinese Communists.

I said I had favored the first course because it seemed the only reasonable choice. I made no effort to hide the fact that some families in our state might have to make sacrifices. I reminded them of the sacrifices that other Americans had made in different circumstances to advance the best interests of their country. I conceded that it was easier to be unselfish amidst the shot and shell and glory of the battlefield than when trying to balance one's own financial ledger. But enlightened world leadership often demanded idealism under many conditions.

I stopped talking. There was silence for a moment. Uneasily I looked out the windows to the blue surface of Yaquima Bay, and to the Pacific, tossing angrily beyond the bar.

Finally a horny-handed fisherman with steel-rimmed spectacles stood up. "My boat has got a mortgage on it," he said, "but I'm not going to pay it off at the expense of the U.S.A. I'm glad now that you voted the way you did."

The others nodded in grave and solemn assent. Their hostile faces softened.

All at once I realized that these men, many of them in hard and perhaps desperate straits financially, were willing to put their personal welfare second and that of the United States first. The so-called greed and selfishness of the American voter, at least as demonstrated here in this county courthouse meeting room, amounted to only a myth and nothing more.

My eyes misted as I drove up the timbered seacoast in the direction of the majestic headlands where Lewis and Clark had brought our flag to the shores of the Western ocean. I thought that every example of gallantry in our country's chronicles had not occurred along the frontiersmen's rugged path or on the field of battle. In my history book these Oregon fishermen also qualified as American heroes.

AMERICANS AT WAR

SALUTE TO AN ENSIGN

ADMIRAL ARLEIGH A. BURKE
Chief of Naval Operations, United States Navy

---

*Admiral Arleigh A. Burke, Chief of Naval Operations of the
United States Navy, is a good man to listen to on the subject
of heroism. He has seen more action than almost any sailor
afloat. His very nickname, "Thirty-One-Knot Burke," is a by-
word for courage in the Navy. He earned it by the way he raced
to battle on a November morning in 1943 when he heard that
the Japanese were evacuating their forces from Buka Island.
"Stand aside!" he radioed a covey of liberty ships in his path,
"I'm coming through at thirty-one knots." And he did. He
got his destroyer squadron to Buka in time to sink three
crowded enemy destroyers transporting key technical personnel. His men still tell of the "order of the day" he issued before they went into combat: "Hold your hats, boys. Here we go
again."*

*In May 1955 President Eisenhower promoted this brilliant,
fifty-four-year-old Coloradoan to be C.N.O. over the heads of
ninety-three senior admirals. He told me about the bravest
naval officer he ever encountered.*

SOME days in battle are so vivid when you think back to them
that you can see the faces of the men who were alongside you.
You can remember to the last detail what they said and how they
looked—living, or lying dead in blotches of their own blood. There
was a day like that during the fight for Okinawa in World War II.

It was vital to our plans for the defeat of Japan that we capture
Okinawa. We had to have it as a base for bombing the Japanese
main islands. More than that, we needed it as a staging area in
the event a land invasion of Japan proved necessary. The Japanese
knew this and they put up a fanatical resistance. You could see in
their stand the death throes of the Japanese empire. Like all such,
they were violent.

We threw everything we had into the attack—180,000 of our best
men, backed by a fleet of 1300 ships. At first it went fairly easily.

Our troops carved out a beachhead and began to drive inland. But the Japanese quickly stiffened. They forced us to pay in corpses for every inch. Night and day, it was hell for the G.I.s and Marines.

The Japanese increased the tempo of their air attacks against our troops ashore—and against the transports and supply ships furnishing the reinforcements, ammunition, and supplies needed by these troops. Enemy planes came by the hundreds. Our losses were mounting and something had to be done—we had to stop those enemy planes before they reached Okinawa.

Picket ships—lone destroyers—were stationed far to the north of Okinawa. These vigilant ships kept radar watch for oncoming enemy planes and, as these planes were detected, vectored Navy fighters from our carriers to intercept and destroy them.

It didn't take the Japanese long to realize that these picket ships were responsible for the heavy losses of Japanese aircraft before they reached their targets—and it didn't take them long to concentrate their attacks on these gallant little ships.

They launched their suicide fliers, the Kamikaze. These sacrificial airmen made human torpedoes of themselves, deliberately driving their bomb-heavy planes right into our picket ships. The toll was terrific. Our pickets took a frightful mauling.

Station No. 1, at the northernmost point on the direct air lane between Japan and Okinawa, was the hottest. Here we had seven destroyers sunk in seven successive days.

On the eighth day we sent another destroyer up there. There was no hesitation by the captain or the crew when they got the assignment. They knew the risks but they gave a cheery "Aye, aye" and set out.

At eleven o'clock that morning I was in the Combat Information Center of my flagship. Suddenly, through some freak of communications, I overheard a radio message from the destroyer at Station No. 1, about one hundred miles away. The destroyer was reporting in, and the report went like this.

"I am an ensign. I am the only officer left alive aboard this ship. The Japanese have hit us hard. All our forward guns have been knocked out. The bridge has been destroyed, and the captain and all the other officers killed. We are afire aft. Now the enemy aircraft are preparing to attack again. I will fight this ship as long as she floats. I am new. Please forgive me the mistakes I am about to make."

I never found out who he was. His destroyer was sunk in the next attack. But I'll always remember him. It is men like this who made it possible for us to take Okinawa and win the war. It is men with his supreme devotion to duty who have written the heritage of our country. I'm proud to have served in the same navy with this ensign.

THE "BATS" OFF GILBERT ISLANDS

ADMIRAL ARTHUR W. RADFORD
Former Chairman, Joint Chiefs of Staff

For four taut years Admiral Arthur W. Radford held the hottest military spot in the world. It was up to him, as chairman of the Joint Chiefs of Staff, to keep our Armed Forces so strong and so ready that the Soviet Union would not dare aggression. In this he succeeded.

Chicago-born in 1896, Radford graduated from the United States Naval Academy in 1916, did battleship duty in World War I, qualified as one of the Navy's first aviators in 1920. In World War II he commanded a task force in the Pacific and won a reputation as a brilliant strategist. In the Korean War he was commander in chief of the Pacific Fleet. Despite his independence of thought, or because of it, Radford was President Eisenhower's immediate choice for chairman of the Joint Chiefs of Staff, the nation's loftiest military post, in 1953. He retired last year after forty-one years of service. Here is the story, as he related it to me, of the navy pilot whose memory he reveres the most.

Lieutenant Commander Edward H. O'Hare was the first Navy pilot to win the Medal of Honor in World War II.

A good-looking, laughing Irishman from St. Louis, Butch O'Hare earned his Medal of Honor in a few brief minutes on February 20, 1942. He was serving aboard the aircraft carrier U.S.S. *Lexington* in a task force operating off New Guinea.

At 1542 hours the *Lexington's* radar spotted a flock of "bandits" approaching fast from the west. Up went the "*Lady Lex's*" pilots to meet them. It was Butch's first flight from the "*Lady*."

As luck would have it, Butch's wingman had to pull out of the scrap; the guns on his plane jammed. Butch was alone against nine enemy planes.

I have before me the official U. S. Navy "battle report" on the action. This is what it says:

"As the enemy flight approached in a broad 'V' formation, O'Hare shot past them out of range, pivoted on a wing tip, and came blazing from the rear to blast the starboard motors out of the last two planes on the enemy's right flank. He ducked under the formation and came up striking at the third plane in the formation. It staggered and fell out. Two more bombers began to smoke, to shed bits of wing covering and to wallow. The enemy's formation was shattered. . . .

". . . Four [others] of the bombers . . . wheeled and were caught in the path of O'Hare's fighter. His control was magnificent, his timing perfect, as he lifted, swooped, darted, and struck like a rapacious eagle. One of the two-engined planes spiraled seaward, then another and still a third. Butch O'Hare had been in action just four minutes—five Jap bombers crashed and three others hit!"

The citation for Butch's Medal of Honor termed this, "One of the most daring, if not the most daring single action in the history of combat aviation."

It was.

Yet I think Butch should have gotten a Medal of Honor for something else. I saw him do something even more heroic.

The greatest hero is not necessarily the man inflamed in the heat of conflict and carried above himself by the dramatic exigencies of the battle. To my mind, it requires much greater courage to undertake dangerous duties when you have an opportunity first to weigh coolly the odds against you, to think of all the things and people you may be giving up, to face your fears and consciously to rise above them.

Butch O'Hare did just this—right in front of me.

It was twenty-one months later. In those months Butch had had some home leave and had been married to a lovely girl. When he came back to the war in the Pacific he had a lot more to live for.

Butch was assigned to the carrier U.S.S. *Yorktown*, the flagship of my task force. We were operating off the Gilbert Islands. Night after night Japanese ships were sending intruder planes out to torment us. We couldn't shoot them down initially as our carrier planes weren't equipped for night fighting.

We had to devise some means to cut the toll, so we organized special night-flying teams, each consisting of two fighters and a TBF torpedo-bomber outfitted with its own radar. Each team was to fight as a unit, with the TBF guiding its companion fighters in through the darkness against the Jap intruders. We dubbed them the "Bats."

This was a new kind of fighting, and of flying, for carrier pilots. Ordinarily we would have spent months training our men in its complex, hazardous techniques. But we didn't have months. Not a single month. Not with the Japs after us.

Butch O'Hare was put in command of the "Bats" team, and he went to work to train his men as best he could in as short a time as he could. We were hoping that he could do it within a couple of weeks.

On the night of November 25, 1943, the Japs came at us in strength. We had to sit and bear it.

On the night of November 26 they came again. It was very late in the afternoon—twilight—when our radar first picked them up. Close to forty Japanese planes were heading in on us. The men seemed to sense that was to be another night of harassment. Some of them probably even wondered if there wouldn't be some major damage done to one or more of the ships.

Butch was wondering about that, too. He mounted to the flag bridge and requested permission to lead his half-trained, untried "Bats" team against the Japs that night.

He recognized the odds: three against forty. And he knew that his team had only had three nights' practice so far. He insisted on going up, nonetheless.

"You don't have to do it, Butch," I said. "I know you're not ready."

"I've thought it all over, sir, and I'd like to give it a try," he calmly declared. "I'm sure we can do *some* good."

The lives of twenty-eight ships and thousands of American sailors weighed heavily in a commander's mind. "Permission granted," I stated.

At 1800 they took off. O'Hare was catapulted first in his Hellcat. Next went his wingman, Lieutenant Andy Skon. Lieutenant Commander John L. Phillips and his crew followed them up in the TBF Avenger. It was just turning dark.

Over the squawk box came the reports from the Yorktown's Combat Information Center:

"A large group of bogies on our port. Thirty miles. Closing fast. Now at seventeen miles and breaking into smaller groups. Now fanning out. Closing fast."

The Japs had a devilishly shrewd tactical plan. They would split their planes into two sections and strike at us at a forty-five-degree angle from both sides simultaneously. This meant that in taking evasive action, the task force couldn't turn from one attacking element without getting broadside to the other. No matter which way we veered we could be vulnerable to strikes by enemy torpedoes.

It was different this night, though.

The Japs didn't figure on the "Bats." Before they knew it, O'Hare and his boys were inside their formation. We heard the reports on the squawk box:

"O'Hare and Skon are closing on a bogie. Phillips reports he just shot down a Betty." Then: "Lieutenant Commander O'Hare has shot down a bomber. Lieutenant Commander Phillips has shot down his second bomber." Off in the distance we could see the burning Jap planes plunge into the sea.

Those Japanese pilots didn't know what had hit them. We heard them jabbering excitedly over their radios, asking what was happening. They were so confused that they even began firing at one another. The whole attack was thrown completely out of kilter. Try as he did, the Japanese commander could not get his formations co-ordinated again.

A couple of Jap planes did reach my task group. The skies burst into white light as they dropped flares that silhouetted our ships against the night. One of the Japs even let go with his torpedo and it missed the bow of the U.S.S. *Belleau Wood* by a mere six yards.

However, the Japs were unable to complete their attack, and we were able to outmaneuver them. They soon gave up and flew home without damaging one of our ships. They had to. The "Bats' " attack had cost them so many precious flying minutes that they'd run low on fuel.

And the "Bats"?

Phillips got back safely. And Skon. Not Butch O'Hare. In the melee, some Japanese plane probably shot him down from behind.

He was a wonderful combat officer; only twenty-nine years of age.

HOMAGE TO A DEAD HERO

CAPTAIN BENJAMIN F. WILSON
Winner of the Medal of Honor

Highest of any decoration this nation awards for valor above and beyond the call of duty is the Medal of Honor. Captain Benjamin F. Wilson won it in Korea on June 5, 1951. This thirty-three-year-old infantryman knocked out a machine-gun nest, led a bayonet attack that cost the Communists twenty-seven dead, and broke up an enemy counterattack with a lone-man charge in which he killed seven Reds, wounded two, and routed the rest. Then he led a new assault on the enemy. It failed of its objective, and his platoon had to withdraw. Painfully wounded though he was, he stayed behind to cover the retreat. The Communists counterattacked once more, and again he charged them all by himself. He killed three with his rifle before it was wrested from him, and bludgeoned four others to death with his entrenching tool. Although he'd been wounded a second time, he held his ground until all his men had reached safety.

Born in Vashon, Washington, Wilson enlisted in the Regular Army in 1940, went to Officer Candidate School, and obtained a commission. He left the Army in 1945 and missed it so much that he re-enlisted the following year. At the start of the Korean War he volunteered for combat and refused rotation on four occasions. A master sergeant on the day he won the Medal of Honor, he was quickly given a commission. Today he is a captain on duty with the Army in Germany. This is his tribute, which he wrote himself, to a fellow fighting man.

IT had been a terrible two weeks in Korea, and this day was the worst.

We'd been trying to drive the Chinese Communists out of "The Iron Triangle," and the going had been rough. We'd taken fearful punishment. Almost a third of the men in our company had been killed or wounded. Only one of the six officers we'd started with was left. Our company hadn't faltered. Its morale had remained excellent, its fighting power high.

Until now.

This day—it was June 9, 1951—we'd forded a swirling river, scaled a jagged mountain ridge, and gone through a grueling four-hour fire fight as we shoved, inch by inch, toward our mountaintop objective.

The casualties had been even higher than usual. Every few minutes you'd hear someone call for the medics. We were badly shaken. And deathly weary.

About four in the afternoon, we launched the final assault on Nodong-ni. This was the place we were bleeding to reach.

It was murder. The Chinese subjected us to an absolute hail of mortar shells, machine-gun bullets, and grenades. No words can describe the blasting, hellish intensity of their fire.

We could endure no more. The time had come when we'd had as much as the human spirit could stand.

Up in the lead, the Second Platoon slowed, came to a halt, and broke. Its men were pinned. That left the other two rifle platoons critically exposed. The entire company was in desperate shape, dying fast.

Huddled in a ditch, I searched within myself for the courage to get up and rally the men of the Second Platoon. I just couldn't. I cowered there, unable to move.

Almost always, in each U. S. Army unit, there is a soldier with a certain something that I cannot define. Something that has its taproot in our American pattern of freedom. It embodies an initiative and an ingenuity, which, when coupled with an uninhibited conscience, does not let the man admit defeat.

There was such a man at Nodong-ni—Sergeant Arnold W. Graham of Marysville, Montana.

He wasn't even in the Second Platoon. But he saw what was going on.

Up he came to help. Without a backward glance, he stepped out in front of the Second Platoon. Firing his rifle and hurling grenades, he strode toward the enemy. Ashamed of my own hesitation, I followed.

Right up to the Chinese position Sergeant Graham walked. Then, totally disregarding the Chinese fire, he turned around and in a voice that could be clearly heard above the shooting, he yelled:

"All right, damn it, get going. There ain't nobody here but us soldiers."

The Chinese didn't have a chance after that. As one man, the

Second Platoon came alive. It got up, ran forward, and took the objective.

Unfortunately Sergeant Graham never knew it. A bullet struck him over the heart and slammed him to the ground with a force which sent his helmet flying for yards.

He died well, of course. When he was hit I dropped to his side and hollered for the medic. Graham looked up at me and slowly, painfully, shook his head.

"Don't take the medic away from his work," he said. "I've had it."

A few days after, I turned Graham's few personal effects over to the supply officer. Among them was his baby's picture, which he had received in a recent letter—the child he'd never seen.

CRASH LANDING

COLONEL CHESLEY G. PETERSON
Chief of Tactical Division, Directorate of Operations, U.S.A.F.

---

*At twenty-three Chesley G. Peterson was a "chicken colonel"
in the United States Army. Born in Idaho in 1920, he quit
college upon the outbreak of World War II to enlist in the
Air Corps. He was "washed out" during basic training, but
it didn't ground him. He joined the British Royal Air Force,
made pilot there, and rose to be commander of the R.A.F.'s
famous Eagle Squadron of American volunteers. In 1942 he
was transferred to the U. S. Army as a major, Within a year he
was a full colonel. In all, he flew a hundred and fifty combat
missions, shot down fourteen German planes, destroyed an
ammunition train, and collected most of the decorations the
British and American Governments had to offer. Twice he had
to bail out into the icy waters of the English Channel. The last
time, he hit the water with such a terrific blow that it temporarily blinded him. Still he managed to stay afloat for several
hours until rescuers came.*

*Since the war, Colonel Peterson has commanded some of the
top fighter-bomber groups in the U. S. Air Force, held a variety
of high-level posts in the Pentagon, and done a tour as an air
attaché in the Union of South Africa. This is his story, as he
gave it to me, of what it was that kept another American pilot
going.*

STEVE Pisanos has no right to be alive today. By all the odds,
he should be tucked away, in small, mangled pieces, under-
neath the Normandy sod. But Steve didn't want to die the July
afternoon in 1944 that he crashed behind the German lines in
France. He had a very special reason for wanting to go on living.

It all began in Greece. Steve was born in Athens around 1920,
the son of an impoverished Greek grocer. When he was fourteen
years old his father sent him out to the airport one day, to deliver
an order of vegetables to a British Royal Air Force squadron. It was
the first time the skinny, dark-haired kid had ever seen an airplane

close up, and he couldn't get over it. Leaving his vegetables to rot, he went off to talk with the R.A.F. pilots.

"Teach me how to fly," he begged them.

They said no, of course. He was far too young.

He kept on asking them. Month after month, he wrote the R.A.F. commander. He also wrote the head of the Greek Army, the head of the Greek Navy, and most of the Greek Government, pleading for a chance to become a pilot. Naturally, they also said no.

Little Steve had the flying bug bad. So he continued writing letters, to everyone of importance in Greece. He even wrote Joannes Metaxas, the Greek dictator.

General Metaxas granted the boy a personal interview, and some good advice.

"Young man," he declared, "if you ever want to be a pilot, you'll need a lot more education than you have now."

Steve didn't know what to do. He was more than willing to go to school, but his family hadn't the money for it. He was miserable until a friend of his father spoke to him about the United States.

"There are fine schools in America," he said. "You can get the best education in the world there—free."

Steve was very impressed. A country where you could get an education free! It sounded like heaven. So he got aboard a ship for New York. I'm not saying how he contrived it.

The United States turned out to be as wonderful as Steve had hoped. He got ashore, got a job, and got an education. He worked all day shucking oysters at a fish store near Floyd Bennett Field, in Brooklyn, and went to school nights. He was one happy youngster.

As soon as he'd saved enough money, Steve started taking flying lessons. In a Piper Cub. He grew to be pretty good at it, too. He had over two hundred hours to his credit when World War II erupted in Europe by courtesy of Adolf Hitler and his Nazi pals.

Steve didn't like Hitler nor his pals. Young as he was, he'd come to realize that the Nazis endangered all the things he'd learned to love about America.

So he went up to Canada and enlisted in the Royal Canadian Air Force to fight them. He became a fighter pilot.

I met him in England. Immediately that he got there, he'd asked to be transferred to the Eagle Squadron, an outfit made up of Americans who had volunteered to fly for the R.A.F. A grand bunch of guys whom I had the honor to command.

What a pilot that boy was! He was really hot. He shot down fifteen German planes over Britain and on raids to the Continent. Nothing fazed him. He would zoom his Spitfire up and attack three German planes at a time. I saw him do it.

Once the United States entered the war, this Greek boy had a single dream: to fly under the Stars and Stripes. The dream came true. In September 1942 the Eagle Squadron was transferred from the R.A.F. to the Eighth U. S. Air Force.

Then Congress passed a law providing that any alien serving with our Armed Forces could qualify for American citizenship. Steve couldn't contain himself. The moment he read about the new law he ran to my headquarters.

"Colonel, please, I want to apply to be a United States citizen," he said.

I agreed to put his application through channels. That didn't satisfy him. Following regulations might take too long.

"We have to do it faster," he insisted.

"What's the hurry?" I asked.

He explained. Fighter pilots weren't living long those days, and he was afraid he might be shot down before his citizenship came through.

"I know I'm going to get it in the end," he declared, "but, Colonel, when I die, I want to die an American."

Gosh, I gulped.

John Winant, the U. S. Ambassador to Great Britian, was an old friend of the Eagle Squadron. I filled him in on the situation and he said he'd fix matters up. Two weeks later an official of the U. S. Naturalization Bureau arrived in England. He'd flown over from Washington just to help Captain Stephen Pisanos become a citizen of the United States.

We made a real ceremony out of it. We scheduled a formal squadron parade and arranged for Ambassador Winant to present Steve with his citizenship papers. We also invited the Duchess of Kent to take the review. She was born a Greek.

Poor Steve. He couldn't wait for the day. "It'll be just my luck to get killed before it comes off," he fretted.

Came the day, and he was present and accounted for. He was the proudest boy on the field. He couldn't speak, he was so thrilled.

He'd been right, however. His number was up. Shortly after D-Day, we took off for a bombing raid in Bordeaux. We were escorting some B-17s. We hadn't gotten far when Steve reported that he was having engine trouble with his P-51 Mustang. I told him to drop out and return to the base. However, he said the trouble wasn't bad enough to wash out the mission, and I let him go on with us.

On the way back from Bordeaux, Steve's engine conked out completely. "This is it," he reported.

I was plenty worried but I couldn't stay around. Our job was to stick with those bombers. I had to wave him good-by. He was losing altitude fast as we flew away.

There Steve was, over enemy-held France, with a dead plane. His big problem was whether he should bail out or try a forced landing. He chose the forced landing. He was afraid that the Germans might spot him coming down by chute and capture him.

Using every bit of piloting skill he had, he kept that crippled plane limping along in the air while he searched for a landing place. He wanted to get as close to the front as he could. It would make it easier to sneak back to the Allied lines.

At last he spied a meadow that looked good. Down he went to two thousand feet and got set to go in. As he drew closer he saw that the meadow wasn't big enough. He'd have to bail out anyway, and now he was very low. Rapidly he climbed out on the wing, holding the stick with one hand, and prepared to jump. It was too late. The plane smashed into the ground. He was thrown a good thousand feet.

Steve should have been killed instantly. For some fantastic reason, he wasn't. He landed on his shoulder, cracking it to smithereens. But he was alive. Temporarily, at least. The Jerries had watched him crash, and they came racing up. Bruised and bleeding, his shoulder hurting like the blazes, he ran into a nearby woods. The Jerries were fast on his heels, their Tommy guns spitting lead about him.

He was still in a daze from the crash, and he wanted more than anything to lie down. To stretch out and sleep. It would have been so easy to stop running and let those German bullets take effect. That searing gasping for breath would have stopped. That hellish pain in his shoulder would have ended.

He didn't quit running. All night he ran, and in the morning he made contact with the Resistance. They bandaged him up, took him to Paris, and hid him for a month until the Allies liberated the city.

The Resistance boys tried to keep him in bed for that month. Swell chance. He spent it operating a radio for them. And when we got there he wanted to go right up in a plane. I had to order him to the hospital.

Later I asked Steve how he'd ever managed to find the strength to keep running from the Germans.

"I'll tell you, Colonel," he answered. "I didn't want to die. I liked being an American too much."

What's befallen Steve since the war? He wished to remain in the Air Force, but he knew he didn't have enough education for a permanent commission. So he obtained a job as a pilot with T.W.A. and went to the University of Maryland on the side. In 1948 he graduated. Promptly he applied to the Air Force for that commission. In 1949 he got it. Today, it's Major Stephen Pisanos, United States Air Force.

SOMETHING FOR THE BOYS

ROSALIND RUSSELL
Stage and Screen Star

Rosalind Russell was the first film actress to go on a camp tour in World War II and, for the duration, she never missed an opportunity to entertain the troops.

A Connecticut girl, born in 1912, Miss Russell has been en-rapturing audiences with her comic antics—and in serious roles as well—since the middle thirties. She has starred in such movies as The Women, Mourning Becomes Electra, Sister Kenny, *and* Never Wave at a Wac. *In 1953 she scored a Broadway triumph in the musical comedy* Wonderful Town, *and repeated it in 1956 with* Auntie Mame.

Away from the spotlight, Miss Russell is a hard worker for many good causes. She was one of the founders of the Sister Kenny Institute and is still a director. She is also an official of the Arthritis and Rheumatism Foundation. Her wartime activities were particularly close to her heart. Not only her husband but all three of her brothers were in uniform overseas. She told me this story.

THE sandy stew did it.

I took one taste of the concoction that the boys at the Desert Training Center were getting for lunch and I could see right off they needed cheering up. The poor kids not only had to walk through sand all day, sleep on it all night, and comb it out of their hair in the morning. They got it to eat, too.

I realized that this outfit—the 6th Armored Division—was here in the California wastelands, 125 miles from anywhere, to be hardened up for combat. But how hard is a guy supposed to get?

Something had to be done, and I decided that I was the one to do it. I'm the impulsive type.

The commanding officer of the Desert Training Center, a friendly gent named Major General Walton H. Walker, was showing me around. "General," I said to him, "I want to do something for your boys."

He stared at me dubiously. "What do you have in mind, Miss Russell?"

"A party. A real humdinger of a Christmas party."

"That's a grand idea." He beamed. "What sort of a Christmas party would you want to give?"

I looked him straight in the eye. "General, let's be frank. What do boys want most? You know and I know. Women, liquor, and money. Isn't that so?"

He had to say yes. What else could he say?

"O. K., I'm going to give them all three."

The poor general gulped. "Just how many men did you figure on inviting?"

"Oh," I said casually, "let's invite the whole division."

How was I to know that an armored division had fourteen thousand men on its rolls?

This was in December 1942, and I should tell you that I had a good reason for making Christmas merry for the 6th Armored. My brother George was a G.I. in the division. The only trouble was that he got transferred two weeks before Christmas.

George or no George, I'd promised the division a party, and I made up my mind that it was going to be the best party in history. No one was ever going to say that Ros Russell couldn't cope with a few thousand extra guests.

On the drive back to Hollywood I drew up my plans. I would have loads of girls, two dance bands, some crack entertainment, a tasty meal, and enough to drink for everybody. Beer, that is. The general and I had compromised on that score.

The first problem was to raise the money. I started off by telephoning a top executive at my studio.

"I need some money," I said.

"What? Again?" he growled. "We just gave you an increase in salary."

"This is different. I'm giving a party for some soldier friends of mine. Fourteen thousand of them."

"My, an intimate little affair."

Finally he asked me how much I wanted from him. I was hoping for one hundred dollars so, naturally, I said two hundred. In the movie business we always start high.

"Two hundred dollars for a Christmas party!" he exclaimed. "Say, this is a party for the G. I.s. It's got to be good."

He sent me five hundred dollars.

You won't believe it but in four days I collected twelve thousand dollars. "Nothing's too good for the G.I.s," everybody said, and who was I to contradict them.

Next on the agenda was the entertainment. I rang up Red Skelton. He's an old friend.

"Red, what are your plans for Christmas?" I asked.

"We'll be delighted to come to dinner at your house," he said. "What time?"

"No dinner," I said. "At least, not at my house. I want you to do a show for some G.I.s."

There was a pause. A very understandable one. No one likes to go off and leave his family on Christmas Day. Then Red declared, "If the G.I.s can take it, I can."

Betty Grable was just as nice. And Pat O'Brien. And Peter Lind Hayes, as well as a slew of other fine stars.

That left the most important item to be accounted for. Girls. Good-looking ones, and a lot of them.

I called together representatives of every major studio. "Gentlemen," I stated, "I want you to trot out all your starlets on Christmas Day, and your secretaries, and all the other girls you can round up. I want six hundred of them."

While they were gasping over that I went on in my most official manner. "And, listen to me, this is for the troops, so only pretty girls. No dogs. Get it?"

They got it.

A hectic couple of weeks followed. There was the show to line up, the musicians to hire, the food and the beer to order. I had to arrange for busses—thirty of them—to transport the girls. I even had to arrange for powder rooms along the way. After all, it was a ten-hour drive.

Christmas morning, I arrived at the Desert Training Center bright and early. I wanted to see how many things had gone wrong.

Can you imagine my surprise? Everything was working out splendidly.

There was the food, and the kegs of beer, enough to float a battleship (or an armored division). There was the dance floor we'd shipped in. I'll bet it was the biggest in the history of Terpsichore. Spread out on the sand, it was a good half mile long. There was the towering Christmas tree we'd trucked down all the way from Lake

Arrowhead. It was the swankiest Christmas tree in those parts. In fact, it was the only tree.

The division had lined up all its tanks, hundreds of them, on the four sides of the dance floor. The G.I.s, fourteen thousand of them, were sitting on top of the tanks.

You should have seen those boys. I was used to them in their dirty, oil-streaked fatigues, unshaven and covered with chiggers. Not today. Each one was dolled up in his dress khakis, with his shoes shined and his overseas cap at a jaunty angle. I could have hugged them.

They weren't thinking of me, though. (Perhaps I should mention that I was somewhat pregnant at the time.) Those boys had their eyes fixed on the road. They were waiting for the girls.

The caravan was due at two o'clock. Red Skelton, Betty Grable, and the other performers got there promptly. The two orchestras got there promptly. Everybody did. Except the girls.

Two-thirty came. No girls. Three o'clock. No girls.

The thoughts I had! I was certain someone had kidnaped all six hundred girls.

The thoughts those G.I.s had. "It's a phony," I overheard one say. "There ain't gonna be no dames. It'll be like all them other shows. A couple of songs, then they'll hand us a pack of cigarettes and send us to bed."

I could have sunk through the sand.

At last the busses pulled into sight. Anxiously I waited to see how the girls looked. Almost as anxiously as the boys.

We needn't have worried. The girls were honeys. Maybe a few weren't exactly exotic by Hollywood standards, but down in the wilderness they all seemed like Dietrichs.

I'd given careful instructions to dress sensibly. High necklines and long sleeves, I'd urged, because it gets cold at night on the desert. And I'd specifically said, "No open-toe shoes," on account of the sand.

For all the effect I'd had I might as well have kept quiet. The girls were wearing their glamorous best, with dainty shoes and necklines down to there.

They wanted to raise the G.I.s' morale, too.

As the girls walked onto the dance floor, there wasn't a single wolf call. Nor a fresh remark from the G.I.s. Then and for the rest of the day those G.I.s were the most gentlemanly gentlemen I've known.

It was quite a party. The girls danced, and danced, and danced, with more than twenty different partners apiece. By the end of the afternoon some of them were so footsore they could scarcely walk, but they went right on dancing.

I suggested to one little blonde that she take a rest. She wouldn't hear of it.

"Oh no, Miss Russell," she said. "That would be desertion in the line of duty."

Along with the dancing, we served beer. And money. We gave away door prizes of up to a thousand dollars.

Then came dinner. It was a mighty good one, if I do say so myself. Anyway, it didn't have sand in it.

The show was the climax of the evening. What a setting it had. The G.I.s and girls were sitting together on the dance floor, while the tanks, in the background, all turned on their headlights and focused them on the stage. Up above, in a cloudless, black-blue sky, were millions of twinkling stars.

Before the overture began, something happened that I'll never forget. I was sitting with General Walker on a bench up front when a young G.I. walked over, searching for a place to sit on the floor. Down he squatted in front of the general and, without so much as a by-your-leave, leaned his back against the general's legs.

The general didn't even blink. He merely shifted his legs a little to give the boy better support.

"Are you comfortable, son?" he asked.

"Yes, sir. Thank you."

"I'm afraid my legs are a little bony."

"They're just fine, sir," the G.I. said reassuringly.

Cite me any other army in which a soldier can use a general as a back rest.

It was a great show. The performers knocked themselves out for the G.I.s. Red Skelton, dressed as Santa Claus, was never funnier, and Betty Grable was a dancing dream. The only thing bad about the show was that, eventually, it had to end.

Sadly the boys walked the girls back to the busses. "Gee," I heard one say to a girl, "it was nice of you to give up your Christmas for us G.I.s."

"Soldier," the girl said, "if it wasn't for you G.I.s, we might not have any more Christmases."

What with one thing and another, including a long breakfast stop, it was the next afternoon before we got the girls back to Hollywood. For some it meant the loss of a day's pay.

They didn't mind. "It was worth it," one of them said. "It was for the G.I.s, wasn't it?"

I knew just how she felt.

Those G.I.s in the 6th Armored were worth it. They fought through Normandy, northern France, the Rhineland, the Ardennes. One thousand and four of them didn't come home. Neither did my friend General Walker. He was killed in Korea.

THIS WAS THE ARMY

IRVING BERLIN

America's Song Writer

---

*Between February 1943 and V-J Day in August 1945 Irving
Berlin visited every American fighting front throughout the
world. He put on his rousing revue,* This Is the Army, *in camps,
air bases, rest areas, any place where there were lonesome,
homesick G.I.s who could use some cheering up.*

*Tin Pan Alley's most famous son, Berlin has done over eight
hundred songs, including some of the biggest hits in musical
history. "Alexander's Ragtime Band" is his. So are "Oh, How
I Hate To Get Up in the Morning," "All Alone," "Blue Skies,"
"Easter Parade," "White Christmas." And the song that has
virtually become a national anthem, "God Bless America." He
has written scores for dozens of Broadway and Hollywood
successes.*

*The friendliest and most unassuming of men, Berlin, who
was born in Russia in 1886, is also a most generous person.
He turned over all of his royalties from "God Bless America"
to the Boy Scouts and the Girl Scouts of America, earning for
them over $267,000. He never took a penny for writing "This
Is the Army." The $10,000,000 it grossed went to Army Emer-
gency Relief.*

He told me this story.

IT was at the height of the big push north from Cassino in
May 1944.

We were touring with the soldier show *This Is the Army*. We had
played in the United Kingdom and Africa, and now we were doing
the show for the U. S. Fifth Army in Italy. After playing Naples and
Santa Maria, we'd appeared at the Royal Opera House in Rome.
Then we'd returned to Bagnoli to play the hospital there. It was
packed with our wounded.

A makeshift stage had been rigged in the central hall and the
patients came trooping in from the wards. There were hundreds of

them. Down front, near the orchestra, was a row of wheel-chair cases. They were G.I.s who'd lost their legs in battle.

We managed to give the whole two-hour show, scenery and all. It was one of the best audiences we ever had. Especially the boys in the wheel chairs.

Came the finale—a number entitled "This Time Is the Last Time." Slowly, the curtain fell. A moment later, it rose again, the orchestra swung into "The Star-Spangled Banner," and the entire house jumped to its feet.

Those of us on stage could clearly see that front row of wheel-chair cases as the orchestra started the national anthem. Instinctively every one of those legless boys attempted to rise.

It made us all stand a little more erect.

TOP SECRET FROM WASHINGTON

DOUGLAS MACARTHUR II

U. S. Ambassador to Japan

Twenty-three years in the U. S. Foreign Service have given Douglas MacArthur II an unparalleled opportunity to see history made, and to make a lot of it himself. This keen, forty-nine-year-old diplomat helped to organize the North Atlantic Treaty Organization, did much to design the Southeast Asia Treaty Organization, was a close adviser to President Eisenhower at the "Summit Conference" with Messrs. Khrushchev, Bulganin & Co.

A nephew of General Douglas MacArthur, "Young Doug" was born in Pennsylvania, educated at Yale, and served as an Army officer for two and a half years before he entered the Foreign Service. After assignments in Naples, Paris, and Lisbon, he was sent to Vichy, France, where he was U. S. Ambassador William D. Leahy's right-hand man in his dealings with the Pétain government.

In recent years MacArthur has held such top posts as political advisor to General Eisenhower at SHAPE, counselor of the State Department, and, since 1957, U. S. Ambassador to Tokyo. Admiral Leahy calls him "the best diplomat I ever met." It is a widely held estimate.

THE United States Government expects a lot from the members of the Foreign Service. It asks for diplomatic skill, devotion to duty, disregard of danger, sometimes sacrifice. It gets them in large measure.

The widow of the United States consul general in Jerusalem who was killed in the Arab-Israeli war can testify to that. The U. S. consul who was kept prisoner in Mukden for eighteen months by the Chinese Communists can testify to it. The Foreign Service men and women who braved the anti-Western rioting that swept Taipei, Baghdad, and Cairo over recent years can testify to it.

Douglas MacArthur II, now U. S. Ambassador to Japan, is another who can testify to it. He also has seen the Foreign Service in times of crisis.

MacArthur was assigned to the American Embassy in Vichy, France, during the early years of World War II. This was after France had been overrun by the armies of Nazi Germany. The country was split in two, and Vichy was the capital of the unoccupied portion.

It was a ticklish spot for the tiny group of American diplomats stationed there—fourteen in all. The United States was at war with Hitler, and it was well known that our people were actively working to stir up anti-German feeling among the French. They were allowed to stay, since unoccupied France was ostensibly independent, but their every move was watched, their every phone call tapped, by Gestapo spies.

One day in the latter part of October 1942 a message arrived at the small villa that served as the American Embassy. It was from the Department of State in Washington, and it was marked Top Secret.

Hastily the Embassy men decoded it. It bore big news. It notified them that the first great Allied military offensive against the Axis was about to be launched. Operation Torch, the Anglo-American landings in French North Africa, was to get under way on November 8.

The little Embassy staff in Vichy had a role to play in the operation, the message went on. In his quiet way MacArthur describes it.

"It was recognized in Washington that, following the landings, the Nazi authorities would almost certainly take action against our Embassy in Vichy, seize our archives, and arrest our Embassy people. Our instructions were, therefore, to dispose of our classified material discreetly, but to carry on as usual as a cover for the landings. It was quite clear that the prospect was that we would be transported to Germany by the Nazi authorities and might remain there indefinitely, if not forever. In other words, our small group of Foreign Service personnel, with our fine military and naval attachés, was rightly considered expendable. Our mission was equivalent to that of a rear-guard detachment which is left behind to cover a retreat with no hope of being able to extricate itself."

The thought of years in a Nazi internment camp was not a pretty one to those Foreign Service men. They knew vividly how Nazi storm troopers treated their captives. And it was not merely of themselves that they had to think. Some of the men had their wives and children in Vichy. The Nazis would grab them too.

There was an out. Those who wished might ask for permission to proceed to Spain, where they'd be out of the Nazis' reach. But that might arouse the Nazis' suspicions.

A meeting of the key people on the Embassy staff was called in the converted bedroom that S. Pinckney Tuck, the chargé d'affaires, used as an office.

As MacArthur tells it, "Mr. Tuck informed them of the situation as well as of the prospects for the future, which certainly were not bright."

Then Mr. Tuck waited to hear how many would want to run for it to safety in Spain.

Not a person suggested it. Says MacArthur:

"All cheerfully accepted the mission that had been assigned by Washington." Every one was ready to do his bit to help cover the landings.

"That's the least we can do," the thinking was.

It continued so even when they all were seized by a Nazi S.S. detachment and transported to Germany. And MacArthur says he never heard one word of complaint during the year and a half they spent in an internment camp near Baden-Baden.

"It made me very proud to be working with such wonderfully dedicated American men and women as those in our Foreign Service."

LOOKING BACK

GENERAL OMAR N. BRADLEY
Former Chairman, Joint Chiefs of Staff

General Omar N. Bradley has commanded more American troops in the field—four armies, forty-three divisions and 1,300,000 men—than any other man. He did it well. He led a corps into Sicily, an army into Normandy, and a huge army group into the heart of Nazi Germany, smashing the Wehrmacht to shreds in the process. Throughout, he had the love and respect of his soldiers. No more gentle, considerate, and democratic man ever wore a general's stars.

A Missourian, born in 1893, he applied for West Point because it provided a free education. Graduating in 1915, he had a humdrum, obscure career until 1941. But then he rose fast. After the war he served as head of the Veterans Administration, as Army Chief of Staff, and, from 1949 to 1953, as chairman of the Joint Chiefs of Staff. He set military policy for the United Nations forces in the Korean War. Since his retirement in 1953 he has been associated with the Bulova Watch Company. He recapitulated for me the highest spots of his forty-two Army years.

IT was a long road from the rocky crags of West Point to that final review on the grassy parade ground at Fort McNair in Washington. It took me forty-two years to travel it, from my first scary morning as a cadet to the afternoon I retired—not without a feeling of sadness—from the U. S. Army. I still can hear the bugler sounding "Retreat" that day, and see the flag come fluttering down.

In forty-two years of soldiering one accumulates a wide store of proud memories. That's a fine thing about the profession of arms. It may have its dull stretches, but it also has more than its share of big moments—times when you see men, armies, and nations at their best.

I can think back to many in my military career. There was an occasion in Tunisia, for example . . .

It was May 9, 1943. I was standing on a hilltop near Mateur. Below, a long stream of German prisoners of war was marching by, thousands upon thousands of them, stretching out as far as the eye could note.

I looked down at Hitler's "supermen." Only a few days before, we'd considered ourselves lucky if we destroyed or captured a few dozen of them. Now, Rommel's crack Afrika Korps had surrendered en masse.

I thought to myself, "Who said Americans were green and not well trained?"

Then there was D-Day, June 6, 1944. I was on the U. S. S. *Augusta* off the Normandy coast. At 3:35 A.M. the gong outside my cabin rang "Battle Stations." Hurriedly I buckled on my Mae West, grabbed my helmet, and mounted to the bridge.

The night was misty black, so dark one could scarcely see another vessel in the invasion fleet. Impatiently I waited for morning and the start of our landing to liberate Western Europe from Nazi slavery.

First light broke the night at five thirty. The mist cleared, and, at last, I could see around us.

The sea was filled with our ships—battleships, cruisers, destroyers, troop transports, landing craft, supply ships, and we were only one of five enormous columns of them, all steaming toward France.

I knew what was in those ships. One hundred and seventy-six thousand men, each of whom had been trained to a "t." Three thousand guns. Fifteen hundred tanks. More than sixteen thousand other vehicles. It was the most powerful amphibious force ever assembled.

I smiled to myself. "And Hitler figured the democracies were too decadent to defend themselves!"

It's not only military might that makes for big moments in a soldier's life, though. Occasions arise when our country is perilously weak but still acts to defend our principles of freedom, despite terrible risks. Such occasions count a lot to a soldier.

Take the night of June 26, 1950. The North Korean Communists had just invaded South Korea, in flagrant violation of international law and morality, and President Harry S. Truman had summoned an emergency conference to decide on a course of action for the United States.

Every man at Blair House that evening—the President, Secretary of State Dean Acheson and four of his aides, the Secretary of Defense, the Secretaries of the three Services, and the Joint Chiefs of

Staff—realized that the United States' armed forces, which had been dismantled after the war, were pitifully small. They fully recognized, too, that Soviet Russia might well use intervention in Korea as a pretext for launching an all-out, total war against us. Even so, Secretary of State Acheson immediately proposed that we go to South Korea's asssitance.

There was not one dissenting voice, regardless of all the dangers concerned.

Yet if I had to pick the biggest of my big moments, they would revolve around men. In a democracy man matters more than any government or any army. That's what governments and armies are for: to enhance and protect the importance of individual men.

It has been a wonderfully rewarding experience to know, and serve with, the kind of men our American Army produces. Heroes like the two G.I.s who voluntarily stayed behind when their company was forced out of the Normandy village it was supposed to hold.

Completely alone, those two G.I.s went on fighting against an entire German battalion. After they used up their own ammunition, they took cartridges from dead soldiers lying about them. Then they picked up German rifles and fired German bullets.

By themselves, the two G.I.s held off the German battalion until their company rallied and won back the village.

And other marvelously brave men. Like Jim Gavin. I was visiting a divisional command post early in the Sicilian campaign when Gavin—now a lieutenant general but at the time a paratrooper colonel—came in, seeking artillery support to knock out a German tank that was delaying his advance. He said his bazookas couldn't make a dent in the tank's heavy armor.

Minus the slightest awareness that he'd done something exceptional, he declared, "Why, I myself walked up to within ten feet of that tank and my bazooka just bounced off."

He got the artillery support he wanted.

There have been colorful men, like George S. Patton. Most of the world regarded him as a hard-boiled, bombastic battler. I knew him as a sentimentalist as well.

Patton felt fear as much as the rest of us but he made a big point of never showing it. Which is more than can be said for his bulldog, Willie. Willie used to go almost wild with fright when bombs and shells dropped nearby. He'd race around madly trying to hide under a chair or a bed.

One night in the fall of 1944, a Nazi battery zeroed in on Patton's CP in Luxembourg and a shell landed in the courtyard of his château, killing a half-dozen men.

Ordinarily, when enemy artillery got our range, we could send up a spotter plane, locate the battery, and have our guns put it out of of business. Or we'd send over bombers to do the job. But this time we couldn't find it, and it kept on firing.

Patton telephoned me at my headquarters nearby. "Brad," he said, "for God's sake, you've got to do something about this Kraut battery. They're really banging us around. Please don't misunderstand me, it's not that I'm frightened, but Willie's scared."

Best of all, there have been some very great men. Like General George C. Marshall, Chief of Staff of our Army in World War II.

No soldier has so exemplified the finest traditions of America and the American Army as General George Marshall. He is a magnificent leader, a brilliant, honest thinker, and, always, a true democrat in heart.

I learned a lot from General Marshall—fast. While I was a young lieutenant colonel I was assigned to his staff as a junior assistant. After my first week on duty he called me and two other assistants into his office. "Gentlemen," he said, "I'm disappointed in you. You haven't disagreed yet with a single decision I've made."

"General," I defended us, "it's just because there has been no cause for disagreement. When we differ with you on a decision, sir, we'll tell you so."

"See that you do." He dismissed us.

The following morning we did dare to disagree with a decision of his.

"That's better," he said.

With men like that at the head, there'll never be any Prussianism in our Army. It will always be, as it always has been, a reflection of the American democratic spirit.

I'm grateful for the forty-two good years it gave me.

SAVED—1,000,000 CASUALTIES

GENERAL CURTIS E. LEMAY
Vice Chief of Staff, U. S. Air Force

Tough, blunt-speaking General Curtis E. LeMay gave America its "Sunday punch." The Strategic Air Command is his baby. He built it up into the crack, ultrapowerful bombing force that it is today. In many people's opinion it is the chief deterrent to World War III.

A long-time exponent of strategic air power, "Curt" LeMay was born in Columbus, Ohio, in 1906, the son of an iron worker. He couldn't get an appointment to West Point so he accepted a reserve commission in the Army when he graduated from Ohio State University. He began his military career in the Artillery, switched to the Air Corps in 1928, and took pilot training. He was no sit-at-home commander in World War II. Once, while commanding the 305th Bomber Group, he became dissatisfied with the amount of damage his men were doing to the Germans. There would be no more zigzagging to dodge antiaircraft fire, he announced, and he led the next raid on Saint-Nazaire himself, keeping his plane on a dead-straight course for seven minutes through lethal ack-ack. Transferred to the Pacific, he directed the final air assault on Japan. In 1948 he organized and ran the famous Air Lift that broke the Berlin Blockade. These achievements brought him command of S.A.C. His work with S.A.C. made him Vice Chief of Staff of the Air Force in 1957. Here is the account that he wrote of the day American air power proved itself.

WE were busy in the Marianas, mounting the B-29 strikes against Japan, when I first clearly realized that America's newest weapon—strategic air power—could save a quarter of a million American lives.

I had been in the bombing business a bit over ten years at the time. I had lived through the frustrations of our slow, torturous build-up of air power during the early days of World War II. After that, I'd been in England, helping in the combined endeavors of the Royal Air Force and our U. S. Army Air Force to smash, forever, Hitler's

Festung Europa. Finally, in the fall of 1944, I'd been transferred to the Pacific.

The biggest push of the war was under way then. Up and down the Pacific, and throughout the United States, preparations were in progress for the invasion of the Japanese homeland.

It was going to be a terribly costly campaign. We knew that. There was a fresh army of two million men in the Japanese main islands, and it was certain to make a fanatical, last-ditch stand. The best intelligence estimates indicated a casualty list of more than one million American dead and wounded.

Our job in the XXI Bomber Command was to soften up Japan for the landings and, for once, we had the tools to work with. The new B-29 Superfortresses were being rushed to the theater in increasing numbers and, with the capture of the Marianas, at last we had bases in bombing range of Japan.

But how to use the B-29s? That was the question.

We were supposed to fly them at twenty-five thousand feet and up. We soon found, though, that our bomb sights weren't good enough for that height. Worse yet, at those altitudes we ran into 180-miles-an-hour winds over Japan. Again and again our planes missed their targets.

Desperately we tried to work out a new bombing approach. We experimented with different flight levels, different bomb loads, different tactics.

I made up my mind to take a chance. A real chance. I was convinced that Japanese fighter opposition would be ineffective against low-level night attacks. And I was reasonably sure that enemy anti-aircraft fire would be no large hazard since the Japanese lacked the accurate gun-laying radar of the Germans.

So I ordered our bombers to go in at night at seven thousand feet. Not only that but I had every shred of defensive armament stripped out. The guns, ammunition, and gunners were removed from each plane. This allowed additional thousands of pounds of bombs per airplane.

I went further. I decided not to employ the conventional high-explosive bombs. Because Japan's industrial facilities are so widely dispersed, I resolved on using incendiaries. We would burn out Japan's war plants.

On the night of March 9, 1945, we made our first strike. Three hundred and thirty-four B-29s were sent against Tokyo.

Anxiously we awaited reports on the raid.

It turned out to be the most devastating air attack of the entire war, not excluding the later atomic-bomb strikes. Industrial Tokyo was gone—fifteen and eight tenths square miles completely burned away. More than 250,000 buildings were destroyed. Their flimsy construction left little or no rubble; the area was leveled.

Our losses? They were minuscule.

Next we hit Nagoya. Kobe. Osaka. Target by target, we destroyed Japan's war-making capacity.

I knew the greatest, most satisfying secret of the war then. An invasion of Japan would not be necessary. American air power alone could force the Japanese to surrender.

I went on record with this belief. I put through an official memorandum, stating:

"The destruction of Japan's ability to wage war lies within the capability of this command."

The day I came to this realization—I can't give the exact date, but I know it was in mid-April 1945—was the best I've ever had.

The land invasion had been set for November 1, 1945. That meant we had only six months to complete the job by air. In a race against time, with the lives of men in the balance, the air crews applied themselves untiringly. Leaves were canceled. So were the restrictions on the number of missions a crew could fly. We doubled the number of flights normally made by the bombers. Before long we were dropping bombs on Japan as fast as the supply ships could bring them.

The six-month period was shortened by the atomic blows on Hiroshima and Nagasaki. But the end was already guaranteed.

For the first time in history a major power capitulated without being invaded. The men of the U. S. Air Force had demonstrated the decisive potential of America's new military force—strategic air power. And they had spared our nation the toll of an invasion of Japan.

"TELL IT TO SWEENEY"

LIEUTENANT COLONEL DAVID F. MACGHEE
Former Prisoner of War in Korea

"If I got clobbered right now," Lieutenant Colonel David F. MacGhee declares, "I can say I've been around." It would be no exaggeration. MacGhee holds the distinction of having spent the longest time as a prisoner of war in Korea—and still survived—of any man in the U. S. Air Force. He was also tortured the most by the Communists.

A New Yorker, born in 1919, MacGhee enlisted in the Air Corps in 1941 and helped bomb the Nazis into submission. He remained in the service and was sent to the Far East early in the Korean War. A B-17 navigator, he was shot down over the Yalu on November 10, 1950. For thirty-four months the Communists beat him, hung him by his wrists, closeted him in ice, cut off his food. His weight dropped from 234 pounds to 117. But he didn't give in to them. He continued to sabotage the Reds' "brain-washing" programs and to organize the other POWs against them. "Colonel MacGhee," the citation for his Legion of Merit reads, "never ceased to harass the enemy with every means of his disposal." Recovered from his ordeal, MacGhee is now assigned to the Air Staff in Washington where he told me about these experiences of his as a POW.

There's been a lot of talk about American prisoners of war who caved in to the Communists. Let me tell you about some American POWs that didn't. . . .

"I've been in horrible places but Prisoner of War Camp No. 2 in North Korea was among the worst. The Chinese Communists beat us POWs bloody, strung us up by our wrists, cooped us up in abnormal positions, starved us until we were just bags of bones. If you protested their brutalities, they threw you in a hole or an abandoned bathhouse filled with ice, and kept you there for months, alone in the freezing darkness.

Often they went the rest of the way. They'd take POWs out and cold-bloodedly shoot them.

The camp was at Pyonggo-dong, five miles from the Chinese

border. In it were packed 316 officers and enlisted men, so many
that each man was allowed only eighteen inches to sleep on. No
more, not even if a hungry rat tried to share it with him.

Ding Chan, a Chinese Communist with the rank of brigadier
general, was camp commandant. We nicknamed him "The Snake."
He looked like one. He acted like one, too.

Ding made just one bad mistake. He thought he had us POWs
cowed.

It was Christmas Eve 1951 when the showdown began. We were
having a makeshift little party, seeking somehow to forget the
memory of Christmas at home. We had songs, stunts, skits and a
Christmas Eve service. I can remember one of the skits. It matched
a six-foot-four giant against a five-foot-three shrimp for the heavy-
weight championship of the world. The shrimp won.

In the middle of the party another man and I were called out.
A Chinese officer had orders for us.

"You are to make up a fancy Christmas card in the name of all
the POWs thanking the Supreme Commander of the Chinese
People's Army for the fine care you have received."

I was to write the message and Nick, the other guy, was to do a
drawing to go with it.

It meant "the hole" if we refused. And the thermometer was way
down below zero, what the POWs called a "full crisp" for the effect
it had on your ears.

Nick looked over at me. "You can write it," he grimly declared,
"but I won't draw it."

I reached out and shook his hand. "That's good enough for me,"
I said.

The Chinese were furious. They didn't jump us, though. Not yet.
They went to work on our senior officer instead. They told him to
command us to make the card.

He wouldn't.

All night long they worked this colonel over. He still wouldn't do
it.

The Chinese were wild. They issued a point-blank order the next
day that every POW in the camp send in a Christmas greeting, or
take the consequences.

The cards they got were honeys. I can recall one, word for word.
It was prepared by a little captain named Joe Manto.

"I wish to send Christmas greetings to our camp commandant,

and I also want to wish Li'l Abner, Daisy Mae, and all the people in Dogpatch a Merry Christmas, and be sure you also tell it to Sweeney."

Were those Chinese mad!

Now they really set out to break us POWs. Christmas night, they pulled out two officers, Captain Bob Wise and Captain Bill Shadish, and stood them barefooted on ice cakes until morning. They wanted "quotes" from them backing Communism.

In POW lingo "they got zilch"—nothing.

A couple of nights later, they did it to three other officers. Again they got "zilch."

That same night an Air Force pilot sneaked out of the barracks and stamped "P-O-W" in huge letters in the snow. The Chinese were almost beside themselves. They'd been trying desperately to keep the location of the camp a secret.

Things moved fast then. At ten o'clock in the morning every POW was summoned to a meeting.

We were plenty worried. The Chinese had never called a meeting like this before—armed guards at all entrances and "burp" guns and light machine guns set up outside—and we didn't know what they were up to, but it just couldn't be good. So we took precautions. Word was passed that no POW was to answer any question if our senior officer had on his hat. It didn't matter how the POW got out of it; he was to say nothing. Only if the senior officer took his hat off could a question be answered.

We met in "the library." This was an unheated room, about forty feet long and fifteen feet wide, with crumbling walls, broken windows, and a floor that was rotted through.

Quickly we learned what the meeting was about. It was bad.

Sun, the chief political instructor, wanted us to endorse an official report by Peking denying that the deaths of four thousand American POWs during the winter of 1950–51 had been due to Communist maltreatment. He demanded statements from us that all of these four thousand POWs had died of venereal disease contracted from raping Japanese and Korean women!

He started in on one of the three boys who had just had the ice treatment.

"What have you to say about the deaths of these misguided POWs?" he asked him.

The boy glanced at the senior officer. His hat was on.

"I have nothing to say."

Sun flushed. He turned to another boy who'd been given the ice treatment. This one was a small Puerto Rican lieutenant named Cordero. Although he was wrapped in three overcoats, he was still shaking all over.

"You have something to say, don't you, Cordero?" Sun smiled.

Cordero just laughed at him. "I'm too sick to answer your question. I guess I must have raped some of those women myself."

Squatting there on the floor, the cold was almost unbearable. It was like rising ice water. It crept numbingly up your legs, your buttocks, your back. You felt paralyzed. But not a POW would answer Sun's questions. The meeting lapsed into absolute silence.

Ding himself finally came in. He was in a black rage. As we later found out, he'd had a directive right from Supreme Headquarters to get propaganda material from us.

Angrily he broke up the meeting. He didn't give up, though. Not Ding. We had to meet again. Repeatedly. And from then on we met in small groups. Ding was smart. This way there could be no control by the senior officer.

We were smarter. We managed to get word to each group how to answer the day's question.

The first time, the question was, "Do you believe that the men who died in the winter of 1950–51 perished from venereal disease contracted by raping Japanese and Korean women?"

Three hundred and sixteen men answered, "No."

At the second meeting the question was "Do you think that the lenient policy of the Chinese People's Army toward POWs is an improvement on the Geneva Convention?"

Three hundred and sixteen men answered, "No."

The Chinese went practically berserk. For four days there were many talks on what to do with us, threats, harassment, intimidation. We were warned that things could be much worse for us, reminded that the whole camp could be shot for mutiny.

Anxiously we awaited the next question. It came on January eleventh. When we read it we realized we'd won.

"Haven't you received any lenient treatment at all?" the Chinese meekly asked.

With true joy I walked through the squad rooms that day. We'd decreed this "a free question." The boys could answer it in any fashion they desired.

They didn't miss a trick. They listed every case of torture, denial of medical care, bad food, illegal incarceration, prohibition against religious services.

It was more than the Chinese could take. We will never know for sure what was said by those frustrated "slant-eyed apes" in their almost continuous conferences in Ding's headquarters and in the meetings among the political instructors, but we knew—and they knew—one thing for sure: the Supreme Commander wasn't going to get any propaganda from this camp.

As one POW put it to Sun, "You just don't understand Americans!"

EASTER IN KOREA

MAJOR GENERAL CHARLES I. CARPENTER
Chief of Chaplains, U.S.A.F.

G.I.s, airmen, and sailors are never abashed by Major General Charles I. Carpenter's stars. They call him "Chappie" and treat him like the regular guy they know he is. He probably has more friends in uniform than any other general officer.

Chaplain Carpenter was born in Wilmington, Delaware, in 1906. He graduated from Bucknell University in 1927 and received his Bachelor of Divinity degree from Drew Theological Seminary in 1931. The following five years he was a Methodist minister with pastorates in Delaware and Maryland. Military life appealed to him, and in 1936 he obtained a commission as a first lieutenant in the Chaplain Corps of the Regular Army. When the Air Force was established as a separate service, he was made its Chief of Chaplains. Now he is a true "flying minister." Any day he's likely to land on any U.S. air base in the world, just to "talk things over with the fellows." Between flights, he "taped" this story of Easter in Korea.

EASTER SUNDAY 1951 was a busy day for me. I spent it in war-struck Korea.

The morning began with a stirring sunrise service at Seoul. There were thousands there, prayerfully happy just to be alive and free. At the conclusion, I flew to a nearby air base for a nine-o'clock service. The moment it was over I took off for an air base up north and an eleven-o'clock service. A service punctuated by the snarl of cannon in the distance. After that I raced back to Seoul. I had a party to go to.

It was no ordinary party. The commanding general of the Fifth Air Force was playing host to a swarm of children from a Korean orphanage. An orphanage set up by G.I.s for homeless, starving kids who'd lost their families in the war.

Those kids! Dozens and dozens of little girls, cute as can be. All five and six years old, with shining black eyes and fetching smiles. What a picture they made! Most of them were wearing blouses that had been concocted out of G.I. shirts—shirts that some American soldiers had taken off their own backs to give them. The sleeves still had the insignia on them, chevrons of master sergeants, buck sergeants, corporals, pfc's.

The skirts the little girls had on were "G.I." too. They'd been cut out of army blankets. I'll bet some supply sergeants are still trying to alibi about what happened to those blankets.

It was a real Easter party, run exactly as it would have been in the States. An egg roll to start, in the yard of the commanding general's house. Next games. Then loads of ice cream and cake. Naturally, the youngsters ate much more than was good for them.

They had a grand time.

As the afternoon drew to a close, the woman in charge of the orphanage came up to the commanding general and me.

"We'd like to have our rhythm band play for you," she declared.

Neither the commanding general nor I knew what a rhythm band was, but we said yes.

A tiny tot climbed up onto a chair and rapped a baton against the back of it. Immediately a group of twelve or fifteen other little girls clustered around her with triangles, tambourines, and sticks which they beat together. You should have heard them play. And sing. Unique is the only word for it.

The first number they did was "Old Black Joe." If you recall the lines of the last stanza, the words go, "I hear their gentle voices calling 'Old Black Joe.'" The youngsters didn't sing it that way. They sang it, "I hear their gentle voices calling 'G.I. Joe.'"

Somehow, it didn't sound unusual. These kids knew nothing of "Old Black Joe." They knew nothing of the War between the States, the slave days of the South. They knew nothing of the music that lilted out of plantation cabins to add to the musical culture of America.

But G.I. Joe, that was different. They knew G.I. Joe. He was an American soldier who'd come in through the beleaguered port of Pusan and fought his way north, pushing back the Communist invaders who'd slaughtered their parents. This G.I. Joe was the fellow who moved into a town with his tanks, his rifles and his grenades, and dislodged the enemy. While he was doing it, he would spy some frightened, little tyke, all alone, cowering in a corner or hiding in a barrel. He'd pause long enough to take the child in his arms, pet her a bit, and give her a bar of chocolate. Then he'd hunt up a chaplain, slip him a few bills, and say, "Chappie, you take care of this child, and when I get a chance, I'll see that you get some money."

He wouldn't forget. He'd shove on but he'd keep sending back money to care for the child.

On this basis, orphanages had sprung up all over Korea. Through G.I. generosity, tens of thousands of war-made orphans, from whose lives love and security had vanished, found new homes and new affection.

The Korean kids ended their program that Easter Sunday with a song for the country from which their friend, G.I. Joe, had come— "God Bless America."

There wasn't a dry American eye in the place.

PEARL HARBOR, FIFTEEN YEARS AFTER

WILBER M. BRUCKER
Secretary of the Army

Staunch is the word for Wilber M. Brucker. When the U. S. Army was under heavy attack by the late Senator Joseph R. McCarthy, Brucker—then general counsel for the Department —refused to kowtow to the Wisconsin demagogue. He insisted that there be an end to the abuse of Service men by politicians. Since his appointment as Secretary of the Army in 1955, he has been equally staunch in defense of Army and Army men's interests.

Brucker was an Army man himself once. A very brave one. He received the Silver Star for gallantry in action in World War I. Born in Michigan in 1894, he took a law degree at the University of Michigan, served as a prosecuting attorney, as attorney general, and at the age of thirty-seven was elected governor of the state. After his term of office he practiced law and headed Republican party affairs until his selection for the Defense Department post in 1954. His tenure as Secretary of the Army has been noted by his efforts to improve G.I. pay and conditions. I heard this story of his trip to Pearl Harbor at the Pentagon.

IT'S easy to forget the dead. Even those who have died for us. They're gone, and their sacrifices fade into the past. So we stop thinking about them. And of what they've done that we might live. Throughout history it's been that way.

But not always.

In the course of an inspection trip to the Far East, Secretary of the Army Wilber M. Brucker happened to be in Hawaii in December 1955—almost fourteen years to the day after the Japanese assault on Pearl Harbor. Curious, he set out to visit the scene of the attack.

The Navy men on duty at the base told him much about that brutal morning when the Japanese sneaked in on them. They related how a hundred and more planes came out of the skies, without warning, and started dropping bombs. They recounted how eight of the United States' giant battleships were sunk or damaged. How 2004 American sailors were killed.

Then they told him something else, something that startled him.

Pointing below the blue waters of the bay, they said, "Over nine hundred of those sailors are still down there."

"Still down there!" Brucker exclaimed. "Why? Couldn't you get them out?"

The admiral who was guiding him around explained.

The Navy was able to salvage all the battleships it lost that day except the U.S.S. *Utah*, the U.S.S. *Oklahoma*, and the U.S.S. *Arizona*. The latter was so horribly mangled that there was no possibility of raising her.

A diver was sent down to bring up the bodies of the officers and enlisted men trapped inside the shattered hull. His lines got tangled in the wreckage and he never came up. Another diver was sent down after him. He met the same fate.

It was self-evident, the Navy felt, that Providence intended that those men remain with their ship. They were therefore left where they'd fallen.

Brucker asked the admiral whether he might see the *Arizona*. Together they went out into Pearl Harbor in a small boat.

Only the blackened bridge of the battleship could be seen. The rest of her, tortured and twisted, lay fifteen feet below the water. A string of small floats marked the outline.

Their boat pulled close to the bridge and Brucker looked down into the wreckage. The water seemed different here from the rest, and he wondered why.

"That, Mr. Secretary," said the admiral, "is oil—oil, the lifeblood of the *Arizona*, still coming to the surface after all these years."

Up they climbed on the bridge. There was something that touched Brucker more even than anything else he'd seen. At the stern the American flag was flying.

"Why is the flag flying out here?" he asked.

The admiral drew himself up proudly. "We like to think of the *Arizona* and her crew as still on the active list of the Navy," he said. "We come out every morning and raise her flag, and every evening we take it down."

Americans remember.

AMERICANS AT WORK

BRIDGE OVER THE GOLDEN GATE

ERNEST G. SWIGERT

Past President, National Association of Manufacturers

Ernest G. Swigert is a two-fisted, hard-swinging industrialist dedicated to the concept that the free-enterprise system should, and can, produce more, better, and lower-priced goods than any other economic system known to man. Last year he held the highest elective office American industry can tender—president of the National Association of Manufacturers, whose twenty thousand member companies include the biggest in the United States and employ a majority of the country's working force.

A sixty-six-year-old Oregonian, Swigert heads a concern devoted to the task of lifting heavy burdens from men's backs. It is the Hyster Company, manufacturers of hoists, cranes, and other lifting equipment with plants in Portland, Oregon, Europe, and South America. He studied at Harvard and served as a pilot in World War I before he settled down to his industrial career. Here is the story he told me about the free-enterprise system at its best.

I T doesn't matter whether he's a corner grocer, a small-town contractor, or a great industrial tycoon. In America each businessman usually has a dream that he is pursuing. Not of sitting back on his haunches, playing things safe, but of growing, of making more and finer products, of doing a bigger, better job.

That is the hallmark of American business. Nothing is too tough for most American businessmen to tackle. And if they should be knocked about a bit in the process, they pick themselves up and start all over again. Trying even harder.

I've seen it happen hundreds of times. I saw it with my own father.

Dad was quite a guy. Anybody who knew Charles F. Swigert will tell you that. He was a typically daring, resilient kind of American businessman. There are monuments to his enterprise up and down the West. Boulder Dam, for example. And the Golden Gate Bridge.

The Golden Gate Bridge job is a good case in point. Some people thought it too much for Dad's company to handle. He went ahead anyway. Later it looked for a spell as though he were going to be licked. But he didn't quit. Not Dad. That's why the Golden Gate Bridge stands, majestic and beautiful, over San Francisco Bay today.

Before I tell you about it, let me recount a little about Dad himself.

At the time of the Golden Gate project he was seventyish, of medium height, and heavy-set. As a matter of fact, you wouldn't have been wrong to call him fat. He'd let his appetite get away from him and his weight was up to 220. However, he was a fine-looking fellow for all of that, with a splendid head of gray hair and shining blue eyes in a ruddy face. They laughed a lot, those eyes.

He never finished high school. His father died while Dad was a boy in Bowling Green, Kentucky, and he had to go to work. He was a well-educated man, though. An inveterate reader, he knew more about the Civil War, for instance, than most historians. He could tell you what Pickett ate for breakfast the morning of his charge.

From the start, Dad was out to conquer the world. He made his way to San Francisco and persuaded an uncle, who headed the Pacific Bridge Company, a west-coast construction firm, to give him a job. In a few years Dad was president.

Money meant nothing to him. He made and lost several different fortunes. And remade them. He was always ready to take a chance on any construction project so long as there was a challenge to it. He put the first bridge over the Columbia River. And the first one over the Willamette River. His was one of the famous "Six Companies" that banded together to build Boulder Dam.

The wiseacres had said that no one could build so tall a dam—the highest in the world. Dad and his associates did it.

Then came the Golden Gate Bridge. That was the roughest job of them all.

It was to be the longest suspension span in the world—forty-two hundred feet. No one had ever before attempted any bridge anywhere that was nearly as long.

It was to be in an area where terrific winds, thick fogs, and racing, ripping tides would make construction frighteningly perilous. If not impossible.

It was, in short, a construction man's nightmare.

Dad's heart had been acting up and the doctors were urging him to retire. "You have to take life easy from now on," they insisted.

They didn't know Dad.

He went out and bid on the hardest, most dangerous part of the entire Golden Gate job, building the great piers of concrete on which this vast suspension bridge was to stand. It was an eight-million-dollar contract.

He went after it against the advice of his best friends. "You'll go broke on this job," they warned him.

"You don't suppose a little thing like that would worry me," he said.

He got the contract.

There were two piers to be built. The one on the north of the bay was not a serious problem. It was just big. But the one on the San Francisco side was a "killer." Its location was in ninety feet of water, and it was so far out from shore that it was practically in the open sea. The tides here ran from eight to ten knots, four times a day, and there were frequent underwater surges, caused by the narrowing of the land formation at the entrance to the bay, which amounted to virtual submarine tidal waves.

Dad began by erecting an access trestle from the shore out to the site of the pier. It was eleven hundred feet long and twenty-two feet wide.

Scarcely had it been completed when a ship, lost in the San Francisco fog, crashed through it.

No sooner was the trestle repaired than a raging storm blew up and tore a jagged section out of it.

The job really seemed jinxed. "We told you so," Dad's friends said.

The specifications required Dad to build a tremendous steel fender around the site of the pier. This was to serve as a cofferdam during construction work, and, thereafter, to guard the pier against colliding vessels.

It was easier said than accomplished. Those terrible underwater currents—which couldn't even be noticed from the surface—crumpled the twenty-four-inch steel girders like paper. It happened again and again.

Dad was almost beside himself. Somehow he managed to get the fender up, though.

Then the worst setback of all.

The construction program for the pier was based on sinking a "dry caisson" inside the fender. This caisson—a giant pneumatic chamber of steel and reinforced concrete—was to extend up from the bed of the bay and keep out the water while the pier was being built within it.

Dad constructed the caisson according to plans, floated it out to the pier site, and maneuvered it inside the fender through an opening that had been left for the purpose. All that remained was to pump out the water and lower the caisson to the bottom.

That night underwater currents grabbed hold of the caisson as it floated inside the fender and, despite its size, began to toss it about like a canoe caught in a whirlpool. The currents jerked that enormous caisson so violently that it threatened to break down the walls of the fender.

The caisson had to be towed away at once, and the whole plan of construction for the pier abandoned.

"Well, have you had enough yet?" people asked Dad the next morning. "Will you admit now that this thing can't be done?"

I'll always remember Dad's attitude. It was so very American— so characteristic of a system of life where free men lean on themselves.

"Can't be done?" Dad said. "Heck, I haven't even started trying yet."

You should have seen him go. He introduced a totally different method of pier construction to San Francisco. Instead of employing a caisson, he poured liquid concrete right into the bay, using the weight of the concrete to force the water out from under it. A strong foundation was easily laid inside the fender, and the pier went up without any further difficulty.

On May 27, 1937, the Golden Gate Bridge was opened. I only wish that Dad could have been there to see it. He died before it was finished, though. That heart of his couldn't keep up with all the things he wanted to do.

STOCK REPORT

G. KEITH FUNSTON

President, New York Stock Exchange

---

*The reason the capitalist system works so well in America is
that there are so many capitalists. Millions of our people own
stock in corporations and share in the steady growth of the
American economy.*

*G. Keith Funston, the forty-eight-year-old president of the
New York Stock Exchange, has done much to encourage this.
Soon after his appointment in 1951 he inaugurated the Stock
Exchange's famous Monthly Investment Plan, which has en-
abled tens of thousands of "little" people to invest in sound
stocks.*

*An Iowan, Funston got through Trinity College on a scholar-
ship, went to Harvard Business School, did sales work for a time,
served on the War Production Board, then became president
of Trinity in 1944. The New York Stock Exchange, the most
important* bourse *in the world—a normal day's sales are
2,500,000 shares—chose him as president because he "was a man
of such character as to impress the public that the Exchange was
thinking more in terms of the public welfare than the securities
business." Here Funston has written of a special day at the
Stock Exchange.*

Go back and wave. The applause is for you."
Surprised and perplexed, our two visitors moved toward the
railing and glanced down at the noisy demonstration on the floor
below. Applause was something very new to them.

Until an eventful morning ten weeks earlier, these two men had
lived obscure lives without any special recognition. Day after day
they reported for work, attended to their jobs, returned home after
dark. Nothing ever changed the rhythm of their lives.

Even the day it happened began like any other day. In the cab
of the locomotive the engineer peered up the tracks beyond the yard
and eased the throttle open, while the trainman sat quietly in a
wooden passenger car, contemplating a timetable. Soon the train

was rolling west along a familiar route between familiar stations.

At noon one last stop remained. In a tumble of hills the train paused briefly at a siding while strong hands threw a heavy metal switch. All at once the train started moving again, lurched off the main tracks, and sped down an unused spur line rusty with age.

"I tied down the throttle and let her go," the engineer said later.

Whistle screaming, the train hurtled along. Up ahead lay a wooden barrier. As the locomotive crashed through, engineer Yaroslav Konvalinka and trainman Karel Truska, their wives, their children and one hundred other passengers passed from one world to another. A few more thrusts of the drive shaft and Communist Czechoslovakia lay behind.

Now, on the morning of November 21, 1951, these two brave men were touring the New York Stock Exchange. Since their escape they had flown to America, settled their families in a suburban community outside New York City, and obtained jobs with the Lionel Corporation, which manufactures model railways for children.

Dressed in new suits, light shirts, and small-pattern neckties, Konvalinka and Truska looked like any average Americans visiting the Stock Exchange. Yet because of what they were, they amounted to something more. As escapees, they symbolized the deep longing for freedom of the peoples behind the Iron Curtain.

In the accents of central Europe, an interpreter carefully translated for me as I told these fine new Americans about capitalism. I told them how it flourished vigorously in our democracy and why. I told them that an individual's money must be able to move as freely as the individual. I told them how capitalism had endured panics, depressions, and even global war to bring us the highest standard of living man has known.

I spoke of the boundless yield of our free economic system. I told them that it had rolled the first automobiles up our highways, put wings on the airplane, bottled milk, packaged food, inoculated our sick with miracle drugs.

Then I broke capitalism down into human statistics. I told our guests that millions of people owned our great corporations. I told them that the bulk of these share owners earned less than ten thousand dollars a year. I explained that a common-stock certificate represented part ownership of a business.

In one brief sentence I told them why capitalism has no limits: anybody at all can buy shares in American business.

As I spoke, Konvalinka and Truska listened attentively, shaking their heads, occasionally frowning, sometimes visibly startled. They were desperately trying to comprehend a system which had little or no meaning in the land they had fled. But they didn't ask a question. Not one.

After a while the two men walked onto the trading floor. Brokers' numbers appeared on the large black annunciator boards high on the north and south walls, calling members to their telephones. Clerks standing at banks of wall phones listed typical assortments of buy and sell orders for oil, rail, utility, food, automotive, aircraft, chemical stocks.

They kept on across the floor until they reached Post 9. A large wooden U-shaped structure around which brokers gather, Post 9 is much like the seventeen other trading posts except for one thing. Shares in the Lionel Corporation are bought and sold right there.

The two men, the company's newest employees, stood in front of Post 9 for a long time—silently. Then they returned to the long gallery overlooking the trading floor. Now, finally, Yaroslav Konvalinka spoke to the interpreter. He started to say something, paused, started again. At his side, Karl Truska listened to the flow of words.

"He wants to know one thing," the interpreter said to me. "He asks, 'Can even a working man like me buy stocks?' "

"Yes," I replied. "Tell him he can buy all the shares he wants and can afford."

A big radiant smile spread over Konvalinka's face. It made me warm all over. I had the feeling that everything I had said earlier was at last understood.

We walked toward the exit. From somewhere below, as people learned our visitors were departing, a murmur grew. The sound swelled and began to barrel up. Clerks, messengers, tube operators, specialists and brokers clapped their hands, cheered, whistled. For a moment, trading came to a standstill. The sound grew.

Our visitors stood there quietly. A final burst of cheering came up. Tears blurred Konvalinka's vision. Then I told them:

"Go back and wave. The applause is for you."

STARTING WITH A YEAST CAKE

WALTER HARD
Vermont Chronicler

---

*Small towns, especially in Vermont, have their own way of
doing business. To describe this, there's no one better than
Walter Hard. In his seventy-five Vermont years, he has been
a state representative, state senator, town official, storekeeper,
poet, author, newspaper columnist, and confidant of countless
Vermonters. Descendant of a family which helped settle the
state, he had every intention at college of going into journalism.
However, his father died and he had to take over the family
drugstore. He thought it would be temporary; it lasted thirty-
five years. "Paroled" at last, he opened the Johnny Appleseed
Bookstore in Manchester and made it into one of New England's
best. In 1910 he started doing a column for a local newspaper
and missed only two issues in twenty-eight years. He has to his
name six volumes of charming free verse about Vermont, a
volume on the Connecticut in the "Rivers of America" series,
and with his wife, Margaret, a splendid guidebook to Vermont.
Carl Sandburg says, "Walter Hard is poet, annalist, anecdotist.
I find his Yankees more fascinating than most of the Greeks in
Greek mythology." Here is Hard's report of a business transac-
tion in the Green Mountain state.*

FIRST it would be well to get the geography straight. Although
the land area of our township is just the usual six square miles,
there are three villages in it, with three separate post offices bearing
three different names. It can be pretty confusing to a stranger.

The earliest settlement was Manchester. It was founded in 1764
by some independent souls who figured that the big landholders
were getting too oppressive in New York. Somewhat later an industrial community grew up a bit to the north of Manchester which
got the name of Manchester Center. (It really started out as Factory
Point, but folks quickly became tired of that kind of a name.) Then
came the railroad, following the little Battenkill River, a half mile
or so to the east, and around it another village arose that was designated, naturally, as Manchester Depot.

If this has you all mixed up, think what it used to be in the past. When the railroad was still carrying passengers up here (now, it merely totes milk, maple syrup, and things of that ilk), you would alight at a station identified on the timetable as Manchester, but it would turn out to be Manchester Depot, two miles away. And it was uphill most of the distance.

Vermont is like that.

This report has mainly to do with the Village of Manchester. And with an old American habit that is particularly cherished here in Vermont. It is called "co-operation."

Some years ago the Village—that's the way we refer to Manchester —was in a ferment. The cause was, quite logically, a small foil-wrapped square known as a yeast cake. A very important commodity, too. "Boughten bread" was not an article easily come by then, and was viewed by many as evidence of a lack of proper housekeeping skill. Or even virtue.

Don't forget this yeast cake, reader, while we go back a step into the mercantile history of the Village.

For many years there had been the customary general store in Manchester. It was a fine big emporium which offered merchandise of sufficient variety to satisfy the needs of the entire citizenry as to clothing, food, and practically anything else a reasonable person could hanker after. Everything from a needle to a bale of hay. It was a godsend to a community such as ours.

In due course the two owners passed on and the business was taken over by a couple of younger men. Alas, they didn't do so well. Their minds were on other affairs, I guess. They lost so much money that they had to saw their three-story frame building in two, and sell half of it to the Episcopal church, which moved it across the road and consecrated it as St. John's Chapel. (It led one lady to express fear that instead of praying for heavenly grace, she might find herself asking the minister for a yard of black calico.)

Month by month the general store ran down more. It got so you could scarcely find the simplest item there. The shelves were almost empty.

That's how the humble yeast cake entered the picture. One day a desperate woman spoke up at Town Meeting. "When a body has to go to the Center or the Depot just to get a yeast cake, it's about time something was done."

No doubt civic pride was involved.

Nowadays many matters are decided in smoke-filled rooms. So it was in earlier times, too. In this case, the smoke-filled room was the office of a large resort hotel which served as a meeting place for a group of citizens. They were wont to spend a few evenings a week there in the wintertime playing King Pede or poker. Until their money ran out, that is. (One winter, a poor poker player who was a good farmer proposed that the kitty be made up of goods instead of cash. He suggested a quantity of vegetables as his offering. Others were canvassed as to what they could bring. The last to be asked was the local judge, who was the most skillful and/or lucky of the bunch. Without a moment's hesitation he said, "I'll bring a wheel-barrow to cart the stuff home in." That was the end of that idea.)

The question of the yeast cake came up there. "Did you hear what Nellie said at Town Meetin' about the gen'r'l store?" a player asked between hands of five-card draw.

"Yep," the others said.

There was a pause while the hand was played.

"Seems to me that Nellie's right."

"Yep."

Another pause for another hand. Then, "Reckon somethin' ought to be done about it?"

"Yep."

That was all. Vermonters don't talk much. Especially when they're playing cards.

By the next poker night one of the players had talked with the owners of the declining business and learned that they'd be glad to sell out for a fair price. Another had spoken with the man who now owned the building the store was in. He was ready to renew the lease for exactly the same rental. The group had even picked a man to run the new store.

Who? None of the members of the poker club, of course. They wanted to give a young man a chance. So they settled on a young fellow they used to know. You'll be surprised when I tell you that he didn't live in the Village. Or even in Vermont.

This boy had worked his way through the nearby prep school, and put in a spell as assistant to the postmaster. Then luck had gone against him, what with serious illness and such in his family. He'd had to move out to Ohio and take a job in a rubber plant.

He hadn't a shred of retail experience, and everyone realized it. But he'd demonstrated enough courage and ambition under tough circumstances to make him worthy of support. That's what the men in the poker club thought, anyhow.

They got in touch with him right off. They found him willing— willing, nothing; anxious—to come home and take on the new enterprise. And to make a success of it.

He had no money, though. Not a cent with which to purchase the store and rehabilitate it.

It didn't faze these men a whit. " 'Spect as how we'll have to raise the money ourselves," they said.

Mind you, none of them was rich. In Vermont you don't live on income; you live on lack of expense.

Down they went to see the local banker. He listened to their story. "Sure, you can have the money," he said. "This Village needs a good store."

He thereupon agreed to accept the note of the new proprietor, backed by the card-playing group.

It's more than forty years now since that store opened, and it still is flourishing in the Village. I was down there the other day. It certainly pleased me to see that it's doing so well. And that it still sells yeast cakes.

A small business, to be sure, in a small community. But it shows the sort of co-operation that's made America great.

Perhaps it also shows the leavening power one disgruntled citizen can have. That's typical of America, too.

JUSTICE ON THE ASSEMBLY LINE

A. J. HAYES

President, International Association of Machinists

The past two decades have seen trade unions gain acceptance in the United States as a powerful integral force on the industrial and political scene. The result has been a more equitable, peaceful relationship between management and employees.

A. J. Hayes, president of the International Association of Machinists, one of the most progressive, scandal-free unions in the A.F. of L.-C.I.O., has described the meaning of this to the working man. Born in Wisconsin in 1900, Hayes went to work as a youngster for the Milwaukee Railroad. The other apprentices thought they weren't getting a square deal and picked him to argue their case. Ever since, machinists have been asking him to be their spokesman. Climbing up through the union ranks, he became head of the 675,000-man organization in 1949. He is also chairman of the A.F. of L.-C.I.O. Ethical Practices Committee and a vigorous battler against any form of corruption or dictatorship in the labor movement.

ONE of the fine things about our free way of life in the United States is the opportunity it affords all of us, regardless of our station in society, to make the most of our individual talents. Another is the equal opportunity it offers us all for justice if ever our honesty, integrity, or sincerity is questioned.

I hadn't been long in the labor movement when the importance of these two things was brought home to me—hard.

It was back in 1938, at the tail end of the terrible depression. I was working as an organizer for the International Association of Machinists, and I was assigned to service a local union in a little town in northern Wisconsin. As you might expect from the location, the members were largely German. Most of them were dairy farmers who'd turned to employment in a small manufacturing plant nearby in a last-ditch effort to eke out their shrunken farm incomes.

Shortly before I arrived, the plant hired a new employee, and the union took in a new member, in the person of a journeyman machinist "fresh out of the old country." I've forgotten his name now, so I'll call him Konrad Schmidt for purposes of identification.

Konrad had come to the United States for two main reasons. First, he wanted to be with his brothers and sisters who had migrated to the United States earlier. Second, he could not endure the growing tyranny of Hitler's Third Reich. Konrad had strong feelings about dictators.

Being the sort of man he was, Konrad threw himself wholeheartedly into his new life—his job, his community, and his union. The work was different from the broader, more exacting type of skill he was accustomed to in the old country, but he readily adapted himself to the demands of a mass-production industry. Soon he was rated one of the top employees of the company.

Then the local owners sold out to a big corporation. The small plant became just another unit in a vast, multibranch enterprise.

Gone was the fine family feeling that had prevailed. The new management converted to an incentive system of wage payment, and brought in efficiency engineers to speed things up.

A few months after this piecework plan went into effect the plant manager and a couple of his assistants began to show unusual interest in Konrad. No one could understand why.

The reason became clear. All too clear. One morning Konrad was called in to the front office.

"You're fired," he was told. They didn't even give him a week's notice.

"But vy?" he asked. "For vat reason do you fire me?"

"You've been falsifying your production records," they said. "You've been taking money under false pretenses."

Konrad was heartsick. Here he'd been working his hardest, using every bit of know-how his training had given him, and now he found himself accused of lying. Worse, he was accused of stealing. He didn't know what to do.

His fellow members of the machinists' local union didn't know what to do either. The plant manager paid no attention when they protested the discharge.

The officers of the local union requested my help. I must admit I was flabbergasted by the nature of the problem. Unions generally have to guard against management setting production norms too high. Never before had I run across a case of an employee being dismissed for claiming to produce far above the norms set by a company's own efficiency experts.

Was it possible that Konrad was actually faking his records?

There was only one way to find out. I went to management and proposed an objective test of the facts. I suggested that Konrad be given a chance to prove his claims right at his own lathe.

The plant manager wouldn't listen to me. It was utterly ridiculous, he declared, to say that an employee could turn out work at the rate Konrad claimed he'd been doing.

"Perhaps it is," I argued, "but in this country everyone is entitled to a fair trial."

The manager stopped and thought. "Mebbe you've got something there," he said. "He can have his trial."

He agreed that Konrad would be permitted to come into the plant and work three complete shifts under the observation of three persons, one representing the company, one representing the union, and a neutral. In the event that Konrad established the validity of his claims, he was to be immediately restored to his old job and be fully reimbursed for the time he had lost. If he didn't, he would be out for good. And stigmatized forever as a liar and a thief.

The opening day of the trial came. The three observers could scarcely believe their eyes. Konrad turned out more production than he'd ever done before—much more than the efficiency experts said was possible. The second day he did it again. On the third—well, he did still more.

It was quite a spectacle to see the manager's face as he read the observers' reports.

The next morning, Konrad was back on the pay roll. In his pocket was a check for the several weeks he'd been laid off.

"Iss good, dis American system," he remarked to me.

There have been many times in my life when I've been proud to be an American but I think that nothing had made me prouder than the sight of this immigrant, happy in his vindicated skills and confident in the justice which a free country and a free labor movement had gained for him.

It was merely a minor incident involving little people, but it invoked a major principle, a principle which is one of the distinguishing differences between a free, democratic form of government and the many variations of quasi-democratic and totalitarian systems.

A country can remain free and democratic only if all its people are governed by just laws and not by men's whims.

A LETTER BY THE UNION

J. C. RICH

Editor, The Hat Worker

Tears, sweat, and blood went into the building of America's trade unions, and the loyalty of many union members to their organizations can be a stirring thing.

J. C. Rich is well acquainted with union members. A veteran labor journalist (and probably the most gifted writer-reporter of them all), he was born in Russia in 1894, arrived in the United States in 1907, and in no time had won a scholarship to Harvard. He has been reporting the labor scene since 1922 for the venerable Jewish Daily Forward *and, in addition, editing* The Hat Worker, *the official publication of the United Hatters, Cap and Millinery Workers International Union, a monthly news magazine which has won repeated awards for its editorial brilliance. He has also written for* The Saturday Evening Post, The New Leader *and other top magazines. Throughout his career, Jack Rich has been one of the country's most effective, and least demagogic, anti-Communists. He wrote this report on unionism, American style.*

I HEARD it myself. I was visiting a millinery factory in midtown New York when this worker approached the union chairlady in a state of considerable agitation.

"Ha, a union!" he exclaimed. "You call this a union? Some union for you."

The explosion was out of character for the man. I'd known him for years, and he was not given to tempestuous outbursts. A meek little person whose spare frame had been bowed by years of stooping over a whirring sewing machine, his strongest expression was usually a verse of poetry which he recited by heart, his strongest drink a glass of buttermilk, his strongest meat a dish of yogurt. Furthermore, it was altogether unnatural for him to criticize his union. If vegetarianism was his faith, the union was his temple. Poetry, vegetarianism, and trade unionism, not necessarily in this order, were the three mainstays of his life.

"What's wrong, Sam?" the chairlady asked.

"Per cents," he sputtered. "Per cents, they give me."

"Whatever are you talking about?" she said.

"Look, it's right here. Per cents." He produced an envelope with an enclosure of a check. "Yesterday I come home from work, I look in the letter box, is a letter from the union. Not from the union, the local, but the union, the main office. It's a letter from the president, Alex Rose. So I'm very glad to get a letter from the president. Why not? I know him personal; we worked in the same shop together and even belonged to the same society, *Kooltoor un Literatoor*, a long time ago. So now he is the president and is a big *macher* in the politics, and I am an operator by millinery, but does it make a difference? I am still his friend, and even if he is the president I don't hold it against him. But this? It's an insult! A dirty insult!"

The insult, it turned out, consisted of a check totaling some eighteen dollars. The accompanying letter stated that it was in payment of interest on a loan he had made to the union when it was in need of money to conduct an unduly prolonged strike in a men's hat plant in Connecticut. The letter expressed thanks to the member for his generosity and union devotion, and stated that other interest payments would follow until the debt was repaid.

"But there's nothing wrong with that," the chairlady stated. "You loaned the money to the union, so the union is paying you interest on it. Is that anything wrong?"

Sam stepped back a pace in sorrowful astonishment. "You," he said, "you, too? You should say that? Some chairlady, if you say that! What am I, a banker, a loan shark, I should get per cents? Is it a business by me I should give money they should pay me per cents?"

"But, Sam, for goodness' sake, can't you understand? You took the money out of the bank. In the bank the money would earn interest. So the union was up against it in the strike and asked the members to chip in and give it a loan, and that's how it won the strike. But if the members helped the union and put their savings in its strike treasury instead of the bank, should they lose money on it? Suppose the union went to the bank and borrowed the money, wouldn't it have to pay twice as much interest? So what's so terrible if the union makes good at least the bank interest to the members?"

"No, I won't take it," Sam insisted. "It's wrong, all wrong. They make the whole thing a cold business proposition. Was it a business by me I should give money to the union? Could I rest if I didn't give the money? Could I work in the shop, nice and warm, and get steady wages regular, eat protose and nuttose steak every day like a prince, while out there all winter they stand in the cold on the picket line, glad to get a little bite to eat in the soup kitchen, the women asking how long, the children need shoes, the men worried sick, but brave? Could I stand that? It was wrong they should have to ask me for the money. I should have given it myself, no asking. So now they give me interest. A cold business proposition. Per cents, they give me. I won't take it."

He threw the letter and check down in front of the chairlady and returned to his sewing machine.

That's a union man for you—in America.

POLICE STATION

EVA MARIE SAINT
Screen and TV Actress

A man can work where and at what he pleases in this country without interference from the government. It is a right that the people of many other lands don't enjoy.

Eva Marie Saint was deeply stirred when she heard how much this could mean to an immigrant to America, and she told me about it. Miss Saint is the gifted young actress whose performance in the film, On the Waterfront, *won her the 1954 "Oscar" as the best supporting actress of the year. A New Jersey-ite, born in 1929, Miss Saint got into acting while she was a student at the Bowling Green State University in Kentucky. Upon her graduation in 1946 she haunted the casting offices in New York until she broke into radio and TV. Her first Broadway role in* The Trip to Bountiful *brought the critics' acclaim and the female lead in* On the Waterfront. *After that—stardom.*

WE got to talking at a party in New York one night, this man and I. He'd been an immigrant, so I asked him what it'd been like to arrive in America with no money, no job, no friends. This is the story he told me.

✻   ✻   ✻   ✻   ✻   ✻

When we landed in New York the woman who spoke to us on the dock wore an arm band; we knew she must be an official. She sent us to an uptown address, and though we did not trust officials, we went. The room was neat and cheap, so we took it.

Then we waited.

We knew it would not be long. This was 1947, and we had seen it happen everywhere. All those thousands who had gone from the prison camps in Poland to one concentration camp after another in Germany would tell you it was always the same. You had to wait in your quarters till somebody knocked on the door and called, "Police!" In six years you learned what to expect and how to act. You did not try to fight. Those who fought disappeared.

My heart pounded every time we heard somebody come up the steps. But there was no knock. Always the sounds passed.

It was the same the second day, and the third. The police did not come.

My wife and I took turns going to the grocery store at the corner. Once a day we brought back what we needed to see us through the next meal or two—bread, cheese, milk, a few slices of bologna. Even the trip to the grocer seemed a great risk, however, and we always put it off as long as we could.

By the end of the fourth day I began to feel desperate. I walked around in the small room. "Why don't they come?" I kept saying. "What new kind of trick is this. Why must they torment us?"

"Be patient," my wife said.

"Our money will soon be gone," I said. "How long *can* we wait like this? I have to find work!"

She became thoughtful. "What would happen if we did not wait for the police?"

I laughed at that. "Then we would quickly be in their prisons! Who would give me a job as I am, without a card of identity?"

This my wife could not answer.

On the fifth day, after I had bought food, we had only a few cents left. I looked at the coins in my hand and I said, "Ilse, we cannot wait any longer. Who knows? Maybe it will take them weeks to get around to us. No, we cannot wait. I will go to *them*."

This alarmed her. Using the dresser as a table, she had been spreading cheese on bread. Now she turned with a gasp, put a hand on my arm. "No! You cannot go to the police! They may never let you come back! Do you not remember how it was in Warsaw?"

"This is not Warsaw," I said. "Besides, I would as soon go to the police as starve in this room. I am sick of waiting. I will go."

"Then I will go with you!"

I thought, she is right. If she does not go with me, they may hold me alone. And this time we may be separated forever.

"Very well," I said. "We will go together."

Outside, she held my arm tight, and we looked up and down the sunny street.

"Where is their police bureau?" she asked.

"I do not know. Maybe the grocer will tell us."

The grocer was the only man to whom we had talked. He was fat and friendly. "The police station?" he said. "Just one street that way,

then one street to the left. You can't miss it. Two green lights on
the outside."

I said, "Thank you." With my wife still holding tight to my arm,
we walked as the grocer had directed. When we came around a
corner and saw the building with the two green lights I stopped for
a second. I patted her hand on my arm.

She said, "Come. I am not afraid."

But when we went inside, my own heart was pounding again.

A heavy bald man in uniform sat behind a high desk. He said,
"Yes? What is it?"

"Please," I said. "Your men did not come to me, so I had to come
to you. I hope this is not against the regulations."

He looked puzzled. "I don't get it, mister. What is it you want?"

I began to unwrap my passport and my other papers. "I wish
permission to work," I said.

"Who's stopping you?"

"I have no identification card, nothing," I said. I gave him the
papers.

He looked through them, and after a while his brows went up.
"Hey," he said, "prison camps, hospitals, D.P. centers. Poland, Germany, France . . . You two sure have been around, haven't you?"

"Yes."

"What kind of work you looking for?"

"I know sewing machines," I said. "In Poland my people sold
sewing machines. I can repair them, too. I wish to find such work."

The man at the desk gave me back the papers. "Best bet for you,"
he said, "is the garment district. Along Seventh Avenue in the Thirties. Chances are they have hundreds of sewing machines that need
fixing. Couldn't get spare parts during the war. You just go from door
to door. Shouldn't have any trouble finding repair work."

I stared at the papers in my hand. I stared at my wife. Then I
looked up again at the man behind the desk.

"But do I not need a permit? A card?"

"What for?"

"To show I—I'm entitled to be here?"

"You *are* here. What more you want?"

"But when—when I ask for work, will they not want to see an
identity card?"

"Mister, going from door to door to make repairs, you don't need
cards. If you know how to fix sewing machines, that's all anybody is

going to ask." He looked at the clock. "You want my advice, get going. Around here you're just wasting time. *We* got no sewing machines."

My wife and I walked out of the police station, and I was dazed. I still held the papers, but no one wanted to see them, nobody was interested in making us prove anything. The police didn't care about my politics or my religion or where I was born. They didn't care where I lived. All such things belonged in the past, with the years in the prison camps. Here they had not bothered even to register me. And if I wanted work I had only to go find it.

"Ilse——" Outside the police station I looked at my wife, and right there on the street I took her into my arms. "They did not ask us *anything!*" I said. "Ilse, we are Americans!"

❋   ❋   ❋   ❋   ❋   ❋

That man is one of the biggest figures in the ladies' garment industry today.

OPERATION BOOTSTRAP

LUIS MUÑOZ MARÍN
Governor of Puerto Rico

---

*During the past eighteen years the people of Puerto Rico
have done the miraculous. They have pulled themselves up by
their own bootstraps and turned what used to be called "the
pest hole of the Caribbean" into a prospering, happy garden
spot. They have proved what a hard-working people can do
once they're given the light.*

*The man who has illumined the way for the Puerto Ricans
is Luis Muñoz Marín, a sixty-year-old poet with vision, courage,
and the ability to lead. A Puerto Rican by birth, he was brought
up and educated in the United States where he earned his
living, such as it was, writing poetry in English and Spanish.
Stirred by the misery in Puerto Rico, he returned there in 1931,
founded his own political party, and in 1940 ousted the en-
trenched business interests from power. When the Puerto
Ricans were given the right to choose their own governor in
1948, he was elected in a landslide, and re-elected in 1952
and 1956. The gains the island has made under his administration are almost immeasurable. Not the least of them is the
unique commonwealth form of government he devised by
which Puerto Rico, for decades a colony of the United States,
now enjoys almost complete autonomy. Not surprisingly, Muñoz
is idolized by his 2,250,000 countrymen. This is his story as
he told it to me, of one phase of Puerto Rico's "Operation Bootstrap."*

FIFTEEN cents an hour is not much of a wage for a grown man.
Not when he has a wife and children to support. It means that
his family is hungry most of the time. And ragged. And sick.

It can do bad things to a man's spirit to come home after a hard
week's work with only a few dollars' pay and see his famished children cough blood. It can make him give up hope. Tomorrow stands
for just another nightmare. The same nightmare that yesterday was
and today is.

This was life, not so very long ago, for a special group of Americans—the two million and more people on the island of Puerto Rico. Hundreds of thousands of them were unemployed, and those who had work received only a pitifully few pennies. Starvation and squalor were everywhere. And disease. Tuberculosis, malaria, and dysentery in particular. The death rate for tuberculosis was four and a half times that of the continental United States.

The number of babies who died in infancy was pathetic. Life expectancy for the population at large was a puny forty and a half years.

Do you wonder that the people's mood was one of tragic apathy? That homeless waifs roamed the streets, not knowing and not caring who their parents were? That honest men committed crimes—if you can call stealing a loaf of bread a crime—in front of policemen so they could be sent to prison? In prison they could eat.

Now life is something else in Puerto Rico. Since 1940 the island's annual income has climbed from $225,301,000 to nearly $1,006,850,000, while the income of the average family has risen from $120 a year in 1940 to $2,215 a year, almost the highest in all of Latin America.

Men have work at decent wages. They have decent homes instead of hovels. They have decent food. And they have health. Malaria has been completely wiped out, tuberculosis has been bested. As recently as ten years ago tuberculosis was the number-one killer. Today it ranks sixth.

Life expectancy is up to sixty-eight years.

There are schools for the children now and educational facilities for adults, too. There are 129 hospitals where before there were scarcely any, 2786 miles of fine roads, countless parks and public beaches.

Best of all, there is hope.

The people of Puerto Rico can look forward to their future.

From all over the world trained observers come to Puerto Rico now to study the transition that has taken place. Some have said that it is the most rapid example of emergence from underdevelopment in history. They see this commonwealth, flying the United States Flag beside its own, proud of its United States citizenship, sharing free trade and currency and common defense with the United States, yet governing itself. And they know that this is not the imperialist behavior the Soviets would like to have people expect of the U.S. They come to me and they ask, "How did your government do it?" Sometimes I tell them how the Puerto Rican Government planned, how it educated, how it appropriated, how it made difficult decisions. But always in the back of my mind is the deeper realization that the government didn't really do it. That no government can. That only a people themselves can rise above despair and hopelessness.

And that makes me think of a certain barrio.

Barrio Rio Arriba is a tiny section, near a pretty little town in the mountains of central Puerto Rico. A river comes from the peaks above and runs through the barrio past the town.

Ordinarily the river is a small stream that you can ford without the least difficulty. But in the rainy season flash floods make it a torrent, deep, swirling and dangerous.

Until August 1951 there was no way of crossing the river when this occurred. If it rained during the night, the men in the barrio couldn't get over the river to their jobs in the town, the hundred or so children in the barrio couldn't get to school. If it rained during the day, the men and the children couldn't get home. They were stuck in the town with no place to sleep.

Once a schoolboy tried to breast the raging waters. He was swept up and battered almost to death against the rocks that line the stream bed.

The people of the barrio—sickly, largely illiterate and unskilled —had only one notion of a solution. It was to request the government to build them a bridge over the river.

For years they petitioned for it. To no avail, though. The government of Puerto Rico was poor. It took a long time to get around to the most pressing necessities.

It never entered the heads of the people that they might be able to do something about the river themselves.

Then José Rodriguez Rivera, an organizer for the Government's Division of Community Education, arrived in the barrio. His job was to awaken the population to the value of health, sanitation, schooling, things like that.

The people were keenly interested in Rodriguez' movies and booklets, but there was a question which concerned them a lot more. A delegation of twenty-four called on Rodriguez to ask:

"What can be done about this ogre of a stream?"

"What should be done?" Rodriguez inquired.

"The government must build a bridge over it for us," they insisted.

Rodriguez was a wise man who knew his countrymen and had faith in them. "Did you ever think of building the bridge yourselves?" he said quietly.

The very idea was staggering. No one in the area had ever had any training in bridge design. In the whole barrio there was only one man with any construction experience. And how were building materials to be obtained? These were penniless laborers and farmers.

"It is an impossibility," the delegation declared.

But after they got home, they thought about it more. "Perhaps it can be done," they said. "We can at least try."

So they tried.

A hat was passed. Pennies, nickels, and dimes were dropped in. For the barrio, a huge amount—$125.

Urged on by the others, the man with construction experience sat down and drew a plan for a small concrete footbridge—a rather unique one. His specifications called for using two old truck chassis as supports. He'd seen them in a junk yard in the town and thought they might be secured cheap.

Down to the office of the district engineer of the Puerto Rican Department of the Interior he hitchhiked with the plan. The district engineer reviewed it carefully. For its purpose, it was excellent.

Into the town went a group of people from the barrio. They were ready to buy the building materials for their bridge. But $125 doesn't go far when you have a concrete bridge—even a small one—to put up. They didn't have enough.

The people didn't lose courage. Or determination. They sent a delegation to the mayor of the town. They persuaded him to donate eighty bags of cement and six hundred pounds of iron rods from the town's supplies. Another delegation was sent to talk with the head of a school that was being rebuilt. They persuaded him to contribute all the old lumber. A third group visited the owner of the local junk yard. Upon their departure they had those two old truck chassis —as a gift.

Work could start now. But who was to boss the job? The people of the barrio decided that democratically. They held an election to choose a "foreman" from among themselves.

On July 12, 1951, construction began. When the "foreman" called for ten men to volunteer their labor, fifty came. And more came on subsequent days.

Twenty-two days later the bridge was completed. It was dedicated with due pomp and ceremony. But minus oratory by any politician. There was just one real speech. It was delivered by the youngster who'd been swept down the stream the year before.

With people like that, is it any surprise that Puerto Rico is doing so well?

It brings to mind something that happened during the festivities marking the opening of the bridge. A stranger asked a man from the barrio, "How did this bridge come about?"

The local man grinned. "We people here, we didn't know our own strength," he said.

AMERICANS AT SCHOOL

CLASSROOM CRISIS

ISIDORE STARR
New York Schoolteacher

*Geometry is hardly a matter of controversy. No pupil is
likely to dispute the Euclidean theorem. Nor is any student
apt to quarrel with the conjugation of a Latin verb. But it can
happen that the principles of democracy are challenged in the
classroom.*

*Dr. Isidore Starr had this occur and he has written of it
here. A teacher of social studies at Brooklyn Technical High
School, Dr. Starr was born in New York in 1912, graduated
Phi Beta Kappa from City College, and took a Ph.D. at the New
School for Social Research. He has been teaching since 1934
save for three years in the Army during which he helped
liberate the Philippines. In 1952 he was named one of the
country's twenty outstanding high-school teachers and awarded
a John Hay Whitney Fellowship in the Humanities.*

Y EAR in and year out you teach school kids about the tenets of
American democracy. You hope it means something to them. You
never know for sure, though. Then a crisis arises in the classroom
and the principles you've been talking about are put to the test.
This can be tense.

It was in March 1956 at the Brooklyn Technical High School in
New York City. The class was American History 221c.

For several days the class had been discussing the strengths of
American democracy and some of its weaknesses. That morning the
period began with an examination of the reasons for discrimination
against minority groups.

In the midst of the discussion a seventeen-year-old Polish boy by
the name of Zarudni raised his hand. He declared that there were
deep-seated motivations for human hatred, and he bitterly related
how his brother had been stabbed by a Puerto Rican.

His emotional outburst ended with the statement, "All Puerto Ricans are bad."

A moment of terrible, embarrassing silence followed. The one

Puerto Rican in the class, a lad named Garcia, looked as though he'd been struck in the face.

Slowly I walked to the blackboard and wrote down what Zarudni had said: "All Puerto Ricans are bad." With my heart in my mouth, I asked the students to evaluate this all-inclusive judgment.

The comments which ensued led to an alteration of the original remark. The students took statistical inventory and arrived at a different conclusion. It was: "Most Puerto Ricans are bad."

Even Zarudni supported the change.

I acted the role of the gadfly. "How many Puerto Ricans are there? How many do you know?"

This succeeded in eliciting a second switch in the statement. It was agreed: "Some Puerto Ricans are bad."

Zarudni had to concur.

Now I began to press for an analysis of this value judgment, requesting every student to examine each word in the new conclusion. Gradually there emerged a third alteration. It was: "Some people are bad."

Here there was unanimous agreement, Zarudni included.

"How do you judge human decency and indecency?" I pushed on.

The answer was not long in coming from the students. Every person is innocent until proven guilty of indecency, inhumanity, or criminality. And each person should be judged on this scale regardless of race, creed, or color.

The bell rang, ending the period. Gabbing excitedly, the students picked up their books and filed from the room. To my delight, Zarudni, the boy who had started the wrangle, and Garcia, his innocent target, walked out together. They were talking to each other in the friendliest fashion.

I relaxed. "No doubt of it," I said to myself, "these old American ideals can be very convincing."

THE JUVENILE DELINQUENTS

LOUIS N. DEL VECCHIO
New York Schoolteacher

Juvenile delinquency is a sore point these days. Here and abroad it seems to be spreading wider and getting more vicious. Yet there are techniques for handling it that seem to work. Louis N. Del Vecchio has tried them.

Del Vecchio, a thirty-four-year-old New Yorker, is a music teacher in a New York City junior high school, and a talented musician to boot. He plays the oboe and a half-dozen other instruments in various community orchestras. A graduate of New York University, he served with the Air Force in India (where he played in the Calcutta Symphony). He told me this story.

THE three boys slumped in their seats. Ned, the biggest and toughest of them, scowled. "I don't know nuttin' about it."

I turned to the second of the three. "How about you, Joe?"

"Don't know whatcha talkin' about," he said.

"And you, Willie?" I asked the little one.

"Me neither," he whined. "I never even seen the stuff."

Once again I tried to get the truth. "Listen, fellows," I declared. "Richie says you stole them. He said you shoved him around, and took them from him. Now, what about this?"

"Nuts," Ned growled. "Richie's off his rocker."

Frightening them was the only thing left. "Do you fellows realize what'll happen if Richie goes to the police? Have you counted on that at all?"

"Let'm," Ned said. "They can't prove nuttin' on us."

I got up. "O.K., fellows, if that's the way you want to be, go ahead. I can't do anything to you. But let me tell you, I sure am disappointed in you. I figured you for good guys. I was wrong."

The three filed sullenly from the office. They were scarcely beyond the door when I heard one of them say, "Snitchin'! Wait'll I get my hands on Richie. I'll kick his teeth down his throat."

That really got me mad.

Out the door I ran. "If you boys lay a finger on Richie," I shouted, "I swear I'll go after you myself. Stay away from him. Do you hear me?"

"And don't show up for band rehearsals any more," I added. "We don't want boys like you in the school band."

I was miserable as I ate my lunch that day. Our experiment had failed. We'd been hoping that the old American idea of team spirit could redeem some of the more troublesome boys at Patrick Henry Junior High. We'd taught several of these difficult youngsters to play musical instruments—it was no easy task, I can assure you. Then we'd invited them to join the school band. We thought the pride of belonging to the band, of playing with the other school musicians, might offset the bad habits they picked up on the sidewalks of East Harlem.

Ned, Joe, and Willie were among the first we'd worked with. We'd had big expectations of them.

They weren't bad boys at heart. Ned's defiant exterior, I knew, was a shell to ward off the taunts of his companions at the behavior of his alcoholic father. That Joe occasionally indulged in a petty theft was merely because he was a weak boy in a rough neighborhood, seeking to prove he wasn't a "square." Willie did what the older boys in his street club told him to do solely because he was small and afraid not to.

It had seemed as though we were making true progress with them. Ned, the tough guy, had gotten to the point where he was carrying his trumpet home every night and practicing for hours on end. "Just so I can keep up with the other guys." Joe was now the first to volunteer when we needed a boy to pass out the day's music. Wise guy Willie, "never much for readin'," was inordinately proud to be our best drummer.

Obviously we'd failed. The night before, the three of them had backed Richie, another kid in the band, against the wall of his squalid tenement flat and robbed him. They didn't take much—just a fielder's glove and two fountain pens belonging to his mother—but for Richie it was a lot. His family didn't have much. No one does in East Harlem.

"American team spirit," I muttered to myself. "It doesn't mean a thing."

Dejectedly I started back to my office. I never got there. Four boys were waiting for me outside the lunchroom: Ned, Joe, Willie—and Richie.

"We got sump'n for you, Mr. Del Vecchio."

Ned handed me a crumpled note. Suspiciously, I opened it and read its crudely penciled message:

"Receeved frum Willie, Tom and Ned

1 feelders gluv

2 fountin pens,"

It was signed by Richie's mother.

"Now, can we stay in the band?" Willie spoke in a tremulous voice.

"Rehearsal's in ten minutes. You'd better hurry," I replied.

OLD SCHOOL TIES

HOWARD E. WILSON

Dean, School of Education, University of California at Los Angeles

---

The affection that many children feel toward their school-teachers is no fleeting thing. It lasts through the years. Teachers call it their richest emolument.

Dr. Howard E. Wilson has known countless instances of it and recounted a choice one to me. A distinguished educator, Dr. Wilson was appointed dean of the School of Education of the University of California at Los Angeles last year. The fifty-seven-year-old, Harvard-educated Illinoisan has held some of the most influential posts in the field of education. He has been secretary of the Educational Policies Commission of the National Education Association, headed the educational division of the Carnegie Endowment for International Peace, served as co-secretary of the Joint Canadian-U. S. Commission on Education, acted as a consultant to the U. S. Navy, been a Harvard professor, and several times represented the United States to UNESCO.

I'M not going to tell you her real name. Nor the name of the Midwestern city where it happened. She wouldn't want me to. She's a modest little woman who hates to be the center of attention. But I can say that she is the finest kind of schoolteacher, interested in her work, devoted to her pupils, and ever honest.

The whole affair was a shock. To those of us in the teaching profession, it was also something of a thrill. It demonstrated so vividly that wonderful sense of loyalty which American boys and girls, aged seven to seventy, can show their old teachers in times of stress.

For Mrs. Baker (I'm going to call her that), this was certainly a time of stress.

A former student of hers who has grown up to be a successful young lawyer saw her, a wisp of a white-haired woman, walking down the street, crying. He could scarcely credit his eyes. She had always made such a point of hiding her emotions.

He ran after her. "You remember me, don't you, Mrs. Baker?" he said. "I'm . . ."

Hastily brushing her eyes, she said, "Yes, I remember you, John."

"What's wrong?" he asked. "Why are you crying?"

"Nothing is wrong, John."

"C'mon, tell me," he insisted.

"Truly, John, nothing is wrong."

And she kept on walking.

He wouldn't let her go, though, and finally she broke down. After thirty years as a teacher in the high school, she had just been handed her dismissal notice.

The young lawyer practically exploded. "Why?" he spluttered. "What's got into the school board?"

Then it came out. The officials of the local utility had objected to the way Mrs. Baker had discussed the public power issue in her social science classes. They'd denounced her to the school board as a Communist.

"And I'm not," Mrs. Baker wept. "I couldn't be. All I did was give the children both sides of the question."

When he got home that evening the young lawyer went straight to the telephone. He called up a man who had been in his class at high school.

"Did you hear what they're doing to old Mrs. Baker?" he said. "What?"

"They're firing her. The utility boys say she's a Communist. I want you to phone them the first thing in the morning. Tell 'em what you think about it."

"I sure will," the other man said.

"And," the young lawyer continued, "I want you to call everyone else you know who ever studied under Mrs. Baker. And get them to phone everybody they know."

After that, the young lawyer called another man. And another. He didn't get off the phone until long past midnight. Nor did any of the people he called. Nor the people they called.

At nine o'clock the following morning the switchboard started buzzing at the main offices of the utility. Phone calls began to pour in by the hundreds. They went like this:

"What are you doing to Mrs. Baker? She's the best teacher I ever had."

"She's a swell person."

"She's no more Communist than I am."

"She's a real American."

That afternoon the head of the utility telephoned the chairman of the school board.

"I want to apologize," he said. "We were wrong about Mrs. Baker. We've had evidence from hundreds of people that she's a decent citizen and a splendid teacher."

Mrs. Baker got her job back. She was a bit fussed about all the ruckus, though.

"Those children," she muttered. "What will they be up to next?"

THE CHURCH IN AMERICA

THE BISHOP IN DETROIT

REINHOLD NIEBUHR

Vice-President, Union Theological Seminary

---

*No American in recent decades has done more to make
people think Protestantism through than Reinhold Niebuhr.
This sixty-five-year-old theologian has shaken the Protestant
world with his provocative, profound appraisals of modern-
day religion. His great work,* The Nature and Destiny of Man,
is required reading for serious thinkers.

*Missouri-born, Yale-educated, Dr. Niebuhr spent thirteen
years in Detroit, preaching in the slums and battling for labor's
rights. He then moved on to the faculty of the Union Theological Seminary where his course on Applied Christianity became
world famous. He is now vice-president of the Seminary. A
consistant crusader for progressive causes, Dr. Niebuhr is also
vice-chairman of the Liberal party of New York and writes
frequently for the courageous, forward-looking* New Leader.

*Always Dr. Niebuhr has felt that the Church should concern
itself with the economic and social betterment of men regardless of any pressures to the contrary. He has fought hard to
further this in America.*

I heard this story from him.

WHEN Reinhold Niebuhr first arrived in Detroit as a young parson, wages and working conditions for the men in the rapidly
expanding automobile industry were appallingly bad. Hunger was a
commonplace, and the automobile workers burned themselves out at
a pathetically early age as a result of the searing pace of the assembly
lines. Efforts to unionize these workers as a means of improving their
lot invariably foundered. The resistance of the automobile magnates
was too powerful.

In the struggle to better the automobile workers' lives, the churches
of Detroit were no great help. Most of them knuckled under abjectly
to the local industrialists.

Not all, though. Not the Episcopal bishop of the Diocese of Michigan.

Bishop Charles D. Williams was an exponent of the "social gospel" of that day, and one of the best. He had no doctrinaire positions. He was merely a man of extraordinary integrity and courage, and he dared to insist that workers required collective bargaining in a city in which all the new industrialists were insistent that the future of the auto industry required the kind of autocracy that had grown up with the rising industry.

One could not say such things in Detroit then without provoking a crisis. Bishop Williams knew this, but he went on saying them anyway.

The crisis occurred. Some of the wealthy men in the diocese were uncomfortable under a bishop who insisted on speaking about problems of justice in industry. They declared a boycott on the diocesan missionary budget.

"Not another cent," they said, "unless the bishop changes his tune."

A diocesan convention had to be called. Present were the pastor and a lay delegate from every Episcopalian church in the Michigan diocese.

There were those who wondered whether Bishop Williams would backtrack. He didn't.

He offered voluntarily to resign his post as bishop, but he would not curtail, by one whit, his fight for a better life for the automobile workers.

"Inasmuch as I have talked a great deal on public affairs," he said in a moving speech to the convention, "I may have frequently spoken foolishly with my tongue, but as for the main burden of my message, I am sure that the Lord has laid it upon my lips."

The convention agreed. Boycott or no, the delegates voted by an overwhelming margin to refuse his resignation. Bishop Williams and his ideas of justice for the everyday man counted more than "big business" and its money.

It meant a lot to a young parson like Reinhold Niebuhr.

BIBLE IN THE DESERT

NELSON GLUECK
President, Hebrew Union College-Jewish Institute of Religion

Rabbi, educator, distinguished biblical scholar, and world-famous archaeologist—that is Dr. Nelson Glueck. A fifty-eight-year-old Ohioan, Dr. Glueck has rolled several full lives into one. Ordained a rabbi in 1923, he joined the faculty of the Hebrew Union College in 1929, was named its president in 1947. A year later he was made president of the Jewish Institute of Religion. When the two schools merged in 1950, he became president of the combined institution, now the world's oldest Jewish theological seminary. Meanwhile, he won other acclaim by his original research and writings on the Bible. On three occasions he also served as director of the American School of Oriental Research in Jerusalem, and, for five years, as field director of the American School of Oriental Research in Baghdad. During this stretch he was an undercover agent for the Office of Strategic Services.

Throughout, he has been an ardent, active archaeologist. He has discovered more than a thousand lost sites in the Holy Land, and proven that Israel's Negev Desert, long considered as always an irreclaimable wasteland, once used to bloom. His explorations have literally revolutionized the world's knowledge of ancient biblical lands. Just recently he found a stock of flint tools in the Negev dating from the twentieth century B.C., and a petrified shark's tooth seventy million years old. He wrote this story.

IN every archaeologist's life there comes a moment of great wonder and pride.

When it comes it justifies all the years of sweat and suffering. Sometimes it is even wondrous enough to make you forget the thousand times you called yourself a fool for pursuing such dirty, painstaking, dangerous work, isolated from your home and family.

A moment of this sort came to me in searching for King Solomon's Red Sea port of Ezion-geber.

In a way, this search had all the elements of a baffling mystery story.

Historians and biblical scholars knew that King Solomon had built a seaport at Ezion-geber. They knew that according to biblical annals it had flourished and that its name had subsequently become Elath. But more than that they did not know.

For almost twenty-five hundred years the knowledge of Ezion-geber's location had disappeared from the minds of man. It was as if it had been a candle flame that had flickered fitfully in the night and then blown out.

Through the centuries many had sought to find this port city from which Solomon's ships had sailed. None had succeeded.

There were many different theories about where to look for the original site. Commonly accepted was the notion that the Red Sea had retreated during the span of time for some thirty-five kilometers. Consequently it was believed that Ezion-geber was to be found nowhere near the present shore line of the Red Sea. I had another idea.

The Bible specifically states (I Kings 9:26; 10:22, 11):

". . . King Solomon made a fleet of ships in Ezion-geber, which is beside Elath on the shore of the Red sea in the land of Edom. . . . Once in three years the fleet came in bringing gold, silver, ivory, apes, peacocks . . . a very great amount of red sandalwood and precious stones. . . ."

The amazing memory of the Bible has been validated in many ways by archaeological findings. Our previous expedition in the Wâdī Araba and discovery of King Solomon's copper mines were echoes of Deuteronomy (8:9) in which Israel was promised a land "whose stones are iron, and out of whose hills you can dig copper."

Therefore, I decided that Solomon's ancient seaport must have been located on the shore of the Gulf of Aquaba, which is the eastern arm of the Red Sea. The discovery of an insignificant-looking mound, Tell el Kheleifeh, by the German explorer Fritz Frank and our subsequent dating of its fragments of pottery to the time of King Solomon linked the site with Ezion-geber.

Quickly our expedition moved to the task of restoring this long-lost spot to life, and uncovering its buried secrets.

It was a cruel job. Our site was open to the full fury of the winds. Sandstorms reminiscent of the American Dust Bowl frequently made work impossible. It completely baffled us why anyone would have chosen this particular location for a port. That is, if they had.

We had an Arab chief of guides who knew the desert like a book. He could survive under conditions that spelled disaster for others. He could tell from tracks days old who had passed. But he could not figure me out. He always seemed puzzled by this man from a world far away who had come to dig into the land of his ancestors.

In the dark of the night he would sometimes ask me about America and myself. I told him how, as a child of six, my father often took me by the hand to Cincinnati's "Fossil Hill" to examine fossils from a prehistoric sea that once covered my native Ohio. I tried to give him a bit of the flavor of Cincinnati, the city where I had been schooled and later ordained as a rabbi by Hebrew Union College. I related some of my experiences as director of the American School for Oriental Research in Jerusalem. And I described my twenty years of probing antiquity for the meaning it could give to us living in the world of today, and how my interests, my education, my skills were all products of America. I told him that I had been taught in America to believe in the teachings of the Bible, that the laws of America were based upon the commandments of the Bible. He nodded, but it was evident that I remained an enigma.

Then came our big find. Deep down, we excavated a large ten-room building, a totally novel kind of structure, the like of which had not been discovered before in the entire Near East.

It was an ancient copper smelter. Its site had been picked so that the strong winds of the area could furnish a constant draft for the furnace rooms.

Not only was this Ezion-geber, the port city of King Solomon, but also a veritable Pittsburgh of Palestine. Again the Bible had guided us well.

The look of wonderment on the face of our Arab chief was joyous to behold. "He found it," he cried. "The American who believes in the Bible, whose country's laws are based upon the Bible, has found it."

I could have wanted no greater accolade for my country.

MIDNIGHT IS THE ZERO HOUR

ED MARCINIAK
Editor, Work

A citation from the Chicago Commission on Human Relations in 1948 read, "To Edward Marciniak, who, as founder and leader of the Catholic Labor Alliance, has shown how religious groups may advance the principles of Christian behavior and Universal Brotherhood without racial discrimination among all men who work, and who, as editor of the magazine Work, *constantly upholds these same principles, thus giving practical direction to democratic sentiments and faiths." With this in mind, it can be understood how Ed Marciniak came to write this story.*

In addition to editing Work, *for the Catholic Council on Working Life, Marciniak, a forty-one-year-old Chicagoan, has taught labor economics and sociology at Loyola University and the Great Books course at the University of Chicago. He has written widely on Catholicism in America, on labor, and on social affairs.*

H E came to hear their confessions—and stayed to defend their rights.

Father Peter Miller, S.C.J., had just learned that some sixty-five Mexicans were working on farms near Divine Heart Seminary in Donaldson, Indiana, where he is rector. So, one Wednesday in August 1956, he set out to visit the makeshift camps housing the Mexicans, who'd been brought to this country under contract to pick cucumbers.

At the entrance to the camps police told him that "agitators" had stirred up the men, that they were refusing to harvest the pickles, and that it was dangerous to enter.

Father Miller went in anyway.

The men were without food. Only a few had any money. The barrier of language and the distance to the nearest store made things worse.

Digging into his pocket, Father Miller went to the market and got as much bread, meat, potatoes, milk, coffee, and cigarettes as his money would buy. He then went and emptied the seminary ice-box.

The men ate and began to smile.

Why were the men without food? Why were they refusing to work? Father Miller listened.

They showed him their weekly pay checks. Many were for three dollars and four dollars; none for more than fifteen dollars. Most of the Mexicans were family men, with wives and children back home to support.

One man showed him a check for $00.90—for a week's backbreaking work.

The men, paid at piecework rates, charged that their "pick" was short-weighted and downgraded.

Father Miller stopped listening. On Friday and Saturday he began asking public officials what could be done to obtain justice. All he got was a polite brush-off.

He went to a local newspaper. The editor said the story was "too hot" to print. A nearby pastor accused Father Miller of having started the "strike" and told people Father Miller was meddling in matters beyond his authority.

He found that the U. S. Department of Labor had only one farm placement representative to cover four Midwestern states. He learned that the Mexicans worked under an international agreement under which they could be shipped two thousand miles to do farm labor without any guarantee of a basic minimum wage.

On Sunday morning the sixty-five men and another hundred, mostly Texans of Mexican descent, arrived for Mass at the seminary. Together with the celebrant, they praised God and asked that justice be done. This was the first time any of the Mexican farm workers had come to the seminary for Mass. With Father Miller as host, the men stayed for breakfast and dinner.

That evening Father Miller heard the bad news. The sixty-five men were to be deported the next day on charges that they had broken their contract by refusing to work.

This deportation, Father Miller learned, was ordered by the U. S. Labor Department's representative without giving the workers a chance to state their side of the case. As a matter of fact the farm labor representative admitted to Father Miller that he didn't speak Spanish.

Father Miller was deeply disturbed. He believed it a violation of every democratic concept to condemn the Mexicans without a hearing.

Doggedly he set out to protect the human and civil rights of these Mexicans. In so doing he uncovered many friends.

A priest from East Chicago, Indiana, agreed to take signed testimonials from the men regarding their working conditions.

A Jewish merchant friend found an attorney in Plymouth, Indiana, willing to represent the men free.

Bishop Leo Pursely of Fort Wayne, Indiana, induced a lawyer he knew to get in touch with Washington in the hope of delaying the deportation until a fair investigation could be made. It was evident that the local office of the federal farm placement service was not interested in the complaints—just or otherwise—of the migrants.

Working against time, Father Miller himself phoned Monsignor John O'Grady, director of the National Conference of Catholic Charities in Washington. He asked him to carry the problem right to the heads of the Labor Department.

On Monday afternoon busses arrived at the camp to take the sixty-five Mexicans back to the Texas border. When Father Miller and the Plymouth lawyer demanded that a hearing be held first, they got nowhere.

The zero hour was midnight.

Sadly the men gathered their meager belongings for the dismal trek home. Suddenly, that evening, the phone rang in the camp office. It was Washington. The deportation of the Mexicans was called off.

The men were given two alternatives. They could stay in their present camp and work under improved conditions—with guaranteed field jobs at seventy cents an hour, full weight and honest grading. Twelve chose to remain. Or they could sign a new and fair contract to pick potatoes, corn and cucumbers for a canning company in Michigan. Forty-three decided to go there.

The American tradition of justice had won. It meant a lot to Father Miller. And it meant a lot to those of us who watched him demonstrate that other great American tradition: helping the underdog.

BAD NEWS

ARLIN H. ADAMS

Wisconsin Minister

To see man demonstrate real love for his fellow man can make the ministry a wonderfully rewarding profession, as the Reverend Arlin H. Adams points out in this account he wrote of a brother National Guardsman.

Reverend Adams is the pastor of St. John's Evangelical Lutheran Church in Janesville, Wisconsin. "Like Jack Benny," Reverend Adams says, "I'm thirty-nine and refuse to get a day older." However, he confesses that he recently did celebrate his fortieth birthday. A native of Wisconsin, he had several offers of football scholarships on his graduation from high school but chose instead to go to Luther College and on to Wartburg Seminary for theological training. His first parish was at Oconto Falls, Wisconsin. His next was in the South Pacific, where he served for thirty months as an Army chaplain, earning two battle stars. He has done considerable writing, lecturing, and youth work.

THEY say it takes all sorts of people to make a world, and I rather think it's true. However, I must confess that there are some I could do without. These are the folks who say you can't expect much of a soldier. That servicemen are an ungodly lot who do nothing but drink, gamble, and raise Cain.

I wish all the folks that think this way could have been with me at Camp Ripley recently. They would have seen how wrong they are.

My National Guard outfit—the 32nd Division—was on its two-week encampment, hardening up with twenty-mile hikes and battle maneuvers—and with fighting off the Minnesota mosquitoes.

One afternoon I was at division headquarters, loading a truck with PX supplies for the troops. The commanding officer of my regiment came up to me.

"Chaplain," he said, "I've got a toughie for you. One of the men in B Company, Sergeant Brown, has just lost his son through drowning. Will you break it to him as gently as possible. Bring him in and we'll arrange to fly him home."

The colonel loaned me his jeep and driver, and I started off. A Sergeant Jenkins, who was to replace Brown, rode along.

It was a sad drive. Sergeant Jenkins was a close friend of Brown's and he warned me what to anticipate.

"Brownie is going to take this mighty hard," he said. "He sets a lot of store by that boy."

We located B Company miles out in the woods. Sergeant Brown was standing around, laughing and smoking a cigarette.

I walked up to him and said, "Sarge."

He stopped smiling. "What is it, Chaplain?" he asked. "What's wrong?"

"Plenty, son, plenty. It's bad, real bad. Almost as bad as it could be. You're a man so I'll give it to you like a man. Your son's been drowned. You're to come into camp at once, and we'll fly you home to Green Bay."

The sergeant sat down on the ground and began to cry.

I knelt there beside him and said, "Friend, we've got to take the crosses that are laid on us and walk the way of life that is before us. God knows and God helps."

"I'm not complaining to God, Chaplain," he wept, "but I'm think-ing about my wife. What is that poor girl doing? This is the second child we've lost. Both times I've been gone, and she's had to face it all alone. Oh, my poor wife."

We returned to camp. I took the sergeant to his tent to get ready. Then I drove to headquarters to check on the plane. I was just getting out of the jeep when an officer ran up.

"Chaplain," he panted, "we've made a terrible mistake. It wasn't Brownie's boy. The phone operator got the message mixed up. It was a call for Brownie but not about Brownie's boy. Brownie was to get the call and break the news to the fellow whose son really was drowned. Sergeant Jenkins. It is his boy."

I tore over to B Company's area and informed Sergeant Brown. He fell on his knees and gave thanks to God that his son was alive. Not that Jenkin's boy was dead but that his own was alive.

Back I went to headquarters. Sergeant Jenkins was being brought in.

He looked at me inquiringly as his jeep arrived. I laid my hand on his shoulder and told him how it was. He wavered like a man hit with a baseball bat. He was a soldier, though.

I've heard many wonderful things in my life. I've heard the news that Christ is risen! I've heard my beloved say, "I love you." At the end of a terrible war I've heard: Peace. But the finest words I believe I'll ever hear this side of heaven were Sergeant Jenkins',

"Chappie," he said, "I'm glad it wasn't Brownie's kid."

MIRACLE IN SOUTH DAKOTA

ROBERT W. SHIELDS
Minister—Editor—Writer

Interfaith co-operation is the American way. Sometimes obstacles are placed in its road by bias and bigotry, but these can be overcome by men of good will and true religious tolerance. Robert W. Shields demonstrates this in the report he has written on religion in a small Dakota town.

Shields is, very definitely, a man of good will and tolerance. Forty years old, he comes from Indiana, got his theological education at five seminaries, including Harvard University Divinity School, Andover-Newton Theological School, and Drake University College of the Bible. He has held four different Baptist pastorates, four different Methodist pastorates, and four different Congregational pastorates. "Somewhat unusual," as he says himself. While serving in New Hampshire, he conceived, wrote, directed, and produced the Deerfield Bible Pageant, the only full sound-with-color film that shows portions of all sixty-six books of the Bible. In 1954 he left the full-time ministry to teach high school in South Dakota. He then shifted to Chicago and from there to Clarksburg, West Virginia, where he is now an editor in the parent-guidance field.

DURING fifteen years in the ministry, I was never more shocked than when I went to the pastorate of the United Congregational Church in New Underwood, South Dakota, in 1954. Conditions there were disgraceful.

This was the only Protestant organization holding religious services for miles around, but its house of worship was a weather-beaten affair which the Methodists had abandoned years before as hopeless. Even the hymnbooks were dilapidated. The first one I opened fell to pieces, scattering pages all over the rough floor.

The parsonage was never built to be a home at all. It consisted of two sheds nailed together. You scarcely could see out of it. The windows had been hideously paint-smeared by a former pastor, nearly blind, who, all by himself, had made pitiful efforts to tidy up the dingy place.

I tried to raise a window for air, and the frame came apart in my hands.

The congregation was financially wrecked. It even had to have help from the State Conference to pay my meager wages.

Just one thing kept the tiny group going. A handful of members was obsessed with a notion that they had to prevent the town from being "taken over" by another faith.

I asked one member why the church was kept open.

"We've got our pride," he said. "It's to save the town from the Catholics."

The Catholics were in no such difficulties. In Father Charles Quinn they had a fine, energetic priest. He had an excellent, aggressive program and he had developed a strong following.

The man was a human dynamo in an immense body that wore oversizes of everything. With his own hands he had constructed a new parsonage and completely remodeled the church. Over the protests of many of his parishioners, he had sawed the church in two and inserted a substantial addition in the middle. He was an able carpenter and did much of the exquisite finishing work himself.

For all his church activities, Father Quinn was never too busy to participate in community affairs. The remarkable fact is that in the face of prejudice among the non-Catholics, and criticism from his own flock, he managed always to be a friendly, public-minded citizen. He made New Underwood a happier town in which to live.

If he had wished, Father Quinn could have capitalized on our distress, and the Roman Catholic church might have become the only house of worship in the region. He didn't. Instead, he was our friend.

Shortly after my arrival I launched an attendance drive and set a goal of 300 for Easter service. It was sighting high. The official population of New Underwood was exactly 267, and half of the people belonged to Father Quinn's church.

My committee stood aghast. "You'll make fools of us!" one cried.

I argued that our plan would succeed if we promoted it, and I earnestly appealed for the congregation's support.

"We can't do it," was the answer I heard. "We haven't the money to promote it. And even if we got that many people in, we haven't enough pews to seat them. We haven't the hymnals for them either. You must be out of your mind!"

Only one person gave me any real encouragement—Father Quinn. He shook my hand and wished me well.

"You're trying to do something constructive in this town," he said, "and I'm all for it."

He did more. He got his parishioners to support me, too. I needed about fifteen hundred dollars for equipment to print our church bulletins and promotional literature. The president of the town's only bank, a Roman Catholic, let me have the money as a loan. I was stricken with illness from overwork and the town's only doctor, a Catholic, left his own sickbed to treat me, without charge, so I could continue. Often we were late in mailing our programs, on which we depended to build attendance. The town postmistress and her assistant, both Catholics, worked overtime to get our hundreds of folders delivered on schedule. The town's only newspaper, owned and edited exclusively by Catholic families, gave columns of free space to our activities in spite of the fact that our circulars competed with their news and announcements. The superintendent of schools, a Catholic, invited me to join with Father Quinn in officiating at school functions.

My critics were right, in a way. We couldn't seat our Easter attendance. They jammed the church to overflowing, stood in the aisles, and sat on chairs in the basement to hear the service over a loud-speaker system. Most wonderful of all, about fifty persons were baptized that day—the largest number at any service in any church of our denomination in the state that year.

I closed my ministry in New Underwood that August with a special Bible pageant, and I determined to have the greatest attendance ever achieved at a service in New Underwood. I set a target of five hundred.

The church officers remonstrated with me. "It's impossible. People don't have as much interest in going to church in August as they do at Easter. They won't come."

I decided to go ahead anyway, and I reserved the town hall for the program since the church could not accommodate so many.

The room was darkened and the pageant was being shown when a man sat down beside me. I looked at him in the dim light and was astonished to see Father Quinn.

"I just wanted to help you make that attendance goal," he said kindly.

We exceeded the goal. We had five hundred and sixteen.

I can report that the Protestant church in New Underwood was in splendid shape when I left. So was the Roman Catholic church. They were working together in the best American way.

I can also report this: I am a 32nd degree Mason, an ordained minister, and Father Quinn is, and always will be, a devout Roman Catholic priest. But between us there is a common understanding of the meaning and message of the greatest person who ever lived. Such understandings make America great.

If you ever visit New Underwood, Father Quinn may show you his collection of coins. Among these coins is a five-dollar gold piece to which he points with special pride. It is a token of gratitude from his Protestant minister friend.

AMERICA'S HEALTH

FAMILY DOCTOR

DR. DWIGHT H. MURRAY

Past President, American Medical Association

For all the methodization of twentieth-century life, the warm, intimate relationship between people and their family doctors remains the cornerstone of American medical practice. The specialists have their place. The big, marvelously equipped clinics, public and private, have theirs. But it is the family doctor on whom we chiefly lean for counsel and care.

Dr. Dwight H. Murray has had this relationship with tens of thousands of people. Although he has been a top-flight figure in medical organization work for twenty years, he has never lost his identity as a country doctor who will still drive thirty miles to see a patient. He was born in 1888 on a small Indiana farm, began his education in a one-room country schoolhouse. After he obtained his medical degree from the University of Indiana he served as a Navy doctor in World War I, then settled down as a general practitioner in Napa, California. In 1956 he achieved the top position in organized medicine—President of the American Medical Association. Here is his case history of a doctor-patient relationship.

DURING my thirty-five years of general practice in Napa, California, I have had many proud moments—the thrill of bringing a new life into the world, the satisfaction in saving someone from death, and the daily joy of seeing people regain their health.

But perhaps the proudest moment was on a day in 1952 when John Fritski, a migratory worker, came to see me in my office.

It was a hot afternoon and Mr. Fritski was in his shirt sleeves. He was a wiry man of average height with arms that bulged at the muscles. After a firm handshake we sat down.

"How's Tommy?" I inquired about Mr. Fritski's only son.

"Well, the last time I saw him he looked wonderful in his army uniform. That was before he went to Korea."

"G.I.?" I almost shouted in amazement. "It seems like only yesterday that he was playing out in the orchards."

"It sure does. Remember how worried we were that time about Tommy?"

I remembered it well.

Back in 1938 Mr. Fritski came to work as a prune picker in our valley. He pitched his battered old tent near the prune orchards, and settled down with his family for months of hard work.

His household possessions were much like those of other migratory workers in the area—few, drab, and shabby. But he and his wife didn't feel poor. They were devoted to each other and they had a son, a frail, blond youngster whom they adored.

One morning, as the Fritskis were preparing their breakfast on a camp stove in front of the tent, screams of anguish and terror pierced the silence of the little valley.

"Help! Mommy! Daddy!"

The boy came hobbling out. His right leg, just above the ankle, was gushing blood. Quickly Mr. Fritski grabbed up a club and ran into the tent. On the floor he saw a small dark form. With one hard blow he smashed at it.

Outside, Mrs. Fritski was comforting her son. The bleeding had stopped but the bite was deep and required the attention of a doctor.

At my office I treated the wound and asked Mr. Fritski if Tommy had been bitten by a dog.

"No, it was a skunk."

My heart sank. That was strange behavior for a skunk. More than likely, it was rabid. Tests would have to be made.

"Did the skunk get away?"

"No, I killed it."

We were in luck. I asked him to get the skunk and take it to the sheriff's office—fast.

The moment the Fritskis left, I notified the sheriff. He radioed to the University of California at Berkeley that he was sending in the head of a skunk for examination. Then I wired a pharmaceutical laboratory in Oakland to prepare some serum for me.

The next day the report came. The skunk was rabid.

Immediately I telephoned Oakland. The pharmaceutical firm said the serum would be ready as soon as someone could pick it up. A clerk at the local drugstore did that for us. I told him the story of the Fritski boy and he volunteered to drive the forty miles to get the serum.

Within thirty-six hours after the boy had been bitten we were able to start the first of forty-two daily injections—the maximum treatment because the skunk's brain was heavily infected with Negri bodies.

"That siege was almost more'n we could take," Mr. Fritski said. "We were scared every minute of those forty-two days."

The serum was effective and Tommy's life was saved. After that I saw the boy many times—out in the valley with his family or at my office for treatment of minor ailments. Once I removed his tonsils.

"When is he coming home?" I asked Mr. Fritski.

"It's hard to say," he said.

Reaching into his pocket he pulled out some papers. He handed them to me and indicated that I should read them.

The first was a short note scrawled on a rumpled sheet of paper. It was from Tommy.

"Dear Dad," it began.

"I know you have always been grateful to the doc for saving my life when I was six. And I know that he has never billed you or asked you for money for that work or for any of his other visits. I realize you have always wanted to repay him. Since joining the Army I've put away a few dollars a month. Now I have fifty dollars. Please give it to him for both of us, even though it only partially covers what he's done for us.

"The fighting has been fierce here, and I've been out many times on raids.

"This war is something like the way the doc and the others helped to save me. We're here now in a co-operative effort to save a life, too—life in America. . . ."

It was signed "Love, Tommy."

Clipped to the letter was a fifty-dollar bill. As I started to put down the letter I saw that the next paper was a telegram—only a few days old—from the Adjutant General of the Army. Instinctively I knew what it was going to say.

"The Secretary of the Army," it began, "desires that I tender his deepest sympathy to you on the loss of your son, Corporal Tommy Fritski. Report just received states that he was killed in action. . . ."

Years ago, a half-dozen Californians had worked together to save this boy's life; only a few days ago he had given that life for all of us.

Now, here was a man who had lost his only son wanting to repay me in behalf of his son and himself.

I handed everything back to Mr. Fritski.

Repay me? Indeed, how could I ever repay them?

VICTORY OVER POLIO

BASIL O' CONNOR

President, the National Foundation for Infantile Paralysis

American medical researchers have recorded many triumphs in the past two decades. Cortisone is one. Streptomycin, aureomycin and chloromycetin are others. The vaccine against epidemic typhus and the "blue baby" operation are two more; and, just recently, the vaccine that Dr. Jonas E. Salk developed to immunize people against paralytic poliomyelitis. In the United States, it has virtually done away with this virulent disease, and latest reports indicate that it is proving equally effective abroad.

The struggle to defeat polio was a long one that took huge sums of money and, as Basil O'Conner reveals here, vast amounts of scientific courage. O'Connor is President of the National Foundation for Infantile Paralysis, the organization which spearheaded the fight. Now a successful New York lawyer, he was born in Massachusetts in 1892 and became interested in polio when his friend (afterward his law partner), Franklin D. Roosevelt, was stricken with the disease. The two of them took a run-down summer resort and made it into the famous Georgia Warm Springs Foundation for the treatment of polio patients. When President Roosevelt established the National Foundation in 1938, O'Connor became president. He has given it most of his time (without salary) since. From 1944 to 1949 he also served as head of the American National Red Cross. He told me this story.

A TIME of agonizing choice often comes with research into human disease. It is the terrible moment when you must decide whether a medical discovery is safe for general use.

There was such a moment during the long struggle against paralytic poliomyelitis. Its real story has never before been told.

The time of decision in this case was 10 A.M., April 25, 1954. The place was a locked room at the Statler Hotel in Washington D.C. Those present were six of the most distinguished medical scientists in the United States. And two others.

I'd called these six scientists together to resolve a shattering question. Did we at last have the means to save the forty thousand boys, girls and grownups who were being stricken by polio each year. Did we dare risk a broad-scale test? Or were we chancing a deadly public fiasco that could set back the cause of polio research by decades?

As we knew them, the facts were these. Ever since it was established by President Franklin D. Roosevelt in 1938, the National Foundation for Infantile Paralysis had been searching for a vaccine to prevent polio. Finally a team of University of Pittsburgh researchers headed by a young man named Dr. Jonas E. Salk had come up with one that looked promising.

Dr. Salk, as the world now knows, had the theory that if you killed polio virus—all three types—made a vaccine of them, and injected this vaccine into human muscles, it would stimulate the production of antibodies which would create an immunity to paralytic polio.

Operating with Foundation funds, he'd developed a vaccine and tried it on 5,320 children and adults in the Pittsburgh area. Not one got paralytic polio.

So far so good. But then came the scientific doubts.

Could we be positive that it was the vaccine alone which had safeguarded these people? The incidence of polio is so low, statistically speaking, that this might have been a mere coincidence. A ghastly mathematical joke.

Only by a vast field trial involving not a few thousand but hundreds of thousands of persons could we be certain that we'd fulfilled the prayers of every American mother for something that would protect her children against the steel brace, the iron lung, and the wooden coffin.

And that was the searing problem. Had we the moral right to inoculate a half million or so children with the Salk vaccine? Did we know enough about it yet?

I'd asked the scientists on the Foundation's Vaccine Advisory Committee to rule on it. They had the final word.

Tensely the meeting came to order. White-haired Dr. Thomas M. Rivers was presiding. He was director of the Rockefeller Institute and unquestioned dean of the country's virologists. Next to him was Dr. Ernest L. Stebbins, the head of the Johns Hopkins School of Public Health. When he was a boy Dr. Stebbins had polio himself. He still limps. Around the table then were soft-spoken Dr. David E. Price, Assistant U. S. Surgeon General, Dr. Thomas B.

Turner, the Johns Hopkins microbiologist, Dr. Joseph E. Smadel, the
U. S. Army virus expert, and Dr. Norman H. Topping, Vice-President
in charge of Medical Affairs of the University of Pennsylvania. Dr.
Hart E. Van Riper, the medical director of our foundation, and I
sat off in a corner as observers.

It was a horrible responsibility Dr. Rivers and his colleagues bore.
The reputation of every man there was at stake. And they knew it.
More than one of them had spent the preceding night pacing the
floor, wrestling with his conscience.

I could tell what was going on in their minds. Was this vaccine
truly safe? Was it possible that Salk's dead virus might still cause
polio rather than prevent it? As a matter of fact, was it advisable
ever to attempt so huge a field trial, the biggest in medical annals?
By the law of averages, if you gave a half-million children shots of
plain water, two or three might die of shock. Were this to occur in the
first hundred, we could never convince the public that it hadn't been
due to the vaccine. The test would be out the window, and the vaccine permanently discredited. To say nothing of the scientists who'd
recommended it.

There was that awful temptation to play it cautiously. After all,
why not run a number of small-scale tests instead of the big one?
Suppose the final determination on the effectiveness of the vaccine
were postponed another year, or two, or three? Who could object?

Yet every month's delay meant more children being mangled by
polio, more deaths chalked up to polio.

It was a tough choice. I had no idea how the vote would go. All
I knew was that it had to be unanimous. One "Nay" and the test
was off.

"Well, gentlemen," Dr. Rivers said, "we all understand the question
before us: do we go ahead with the field trial or don't we? How do
you vote?"

There wasn't a second's hesitation. "Yes," said Dr. Stebbins.

"Yes," said Dr. Price.

"Yes," said Dr. Turner.

"Yes," said Dr. Smadel.

"Yes," said Dr. Topping.

"And I vote yes," said Dr. Rivers.

The rest is medical history. Within a few months, 440,000 children
were inoculated with the Salk vaccine, and another 210,000 given
dummy shots. On April 12, 1955, the results were announced. The

vaccine had proved to be 60 to 90 per cent effective. And 100 per cent safe. This score turned out even better after the vaccine was released for public use. In September 1956 it was officially reported from Washington that not one child who'd received the full series of injections had died of polio.

The disease had met its master. And all because six (*) great American scientists had the courage, the integrity and the strength of will to stand up and be counted.

* (A seventh member of the Vaccine Advisory Committee, Dr. Thomas P. Murdock, a trustee of the American Medical Association, couldn't attend the Statler Hotel meeting because of a serious heart attack. Dr. Murdock's opinion couldn't be influenced by the voices of his colleagues. There were no faces to be read, no states of mind to be felt. His word came in by mail. He voted, "Yes," too.)

HEART ATTACK

JOSEPH USHKOW

President, Endo Laboratories

It is an American principle now that no sick person should ever go without proper medical care for lack of money. Today hospital doors are open to all people, no matter how poor they may be, and they can be sure that every known aid to recovery will be at their disposal. This is as it should be, for death doesn't wait on dollars and cents.

As a manufacturer of pharmaceuticals, Joseph Ushkow has seen hundreds of hospitals from the inside. He is constantly visiting them to see his products at work. A pharmacist's son, this fifty-six-year-old New Yorker heads Endo Laboratories, Inc., the firm which developed Coumadin, a new miracle drug for treating heart disease.

Two men had severe heart attacks in September 1955. One was the President of the United States. The other was an old, unemployed butcher from Brooklyn, New York. It was touch and go with them both.

The President had the most distinguished physicians in America at his bedside, the best in hospital care, the latest in medications. As for the butcher . . .

I happened to be in the hospital when the butcher was brought in. Drug manufacturers spend a lot of time in hospitals. It is the only way they can see for themselves how their products perform in specific cases.

This was a huge city institution in mid-town Manhattan, a place to which ambulances come shrieking every few minutes with people mangled in accidents or racked by disease. Here the dispensaries are endlessly crowded with poor folk seeking treatment, and the gray, drab wards overflow with ill and dying. Doctors and nurses have never a moment free. They're too busy racing death.

I was standing in the admitting office when this white-haired man was wheeled in on a stretcher. His face was absolutely ashen, and there were rivers of sweat running down his forehead. He was gasping desperately, gratingly, for breath.

The nurse on duty took one glance, "Emergency," she called.

Instantly an intern went to the stretcher. "Where does it hurt you?" he asked.

The old man was whimpering with pain. "I'm . . . William . . . Maloney . . . seventy-one. I'm a butcher. . . ."

"Friend, it doesn't matter to me what you are," the intern said. "Just tell me, where does it hurt you?"

"Here. Here." The old man clutched agonizingly at his chest and shoulder. "Like a cleaver it is. Will I be dyin', Doctor? Will I?"

"You're going to be all right, Mr. Maloney. You're going to be all right. When did you have this pain first?"

"A little while ago. I . . . I was walkin' down the street . . . all of a sudden, it hit me. It was awful."

"Have you had attacks like this before?"

"Never. Doc, I don't want to die. I don't want to die."

In his eyes was a look of abject terror.

The intern loosened the old man's clothing and put a stethoscope to his chest. Then he took his blood pressure.

I heard him murmuring to the nurse. "B.P. one-thirty over eighty. Heartbeat very fast. And irregular."

"You think . . ." she said.

"Coronary occlusion with complications. We'd better get him to the emergency ward. Fast."

Shudderingly the old man tried to lift his head. "Doc. Doc."

"Take it easy, Mr. Maloney," the intern said.

"But, Doc, I want to tell you somethin'."

"Later."

"No, Doc . . . gotta tell you somethin' now. It's . . . that I ain't got no money. I been out of work. I . . . can't pay nothin'."

Gently the intern rested the old man's head back on the pillow. "Don't you worry about that, Mr. Maloney. All that counts is for you to get better."

There was no waiting for an orderly. The intern himself rolled the stretcher up the hall to the emergency ward where critically ill patients are kept until they pass their crisis. Crack, specially trained nurses are on duty around the clock here, and every known kind of drug which might be needed in an emergency is at finger's reach.

A nurse was at the door, ready. Together, she and the intern undressed Mr. Maloney and eased him into bed. By my watch it was only eleven minutes from the time he'd been brought into the hospital.

Scarcely was the old man in bed when another doctor hurried in. He was the intern who was to have personal charge of the case. The admissions office had phoned him.

This second intern didn't waste a motion. As soon as he'd heard the admitting intern's report, he turned to the nurse.

"Oxygen by mask."

The oxygen tank was there, close by the head of the bed. At once the nurse slipped a mask over Maloney's contorted face.

"Morphine. Fifteen milligrams for intramuscular injection."

The nurse was back in an instant with a hypodermic syringe. Deftly she inserted the needle and the old man's gasping sobs gradually began to subside.

The new intern now examined Maloney from top to bottom: his eyes, ears, nose, mouth, body, arms, legs. He paid particular attention to the legs. The ankles were ominously fat with swelling.

Off to the side the two interns discussed the case while I listened in. It seemed to them both that Maloney had a bad clot in one of the arteries supplying blood to the heart, and, to make things blacker, that he was also suffering from congestive heart failure.

They didn't take any chances on a mistaken diagnosis, though. They ordered an electrocardiogram, a photographic record of the heart's action. Within minutes a technician was at the bedside with a portable "E. C. D." machine. And a third doctor, an expert on electrocardiography, was on hand to interpret the findings.

The results were what they'd feared. Death was nudging William Maloney.

"We'd better have Dr.—— look at the patient," I heard one of the three doctors say.

Dr.—— is a world-famous heart specialist, who, like so many other noted physicians, contributes his services free to a public hospital.

Almost immediately the public-address system started up throughout the building. "Calling Dr.—— Calling Dr. ——"

In less than fifteen minutes Dr.—— was in the emergency ward. While he was coming, the two interns were tensely busy, making more vital tests—a blood count, a urinalysis, a check on the clotting time of Maloney's blood, another reading on his blood pressure. They omitted nothing.

Quickly, Dr.—— scanned their reports. After that, he, too, examined the patient.

"It's going to be a tough fight," he said, "but I think we can win it."

He told the interns in detail what to do. I noticed that he prescribed the very same drugs that had been given to President Eisenhower. Expensive ones.

* * * * * *

Six weeks later I was at that hospital again. It was the day Maloney was going home. "How do you feel?" I asked him.

"Like a new man," he grinned. "They couldn't have treated me any better if I was the President of the United States."

It was so true. There wasn't one thing done for President Eisenhower which William Maloney needed that he didn't get from the moment he entered the hospital, poor, friendless and known to absolutely nobody.

AMERICA AND ITS MINORITIES

TRAIN RIDE TO ARKANSAS

MORDECAI W. JOHNSON

President of Howard University

Headlines scream of violence done the constitutional rights of Negroes and members of other minority groups. And justly so, for only by exposure to fresh air can the dark corners of man's mind be cleansed of age-old fears and hatreds. Yet there are other, healthier aspects to the minority question. Step by step, quiet progress is being made toward decency and equality. In Arkansas as elsewhere.

Dr. Mordecai W. Johnson, the first Negro president of the largest Negro University in the United States—Howard University in Washington, D.C.— told me of a case in point. A minister's son, Dr. Johnson was born in Tennessee in 1890, graduated from Morehouse College, and went on to win another A.B. at the University of Chicago, plus a Doctor of Divinity from Howard. He taught at Morehouse for two years, then switched to the clergy, preaching in Charleston, West Virginia, until he was called to Howard in 1929. As president, he has built Howard into a top-notch institution with a spendid faculty, campus, and reputation for academic freedom. For his work Dr. Johnson has been awarded the Spingarn Medal as the American Negro of outstanding achievement.

I saw him the moment I entered the dining car, a handsome, dark-skinned young man sitting alone. He looked as miserable as a boy could be.

"May I sit with you?" I said.

"Help yourself," he muttered. He didn't glance up.

I studied the menu while he stared dejectedly at the table. There was a plateful of food in front of him but he hadn't touched it.

"What's wrong, son?" I asked.

Slowly he turned toward me. His eyes widened. "Why, you're Dr. Johnson," he said. "You don't know me but I know you. My name's Silas Hunt. I'm a friend of Lawyer Scipio Jones of Little Rock, Arkansas."

"Well, I'll be blessed," I exclaimed. "I'm well acquainted with the distinguished Mr. Jones, and I'm happy to meet his friend. Now, tell me, what's the trouble?"

"I'm on my way to the University of Arkansas," he said. "I'm the first Negro ever to be admitted to the law school."

That didn't seem like something to be despondent about, and I said so.

"You don't understand. I don't want to go. I don't want to go at all."

"Why not?"

"It will be awful. The students are going to cut me dead. They won't talk to me, won't have anything to do with me. They're going to treat me like dirt."

"Yes." I had to say it. "That could well happen to you."

The boy went glumly on. "I was all set for a law school in Illinois. Then Mr. Jones got the University of Arkansas to admit a Negro student to the law school for the first time. He wrote me that I had an obligation to my race to go, and I suppose it's so. It's my duty. Somehow I'll try to stick it out."

He paused and drank a little water. "It's going to be dreadful. Those students are going to plain refrigerate me."

What could I say to the boy? I knew how right he might be.

With every turn of the wheels, the more miserable he became, and apprehensive.

Unfortunately, I couldn't stay with him to the end. I had to switch trains.

Weeks later I heard what happened. Someone said to me, "Do you know what took place at the University of Arkansas when the first Negro student entered the law school?"

"Tell me. Quick."

He did.

When the train pulled into Fayetteville, where the university is located, young Hunt saw a crowd of thirty-odd white students standing on the station platform. As he stepped down from the train, they pressed toward him.

Young Hunt's heart sank. His worst fears came to the surface.

A lanky white boy pushed forward right at him. "Is your name Hunt?" he demanded.

"Yes, that's my name," Hunt answered. His forehead was wet with perspiration.

The white boy stuck out his hand. "Shake," he said, "Welcome to the University of Arkansas. And step over here. I want to introduce you to thirty-five of your friends."

It seems that the night before, a number of law-school students had been having a bull session. Suddenly one of them blurted out, "Say, you fellows, how would you feel if you were the first Negro to enter the University of Arkansas Law School? How would you like it?"

They talked it over. They knew that the Negro boy would expect to be "refrigerated." (They actually used the same word young Hunt had employed.) They made up their minds, then and there, to see to it that Hunt had as normal a life at the University of Arkansas as he would have at any law school in America. As a first move, they decided to meet his train.

"These fellows here are not all of your friends," the lanky white boy said to Hunt as he made the introductions. "There are more— many more."

There were.

THE KIDS TAKE A STAND

RICHARD B. KENNAN

*Secretary, National Commission for the Defense of Democracy
Through Education*

---

*"And a little child shall lead them . . ." So it has been in
town after town where the battle over segregation has raged.*

*Dr. Richard B. Kennan, who told me of this incident in
Missouri, is the secretary of the National Commission for the
Defense of Democracy Through Education, an arm of the National Education Association set up to aid school systems and
educators that have been unjustly attacked by special-interest
groups. Massachusetts-born, Dr. Kennan got his Ph.D. from
Columbia, taught in Connecticut and New York, was superintendent of schools in Georgetown, Delaware, and a professor of
education at the University of Vermont. Before he went with the
NEA in 1944, he served five years as executive secretary of the
Maine Teachers Association. He has been on the firing line in
the Pasadena, Houston, Miami, and many other struggles for
academic freedom.*

Lucile Ellison, the assistant secretary of our commission, saw
it first. She brought it to me.

"Here is one of the most important editorials I have seen this
year."

"Where's it from?" I asked her. "The New York *Times? The Manchester Guardian?*"

"You're way off," she declared. "It's from a high-school newspaper
in the town of Mexico, Missouri, population 11,623. Read it carefully.
In fifty-two words it shows better than anything I've seen the true
worth of American youngsters."

The editorial was written by a student editor of the Mexico high-
school's paper, *The Bulldog Growl*. It was published after this
Southern Missouri town had finally moved to end segregation in its
schools.

"We are going to have a new system in our school this year called 'integration,'" the editorial read. "All it means is that we are going to have forty new students here.

"We hope the townspeople will not make a big production out of it because we kids are going to take it in our stride."

That was all. But it was enough. It convinced me that Mrs. Ellison was right.

SHOULDER TO SHOULDER

LESTER B. GRANGER
Executive Director, National Urban League

Men with white skins and black have stood together in the long struggle to affirm the dignity of man in America, regardless of color or race.

Lester B. Granger told me of one such case out of his own background. He is executive director of the National Urban League, an organization of Negroes and whites which has made a splendid contribution, in its quiet, moderate manner, to the easing of discrimination. Born in Virginia in 1896, he graduated from Dartmouth and was in social work until he joined the N.U.L. in 1940. For his wartime services as an advisor to Secretary of the Navy James V. Forrestal, he received the President's Medal for Merit.

ONE of my first assignments with the National Urban League took me deep into the South in the bitter winter of 1936. I was sent to investigate conditions among Negro farmers.

I found things tragic. Everywhere it was the same for rural Negroes: hunger, hovels, and rags.

During the trip I stopped off in Memphis to visit the headquarters of the Southern Tenant Farmers Union, an organization aimed at improving the life of the sharecroppers. It was a depression phenomenon—an anti-Communist one incidentally—born of destitution among Negroes and whites in the delta region.

The union's organizers were glum. They told me they were meeting terrible obstacles in their efforts to recruit new members. Suspicion, for instance. From childhood, the Negroes and whites in that area had been taught to distrust each other and to view darkly any group that urged them to unite to better themselves.

Even worse was the fear.

Day and night it hung over Negroes and whites alike. From painful experience they knew that the local sheriffs could be rough—plenty rough—on anyone who tried to change the miserable status quo.

It was a grim session we had. And a cold one. The potbellied stove went out and there was no more coal to feed it.

Sadly I rose to return to my rooming house. As I moved toward the door, a scrawny, ill-dressed white man, who had been introduced only as Lew, came up. He asked abruptly:

"Wanna go to a T.F.U. meeting tonight?"

I said, "Yes."

"Yuh sure? Might be dangerous."

I still said, "Yes."

Going to the meeting wasn't a matter of walking to a nearby lodge hall. We climbed into a ramshackle Ford and drove west for thirty miles, then north for another fifteen miles or so. After that, we jounced off the highway onto a dirt road, from there over a rain-rutted country lane twisting through trees and underbrush.

Lew drove with grim concentration, hugging the wheel and staring straight forward. He didn't utter a word.

Suddenly he swung off the rutted road and wormed the car far into a clump of trees.

"Don't dare let no one find it," he said, "They'd come lookin' for us—with guns."

We continued on foot—stealthily. Every few yards, Lew would stop and peer behind to make sure that we weren't being followed. Finally we came to a small, weather-beaten cabin. It was in complete darkness.

Lew gave a peremptory triple knock and whistled twice. The door squeaked open.

Some two dozen men and women were seated on the floor with their backs against the walls. The chairman sat on a cot in the corner. A lone candle was covered with a burlap bag, giving just enough light for me to see that the group was about half white and half Negro.

The talk at the meeting was about the pitifully low wages the sharecroppers were getting from their landlords. Two dollars—for twelve hours' work—was the average daily pay.

"My kids are starvin' away in front of my eyes," one woman declared.

"Our baby died last week," another said.

Lew got up. He outlined plans for a county-wide demonstration of sharecroppers to ask a minimum wage of three dollars a day.

"The only hope we got," he said, "is to show the landlords that we're all together in this, whites and Negroes. Whaddya say? Shall we do it?"

They decided to take a vote.

Before they could do it there was another triple knock on the door. And a whistle repeated twice.

A Negro came breathlessly in. He reported that a sheriff's posse at the nearby town of Marked Tree had just surrounded a cabin in which a union meeting was supposed to be in progress, and had fired a fusillade through the cabin walls.

"Thank God there weren't no meetin' goin' on," the Negro said. "The cabin was empty."

"What happened to the posse?" Lew demanded.

"That's what I came to tell yuh," the Negro said. "It's mighty mad, and it's headin' down this way."

I confess that I was scared. Instinctively I pulled away from the wall. I could feel a slug burying itself in my back.

But those twenty-odd white and Negro sharecroppers weren't frightened. They voted to go on with their demonstration.

Then, led by a colored preacher, they sang a song—a "benediction song"—adopted from an old Negro spiritual.

> We're gonna build a union,
> We shall not be moved;
> We're gonna build a union,
> We shall not be moved.
> Just like a tree that's planted by the water,
> We shall not be moved.

I wanted to sing along with them. I couldn't. I was swallowing too hard at the thought of these people who'd broken their ancient bonds of fear, suspicion, and racial hatred, and had joined hands— white and colored—to protect the future of their families and their stake in the American democracy.

Times were bad. As bad as they've ever been in America. But these people were resolved to make them better. And they did.

They held their demonstration, and it won them their raise.

And the posse? It got lost.

A MATTER OF MANNERS

DOROTHY CANFIELD FISHER
Novelist

---

*To many Americans racial prejudice is something far re-
moved from their cosmos. They can not do otherwise than treat
all people as the same. Dorothy Canfield Fisher is one of them.*

*Though she is seventy-nine, Mrs. Fisher looks a beautiful
fifty-nine and has the mental vigor of twenty-nine. She is still
writing superb short stories, to cap a career which has produced
thirty-six distinguished books. She is perhaps best known as a
novelist, for works like* The Squirrel-Cage, The Bent Twig, Her
Son's Wife, *and* The Deepening Stream. *But she has also done
hundreds of short stories and articles, children's books, transla-
tions, and important volumes on education. It was she who
introduced the Montessori method to this country.*

*Mrs. Fisher was born in Kansas, took a Ph.D. at Columbia,
worked on the rehabilitation of the battle-blinded in France during World War I. For over fifty years she and her husband, John
R. Fisher, have lived a gracious, literary life in Arlington, Vermont, a friendly little town which her family founded almost
two centuries ago. Hand in hand, the Fishers walk the wooded
mountain trails together.*

She has written this account.

A KINSWOMAN of mine—if you'd like to know just what relation
she is, my father's second cousin—lives to the north of our town
of Arlington. Her home town is in the section of Vermont where, for
a good many years, Negro children from Harlem have been taken
into farm and village homes, off and on, as summer guests. You may
have read something about this in the newspapers. The Rutland
Herald always has news items about them, and once in a while a
photograph of them and the Vermont family where they are staying. These visiting Negro children from New York are not "fresh-
air" children, you understand. The Harlem kids come from reasonably well-to-do families, with about as much money as the Vermont
farmers and wage earners who are their hosts.

It's always interesting to us to hear about this project—something a little special, different from most places, like that live-wire summer school of music which is so much a part of the community life of the town of Adamant or the other music school of such very fine quality, which, under the direction of Rudolf Serkin and his family and friends, blossoms out in the forest around Marlboro College. So when my elderly cousin comes to visit in our town we always ask her about it.

"Have you heard about the new part of it—the Christmas-vacation plan?" she asked us. "It's quite nice, we think. Some of the fathers and mothers of the children that we have up there in the summer-time have asked the folks in our town who take the children in to come down to New York and spend part of the Christmas vacation with them. Several of our neighbors have gone, and have had an awfully good time. Some of them never would have dreamed of going to New York except for such an invitation. They just see every-thing, St. Patrick's Cathedral, the Bowery, Radio City, the Natural History Museum—oh, you know, what everybody sees in New York—the Statue of Liberty, Chinatown.

"But something sort of queer happened the other day—just before I came down here to visit.

"I was out in our front yard late in the afternoon, talking to our next-door neighbor, just back from work. He and his wife had made one of those trips that way, the Christmas before, and he happened to think of something new to tell me about it. He is a master hand with machinery, and has a good job as maintenance man for the machines in a little factory just down the valley from our town and still had his working clothes on. He'd got out the lawn mower and was leaning on the handle when a summer person came along the sidewalk.

"We don't know her very well, because she has only been coming to the hotel for the last six or seven years in the summertime. But of course we know her by sight and she has always seemed all right, very nice, helps out at food sales for the Girl Scouts and church bazaars—that kind of thing. She saw us there, talking together, and stopped as if she just wanted to pass the time of day. But she evi-dently had something she wanted to say to my neighbor. She looked at him and asked, 'Is it true, Mr. Fitch, that you were one of the people, you and your wife, who accepted an invitation from a Negro family to visit them in New York?'

" 'Yes, ma'am,' said my neighbor—he's quite a mannerly person—
'We're going down again Columbus Day.'

"She stopped smiling and looked very serious. 'I have only just
heard about it and I feel I ought to have a talk with you. I don't
believe you *know* what you were *doing*. If you did, you wouldn't
have.'

"My neighbor looked sort of blank, and I guess I did too, for I had
no idea what she was talking about.

"The summer lady went on, 'I can understand perfectly how, in-
experienced in that world as all you Vermonters are, you could have
made that mistake without meaning any harm. But somebody should
have told you. There's a *very* great difference, you know, between
taking in children from poor families, and giving them a little fresh
air and country food——That's entirely different from accepting an
invitation to *visit* in a Negro's home.'

"My neighbor and I looked at each other. Neither of us could
think of anything to say, so we didn't say anything.

"She probably saw from our faces that we weren't getting her
point, and explained, 'You see, taking poor children in——'

"Here my neighbor interrupted her. 'Those kids weren't *poor*, you
know, Miss Van Deusen. The little boy and girl I had—their father
and mother were both teachers in the public schools. They came
from a good home.'

"Miss Van Deusen took a long breath, 'That doesn't make any
difference,' she said. 'That's not what I'm talking about. It's the *principle* of the thing. When you take the children into your homes that's
charity. Anybody can show charity. It can't do any harm. But when
you accept an invitation from Negro parents, that is Social Equality.'

"The way she pronounced it, she sort of put it in capital letters.
You know how people can. It sounded as though she meant to have
it sound like, 'That's *Assault and Battery*.'

"We two Vermonters must have looked like sap-heads. I know my
mouth fell open and Mr. Fitch's did too.

"He closed his and said in kind of an astonished voice, 'What's
the matter with social equality? I thought that was all right. I thought
that was what we were brought up to believe in. Around here anyhow.'

"She got kind of red in the face and her voice sounded mad. 'Not
with Negroes! Give them an inch and they'll take an ell. You don't
understand, because you haven't had any dealings with them, except

charitable ones and that's all right. If you *knew* them as we South-
erners do, you'd know that that's what they're always scheming for,
to force themselves on us as social equals. You can't be too careful.
We've all got to stand together.'

"About that time Mr. Fitch and I gave up trying to talk to her.
He didn't say anything and neither did I. He just looked down at
his shirt, saw that a button was unbottoned, and fastened it up very
carefully.

"But *she* went on talking, you'd better believe. 'Now, Mr. Fitch,
I can see that you don't take this as seriously as you should. It's a *very*
serious matter. The difference between being charitable and admitting people as social equals is very, very great! And you are not
thinking of other people's rights. When you open the door like that,
you make it much harder for everybody else to keep standards where
they ought to be. You let down the bars, you don't realize that that
makes a lot of trouble for other people. You should bear that in mind.
We all should, and realize that other people depend on our keeping
up standards that will help us all to preserve what we have inherited
from our forefathers in this great country.'

"Mr. Fitch looked at her pretty hard just then, but he still didn't
say anything. We both just stood there, too astonished to speak. I
suppose to her we looked just like country hicks. But our mouths
weren't hanging open any longer. Not much. Mr. Fitch had closed
his tight, till he looked like his grandfather—I remember the old
gentleman when I was a little girl. When he shut his mouth tight,
all we youngsters took to cover.

"But what could he say that would be mannerly to a gray-haired
summer lady? Neither of us wanted to hurt her feelings. And you
know Vermonters aren't very smart about thinking up polite ways
to say what we mean wrapped up so it won't sound like jumping
down the throats of folks who don't agree with us. So we just stood
still and took it.

"After a while she sort of ran out of breath and stopped talking.
My neighbor stood up straighter and took hold of the lawn mower.
But before he started to push it away, he said to her, kind of easygoing as if he was just talking about the weather, 'Well, I see how
it looks to you, Miss Van Deusen. So I'll tell you how it seems to us.
When I was little, my folks didn't try to bring me up to be so awfully
good—Bible-good, you know, doing your duty and so on.' He laughed
a little and said, 'I guess they thought that was too much of a chore

for anybody to do with *me*. I was just an ordinary kind of a boy. So they never said very much to us youngsters about being church members or pious. I guess they took it for granted that any child of theirs would act decent. But they *did* lay it on the line about having manners. Not fancy manners, you know, just plain, ordinary decent manners. That, they were bound their children *would* have. And they always claimed that it wouldn't be manners to do something for somebody that you wouldn't want him to do back for you. We're great up here, you know, Miss Van Deusen, on helping each other out as neighbors. But it is always understood that if we help other people out, they'll help us out and we'll be glad to have 'em. If you ask somebody to come in and eat a bite with you, that means that if he calls you in from his front porch as you go by to have a cookie and a glass of cider, you'll go.'

"He turned around to the lawn mower and took hold of the handle. But sort of over his shoulder he said, 'You see, Miss Van Deusen, to us it don't seem mixed up or hard to understand. Just manners. Just ordinary, decent manners.'

"The lawn mower began to move, and he took a step or two forward. Then he stopped and, kind of as if he'd just thought of something, he called back to the summer lady, 'Anyhow, I've bought the tickets to New York and back for my wife and me. Wouldn't want to waste *that*.' "

VOYAGE TO PUERTO RICO

FERNANDO SIERRA BERDECIA
Secretary of Labor, Commonwealth of Puerto Rico

---

*Tolerance must go two ways. The prejudiced stand in dire
want of it, and the people who suffer discrimination for racial,
religious, and other such causes need it too. Not for a meek acceptance of injustice. That has to be fought. But as an example
for the bigots.*

*Fernando Sierra Berdecia, the far-sighted Secretary of Labor
of the Commonwealth of Puerto Rico, gives a vivid illustration
of this here. A prize-winning journalist, playwright, and short
storyist, Sierra was born in Puerto Rico and educated at its university. He was a newspaperman, labor mediator and head of
the Puerto Rican Labor Relations Board before he was appointed Secretary of Labor in 1947. On several occasions he has
represented the United States at conferences of the International Labor Organization.*

THERE's nothing like a dose of the negative to emphasize the
positive. It's like sickness making you appreciate health.

That's why the day I was proudest to be an American followed
so closely upon, and was so integrally related to, the day I was least
proud to be an American.

We Puerto Ricans are, of course, United States citizens. Particularly loyal ones, too. We sent the greatest percentage of volunteers
to the Korean War, for instance, and they came back with the highest
proportionate number of casualties. Beyond that, we have a devotion to the United States that is based on an innate faith in democracy, and all that it stands for. We believe in freedom, tolerance,
the dignity of the human spirit, and the right of the individual to
be what he is and think what he thinks without molestation or insult.
We cherish the thought that this is the American way, and that in
upholding this way we are being good Americans.

Which brings me to a night late in 1945 aboard the S. S. *Washington*, en route from New York to San Juan, Puerto Rico. As usual,
nearly everybody was gathered in the saloon after dinner, settling

the affairs of everybody else in the world with the intensity that arises out of enforced idleness.

The main table was presided over by a beefy man with a blotched complexion and a raucous voice. Alongside him sat his wife, a tiny woman, so retiring that her face seemed to sink back into its own fatigued features. With them were an old gentleman of pronounced opinions which he always punctuated with an exaggerated blink of the eyes; a prosperous Puerto Rican businessman returning home for a visit after many years in the United States; a middle-aged couple who spoke with a tinge of an unidentifiable accent; and an unrelaxed fellow, a representative of a surgical supply house, who loved to talk about the great advances of medicine and the sorry state of American politics.

I was sitting at the next table with two of my colleagues. We were reviewing plans for Puerto Rico's "Operation Bootstrap," the program that was to double the income of our people within ten years and turn a one-crop country into a balanced economy of thriving factories and modern agriculture. It was difficult to concentrate, though. The discussion at the main table was too loud. And unpleasant.

While we sat there, trying not to listen, a young man came into the saloon. He was a tall chap of thirty to thirty-five, with curly, reddish-blond hair, and an amazingly white complexion. But with deeply etched lines that gave his face an almost incongruous look of toughness.

His name was Dan, and he was very popular aboard. He seldom had much to say—just a few penetrating questions—but he always showed such a sincere interest in other people's views that everyone loved to have him around—and his pretty young wife, although she was so pregnant that I feared she was going to increase the passenger list any minute. As a rule, she went to bed early, and he then would join the other passengers in the saloon.

He was heading for our table when the beefy fellow at the main table suddenly bellowed at him.

"Hey, Dan," he shouted, "come on over here and add your two cents' worth. We're talking about the damned Jews."

To my surprise, Dan turned and sat down with them. However, the beefy fellow didn't give him much chance to put in his "two cents' worth." He was running through the whole score of tiresome shibboleths and stereotypes of anti-Semitism. The others joined in the chorus whenever they could slide in some bigoted cliché of their own.

We finally closed our ears and were carrying on our conversation —for ten minutes or more—when the three of us were brought to an abrupt stop by a new note in the discussion at the other table. It was a voice low-pitched and deliberate, yet so vibrant with fury that it drew everyone's attention like an electromagnet. It took me a time to realize that it was Dan speaking.

"I've had all of this I can take," he was saying. "At first I thought you were kidding, that this was a setup, some kind of a nasty joke, and I was waiting for the pay-off. Well, it looks like I've got to provide the pay-off. These Jews you've been talking about"—he looked at each one of them in turn and each one knew what was coming— "I'm one of them. I'm one of those 'dirty, damned Jews,' You understand?"

The beefy one smiled halfheartedly and began, "Now, Dan, we didn't . . ."

The young man went on as if the beefy one had never spoken.

"I'm going to tell you about some Jews. Five of them, Me and my four brothers. American Jews. We went to war, all five of us. I could say, if I wanted to, that we were fighting for you. I hope we weren't, but I'm afraid we were. Anyway, we were fighting for things we believed in, and to destroy something we hoped all Americans hated.

"Oh, to hell with that," he interrupted himself. For a moment I thought his anger was going to get the best of him, that he'd thunder with rage. But he kept the pitch of his voice low. "Five of us brothers went over. I'm the only one of us who came back."

He paused. None of them said anything. None of them knew what to say.

"I'm going to show you something," he resumed. He reached up to his shirt and ripped it open—literally ripped. Two buttons popped. One dropped noiselessly on the floor, the other fell into a highball glass with a little tinkle that sounded to everyone in the room like a gunshot.

High on his chest, just to the right of the center, was a deep, irregular, still-livid hole, the sort a heavy-caliber bullet makes when it meets the resistance of bone as well as flesh.

"It was damned near unanimous for all five of us. And, sitting here tonight, listening to all of you, I wish for the first time that I hadn't come back. I don't know what we fought for. Not to come back and find this."

He turned on the Puerto Rican with a special anger, though the Puerto Rican had probably contributed the least to the orgy of vilification.

"You," he said, "you ought to be more ashamed of yourself than these"—he swept his hand around the table as a substitute for the word. "I'm married to a Puerto Rican. She's always told me that Puerto Rico was a land of tolerance. She wanted to have our baby in Puerto Rico. That's why we're here. Now—I ought to bust you right in the face."

He shook his fist under the man's nose. Then he stopped and looked at his fist as though it were some curious lump from outer space that didn't belong to him. He seemed to realize that he had reached the point of losing control.

He stood up, came over to our table, and called the steward over for a drink.

I stole a glance at the occupants of the other table. The beefy one had opened his mouth as if to speak, and thought better of it. The rest were staring straight down into their glasses. I could sense their embarrassment so acutely I shared it, and yet I could feel no sympathy for them.

Less than a month later I met the young man at a luncheon in San Juan at which I was speaker. He came up to me afterward.

"Did you two have that baby all right?" I asked.

"Yes, a fine boy," he replied. "But I've been wanting to see you, Mr. Sierra. I came here today just for that. I've been wanting to tell you how much I appreciated your good judgment in ignoring everything that took place that night. And in letting me simmer down at your table by talking of other things. . . ."

I wished to tell him that it was less good judgment than embarrassment, but he was anxious to say more, so I held my tongue.

"I'm sorry I lost my temper that night. I've been in Puerto Rico over three weeks now, and everything my wife told me was true. I've seen no trace of prejudice here, and the truth is that I've seen darned little of it back home either. I suppose there will always be stupid people like that. They just like to hear themselves talk, I guess. I doubt if they even believe all the things they say.

"The point is, I'm not sorry I came back from the war. When I think how few people of that kind there are in America, and how free we Jews are, I realize that everything I went through in the war was really worth while. I had to tell you this. I wouldn't want you to believe I hated America. I'm proud of it."

"So am I," I said.

ADVICE FROM JUSTICE BRANDEIS

MORRIS L. ERNST

Attorney

Hate mongers there always will be. Everywhere. But in America you don't have to cringe before them.

Here Morris L. Ernst reveals the views on this subject of the late, great Supreme Court Justice Louis D. Brandeis. Ernst is one of America's foremost lawyers as well as one of its most telling liberals. The list of his legal triumphs is almost endless. He argued the historic Watson Case before the Supreme Court which led to the validation of the Wagner Act, and he has done more almost than any attorney to defeat attempts at literary censorship. Because of him, the right of general sale was won for James Joyce's Ulysses *and Dr. Marie Stopes'* Married Love.

An Alabaman, Ernst was born in 1888, educated at Williams College and the New York Law School. After three years as a shirt manufacturer he started practicing law in New York City in 1915, and has been at it ever since—except for time out for various government posts, secret wartime missions for President Roosevelt, and countless, payless crusades for liberal causes.

By the hundreds, the letters from the crackpots poured in. They denounced me as "Un-American," "Red," "Disgrace to the Bar." Some called me "Dirty Jew."

"Why don't you go back where you came from?" many shrilled.

I was representing the Congress of Industrial Organizations in a federal suit to force Mayor Frank "I Am the Law" Hague to recognize the right of free speech and assembly in Jersey City. This had gotten the lunatic fringe up in arms.

At that time—the late thirties—much of the nation had not yet been educated to accept trade unionism as an integral part of our economy. John L. Lewis, the head of the C.I.O., was widely looked upon as a devil with horns, and anybody associated with him was subject to attack. Vicious attack.

The longer the trial lasted, the more letters came. And they were not just from bigots. Scores were from decent people—good friends and important clients—upset for another reason. They insisted that a Jew should not be acting as counsel for the C.I.O. They feared that it would arouse ill will against Jews throughout the country. There was then, as there no doubt is now, a group of persons who fail to realize that Jews have no intrinsic right to be liked, that Jews are only people, and as such have simply the right not to be discriminated against, as have all other people.

It was a painful experience to receive a flood of mail like that. I felt then and I still do that, in a democracy like ours, lawyers have a duty to represent people in trouble no matter how unpopular their cause. A man is entitled to counsel whether he is a Communist, an anarchist, a homosexual, or anything else deemed offbeat in the arena of public opinion at any moment in history. The constitutional right to counsel is meaningless unless lawyers are willing to serve regardless of the repercussions.

But mail of that sort makes a man wonder.

I decided to show the letters to Supreme Court Justice Louis D. Brandeis. This great jurist was a Jew too.

After a decade of intellectual debate, Justice Brandeis and I had become fast friends. On many occasions I'd consulted with him on problems. I phoned him now and made an engagement to see him at his apartment in Washington.

He glanced at a few of the letters. No more. In his quiet voice, he said, "Morris, if you ever decide to take a case on the basis of whether or not you are a Jew, I suggest that you first resign from the Jewish race."

He continued, "On further thought, I think you might want to consider resigning from the human race."

I got the point. Needless to say, I stayed in the case. And I won it. The courts ruled that the Constitution of the United States applied to Jersey City, and even Mayor Hague had to comply.

There is another episode involving Justice Brandeis and me which might be worth relating here. This one has no moral, though. Just sentiment.

Shortly before his death in 1941 Mr. Brandeis said that he wanted me to have a keepsake of him—the lamp that he'd used on the bench of the Supreme Court through all his twenty-three years of service.

I was deeply moved, and, upon the judge's death, I wrote the marshal of the Court asking that the lamp be shipped to me. And

I mailed a copy of the letter to Justice Felix Frankfurter, with a request that he facilitate things.

Back came a formal communication from the marshal stating that Justice Brandeis had no authority to dispose of the lamp. It was the property of the United States Government, and the marshal, therefore, could neither give it nor sell it to me.

However, the marshal went on, under an odd, old statute, he could exchange the lamp for one of equal value. As if there were, for me, a lamp of equal value!

Because of Justice Frankfurter's interest in the matter, a copy of this letter was also sent to him. He forwarded it to me with a message scribbled by him in the margin. The message read, "Who said the law ain't wonderful?"

Today the lamp stands on a table in my office in New York. Whenever I'm tempted to condone overbigness—a sure step to statism— I walk over and touch the lamp in hopes of deriving a little of Justice Brandeis' wisdom by osmosis.

AMERICANS ABROAD

VIENNA 1955

JOHN FOSTER DULLES
Secretary of State

In the course of the past sixteen years the United States has sacrificed tens of thousands of lives and spent hundreds of billions of its citizens' dollars for one end—the preservation of freedom in the world. This policy has had many setbacks. It has also had its glorious victories. Secretary of State John Foster Dulles has written here of the one he treasures most.

Dulles has been guiding American foreign relations through five years of constant, searing crises. Born in Washington, D.C., in 1888, he graduated Phi Beta Kappa from Princeton, took a law degree at George Washington University with the highest record ever made, and went to work for the big international law firm, Sullivan & Cromwell. By forty, he was the head of it. From childhood, diplomacy was his goal, though. (His grandfather was a Secretary of State; so was an uncle.) His first appointment came in 1917 as a special State Department agent in Latin America. His next was in 1919 as a special counsel to the U. S. delegation to the Paris Peace Conference. In 1945 President Roosevelt appointed him a delegate to the founding session of the United Nations. Under the Truman Administration he served as an assistant to Secretaries of State Byrnes, Marshall, and Acheson, and negotiated the Japanese peace treaty. Immediately that President Eisenhower was inaugurated in 1953, he chose Dulles for Secretary of State.

A TRIP from the American Embassy in Vienna to the entrance of the Belvedere Palace in that ancient Austrian city is usually a brief one by automobile. But on that Sunday morning of May 15, 1955, it was a slow trip, for the streets were packed with the joyous people of Austria. For this was the day when at long last the state treaty, returning Austrians their freedom, was to be signed. The occupation troops, and above all the Soviet Red Armies, were to be withdrawn. And as we reached the Belvedere Palace we saw in the palace gardens thousands of cheering Austrians braving the rain, waiting for the signing of the treaty.

We Americans are proud of our heritage of freedom. So we understood and shared the joy that came to our Austrian friends when they regained their liberty. And it was deeply moving to me as an American to note the gratitude shown by the people to the United States.

Seventeen years had passed since Hitler had subjugated Austria and imposed servitude upon an entire population. Then came World War II and then after the end of that war there quickly followed a new occupation, prolonged for ten years by the stubborn refusal of the Soviet Union to carry out its 1943 pledge that the Austrians were to be completely free. The courage of the Austrian people was a source of inspiration to the representatives of Britain, France, and the United States during the long postwar years—years in which they sought, through no less than 379 meetings, to bring the Soviet Union to restore Austria's freedom.

On my way through the crowded streets of Vienna I recalled that I had first started work on the Austrian treaty eight years before, in 1947, when I went to Moscow as an adviser to Secretary of State George Marshall. My mind went further back, to the initial loss of Austrian independence in 1938. I thought of all the changes since 1938 that now brought me to Austria in 1955 to place my signature on a document, in behalf of the people of the United States, that would restore liberty to a gallant nation and a courageous people.

In 1938 the United States had still not fully realized its grave responsibilities as a world power. It was generally believed that we could and should stay aloof from the European conflict then threatening.

But by 1943, when we were in the midst of World War II, we realized, as a nation, that henceforth we were inextricably a part of all the world. The Senate then passed a bipartisan resolution pledging our participation in an international organization designed to ensure a peaceful world of free nations.

The United States henceforth took a leading role in helping to develop the United Nations, whose charter provides for equal rights and the self-determination of peoples, for settlement of international disputes by peaceful means and for the protection of the political independence of sovereign nations. We Americans began to devote full energy and thought to carrying out the goals of the Charter.

It soon became clear, however, that peace and freedom were not to be had merely because of the noble principles of the Charter. While we in the West disarmed, the Soviet Union maintained its huge military forces. While we quickly helped the Western nations to regain their strength in freedom, the Soviet Union used military pressure and Communist subversion to make the Eastern European nations into satellites. Continued threats against the free nations of Iran, Turkey, and Greece, the blockade of West Berlin, the war of aggression in Korea, made it imperative that a means be found to create and maintain peace. So we continued to build strength, and to unite our strength with that of others by pacts of collective defense.

Finally it became apparent to the Soviet rulers that their policies of violence would not prevail. So they made a tactical shift in Soviet foreign policy. The first exhibit was the change in the Soviet position on Austria.

All this I realized on the way to Belvedere Palace, and when I climbed the grand staircase on my way to the ceremony I felt proud that the United States and its allies throughout the world had by their fortitude made possible the further extension of freedom. Long years of diplomatic negotiation and the sustained courage of the Austrian people were indispensable. But equally indispensable was the course of world affairs, and in that my country had played a worthy part. So, for the first time since 1945, the Red armies in Europe turned their faces to the east and marched homeward.

I signed the historic document and then went out on the balcony with the four other Foreign Ministers who had signed the treaty. The Austrians assembled in the garden below cheered joyously, for now they knew they were free. At that moment there rang out in the distance the "Pummerin," the tremendous bell of the Cathedral of St. Stephen, the symbol of Austrian love for liberty. Because of the joy we had helped to bring to a great people, because of all that had gone before, and because of the symbolic significance of Austria's new freedom for the future of us all—a "deed" that our country had demanded, instead of "words" in the so-called Cold War—it was for me the day I was proudest to be an American.

THE POWER TO FORGIVE

EZRA TAFT BENSON
Secretary of Agriculture

---

*At war's end a victorious nation can wreak vengeance un-
limited on its prostrate enemy. Or it can be generous and for-
giving. With the United States, it usually has been the latter.
Surely it was so after World War II.*

*Secretary of Agriculture Ezra Taft Benson was in Germany
following the war, saw our policies in operation, and has written
about them. Great-grandson of a pioneer Mormon, Benson was
born on his family's farm in Idaho in 1899 and educated at the
Utah State Agricultural College, Brigham Young University,
and Iowa State College. Agriculture and church work have always been his chief interests. He has run a farm, been a county
agent, headed the department of agricultural economics at the
University of Idaho, and served five years as executive secretary
of the National Council of Farm Co-operatives. He has also been
a leading figure in Mormon affairs, rising to be the eighth rank-
ing apostle of the Church. (In 1946 he directed all Mormon relief activities in Europe.) President Eisenhower appointed him
Secretary of Agriculture in 1953 and he has held the post since.*

As he ran his trembling hands through a container filled with
wheat, letting it sift down between his fingers, I heard him
say almost incredulously, "You mean that you Americans are willing
to do all this for us—your former enemies?"

This expression from a mild-mannered, half-starved German from
the Russian sector of Berlin brought tears to my eyes. I felt like
humbly bowing my head and thanking God from a grateful heart
for the privilege of being an American.

Nearly four months had elapsed since I had arrived in Europe to
supervise the distribution of relief supplies and to get needed rehabilitation activities under way. During this time I had witnessed
the shattered, twisted skeletons of once-famous cities. I had seen
and lived among emaciated human beings, the victims of dread
disease and starvation. I had smelled the stench of decaying, un-

buried bodies. I had visited but recently the infamous Dachau concentration camp and my mind was still tortured by the shocking
evidence of man's shameful bestiality in dealing with his fellow man.

We had succeeded during the first few weeks in getting much-
needed food, clothing, and medical supplies to many critical sections.
Our efforts to extend such assistance to those living in the Russian-
controlled areas, however, encountered heartbreaking delays and
seemingly insurmountable obstacles. Yet an inward peace flooded
my soul and grew into an unshakable assurance that somehow, with
God's help, the way would be opened.

Then came that memorable day when our first relief supplies for
distribution in the Russian zone of Germany reached Berlin. I shall
never forget the sight of entering that large warehouse in the American sector of Berlin to inspect our supplies. Accompanying me were
several German civilians, two of whom were in a critical state of
health. On both sides of us were huge stacks of relief supplies. On
the eager, half-starved faces of those accompanying me I could see
the mixed expressions of thankfulness and wonderment.

As they opened the first large container filled with wheat, tears
of gratitude from swollen red eyes moistened hollow, sunken cheeks.
That is when this overjoyed German paid such a sincere tribute to
his unknown benefactors in America.

These were not ordinary supplies purchased on the open market.
They represented food and clothing produced by the voluntary labor
of thousands of Americans, most of whom lived in small farming
communities in the western United States.

This expression of compassion and encouragement—the product of
humble, rural folks—stirred me to the depths of my soul. As I stood
there I sensed the real strength of America—her power to love and
forgive.

I felt that God would never fail such a people. Never have I
been prouder to be an American.

BERLIN BLOCKADE

ROBERT D. MURPHY

Deputy Undersecretary of State

---

*Moments come in history when nations rise to noble heights.
The Berlin Blockade was one of these.*

*Robert D. Murphy was there. This sixty-four-year-old Wis-
consinite has been in almost every trouble spot. Educated at
Marquette and George Washington University, he has been a
trouble shooter for the U. S. Diplomatic Service for forty years.
When the German troops entered Paris in June 1940 it was Bob
Murphy who met with the German commander to safeguard
American and French interests. When the Allies landed in
North Africa on November 8, 1942, it was Bob Murphy who
greeted them. He did the underground work that made the in-
vasion possible. When the Allied armies advanced into Europe,
Murphy was along as U. S. Political Advisor to General Eisenhower. During the four crucial years following the German surrender he was political advisor to the U. S. Military Government. While the Korean Armistice negotiations were under way
he was political advisor to the United Nations Command.
Murphy has further served as U. S. Ambassador to Belgium and
Japan, and as Assistant Secretary of State for United Nations
Affairs. Now, as Deputy Secretary of State, he holds the highest
office open to a career diplomat. I heard this story of Berlin
under blockade from him.*

BERLIN was a nervous city in the spring of 1948. A strained
look was in people's eyes, uncertainty in their voices. The tension could be felt on the streets, in the homes, everywhere. The
Russians were acting up.

More than anything the Kremlin wanted to drive the American,
British, and French soldiers out of Berlin. If they could do that they
knew that the population of the Western zones of Germany would
lose faith in the ability of the democracies to defend them against
communism. Then all Germany would surely fall into Soviet hands.

It was not only the fate of Germany that was at stake. The prestige
of democracy hung in the balance. All over the world people were

waiting to see whether the United States and its allies would back down to the Soviet.

There was just a small detachment of Americans in Berlin. Surrounding them on all sides were hundreds of thousands of Red Army troops. The Kremlin was confident that under pressure the Americans would crack, as individuals and as a nation.

The method the Kremlin used was typical: a calculated attempt to starve to death the Americans, their allies, and the two million men, women, and little children who lived in the Western sectors of Berlin. On March 31, Russian officials deliberately began to interfere with the movement of U. S. Army trains. They did this in violation of a solemn agreement according the United States unlimited access to Berlin. A few days later they stopped every outgoing passenger train. On June 24 they halted all trains, freight and passenger both, between Berlin and the West. "The railroad requires repairs," they lied. Next, they cut off the highways and canals. By August 4, Berlin was blockaded. The city was left to die.

What ensued is history, one of the few bright pages since World War II. Despite hunger, cold, darkness—electricity could operate only a couple of hours a day—and despite the constant threat of war, the Americans didn't crack. Neither did the British nor the French. Nor did the Berliners. They stood stalwartly with the democracies.

Overnight the greatest airlift on record was organized. Big C-54s raced back and forth from the U.S. Zone, carrying everything from eggs to medicine. Day and night they flew, through fog, snow, and ice. They continued flying even when Russian jets buzzed them. Every thirty seconds one of them would arrive or take off. Berlin needed a minimum of 4000 tons of supplies a day. The airlift pilots got to a point where they were bringing in 8000 tons.

For eleven months the U. S. Air Force kept the airlift going, delivering 1,402,644 tons that Berlin had to have to live. It proved to the people of the entire world that they could rely on America's ingenuity, America's resources, and America's determination to resist tyranny whatever the cost.

It was a crushing propaganda defeat for the Russians, and on May 11, 1949, they admitted it. Ignominiously they called off the blockade.

To those who lived through it, like Robert D. Murphy, some of the days during that blockade are unforgettable. And always will be.

How could he ever forget, for instance, the day the airlift was conceived?

There he was, sitting, with a group of U. S. Military Government officials, in the office of General Lucius D. Clay, the U. S. Military Governor in Germany. Before them was the specter of a foodless Berlin. And, of equal gravity, a coal-less Berlin. That meant no heat, no light, no power to run industry—tragic unemployment.

The railroads, the highways, the canals were blocked. Only the air remained. But how could you move tens of thousands of tons of coal in airplanes?

"It can't be done," the Military Government men said. "Maybe we can get in food. Not coal, though."

General Clay wasn't convinced. He picked up the phone on his desk and put in a call to General Curtis E. LeMay, the U. S. Air Force chief in Europe. Point-blank, he asked him,

"Can you deliver coal by air?"

LeMay gulped. Murphy could hear it at the other end of the line. Then he said, "Will you repeat that question, please?"

"Can you deliver coal by air?"

"Sir," LeMay answered, "the Air Force can deliver anything."

The morning afterward, the airlift was under way.

Another day was unforgettable to Murphy. This was the one on which a Russian officer was watching the endless stream of our airplanes pouring into Berlin. It was more than the Russian could stomach.

In Murphy's presence, he shook his fist at the planes up in the sky.

"Damned Americans," he snarled, "you just don't know when you're beaten."

Yet if Murphy had to choose the day that counted the most to him as an American, it would be neither of these. Actually, it would be a miserable, sleety day in January 1949 when a poor, ragged German mother walked all the way out to Tegel Airport. She wanted to thank a group of American airmen who, in addition to everything else, had been buying candy with their own money and parachuting it down to the underfed Berlin kids. "Operation Little Vittles," they called it.

"*Danke schön, danke schön,*" the woman said, trying to kiss the boys' hands.

"Aw, it's nuttin'," the embarrassed airmen said.

"It iss not nothing," the woman said in broken English. "Here we Germans was your enemies but you giff our children candy."

The boy who commanded the airmen patted the woman on the shoulder. "Lady," he declared, "kids ain't nobody's enemies."

It was so true. And so American.

MY FAVORITE ROLE

IRENE DUNNE

U.S. Alternate Representative to the United Nations

From the day of the United Nations' inception the voices of the famished, the diseased, and the despairing have been heard in its halls, calling for help. How have the nations of the world answered their pleas?

Irene Dunne was deputized to give the United States' response at the U.N. last year, and she told me about it. Miss Dunne was a member of the U. S. delegation to the twelfth U.N. General Assembly. It was a new role for her. Usually she's seen on the screen.

A Kentuckian, Miss Dunne studied to be a concert singer, but found acting more interesting. Her very first movie, Cimarron, won the Motion Picture Academy Award, and she quickly became a Hollywood luminary. In all, she has starred in thirty-three films, among them such hits as Show Boat, Theodora Goes Wild, The Awful Truth, *and* I Remember Mama. *She has been nominated five times for the Academy Award for the most outstanding performance by an actress.*

Interreligious harmony has been a crusade with Miss Dunne, and in 1948 she was given the American Brotherhood Award by the National Conference of Christians and Jews. She was appointed to the U. S. delegation to the U.N. in line with the tradition that our delegation should represent all walks of American life.

WHAT is it like to be a U. S. delegate to the United Nations? After my years in the movies I thought I was somewhat inured to drama and excitement. But Hollywood has nothing that can approach the United Nations in these spheres. For at the United Nations all the problems of the world are paraded before your eyes. You never forget for a moment that war and peace and life itself are at stake.

In the past I have greatly enjoyed making people laugh. Some of my favorite films have been comedies. At the United Nations, however, there is no time for comedy.

What is there time for? Just for measures that will preserve the peace, and help to improve the lot of all the 2,500,000,000 people on this earth or ours. Along these lines the United Nations has done splendidly. It has fed millions of starving people, aided hundreds of thousands of homeless refugees to find new homes and new lives, cured vast numbers of little children of tuberculosis, leprosy, trachoma. And, for thirteen years, it has kept World War III from splattering us with nuclear bombs. President Eisenhower was so right when he called the United Nations "the world's best hope for peace."

The United Nations is, of course, only as strong as its eighty-two member nations make it. The United Nations cannot draft a single soldier. It cannot levy one dollar in taxes. Its vigor depends entirely upon the conscience of its members.

As a delegate to the United Nations I soon found out that some of the member nations have consciences. Others don't.

This was on October 4, 1957. The General Assembly was convened in solemn session to consider the tragic plight of the 900,000 Palestinian refugees, and the 250,000 refugees from Nazi and Communist terror who are still scattered around Europe, Africa, and Asia. Many of them have not been out of a refugee camp since World War II.

The question before the Assembly was how to feed and clothe and house these unfortunates for another year. Would the members pledge enough money to do it?

One by one, delegates stepped to the rostrum to announce the contributions their nations would make for the Palestinians. Later they did it again for the other refugees. I watched the British delegate, the French, the Australian, the Swiss, the Swedish, and the others come forward. They each pledged substantial amounts.

It was truly touching. Even the poorest countries gave something. Poverty-stricken Greece donated $18,000, for example. Tiny Luxembourg, with a population of less than 320,000, still managed $5,000.

Not Soviet Russia, though. Nor any of its satellites. Their delegates were silent that day. They didn't give one single penny toward helping the refugees. They never have given a cent.

It was my assignment to announce to the Assembly what the United States would contribute to both the refugee programs. Eagerly I awaited my instructions from the State Department.

Thank heavens, I did not have to stay mute like the Russians and other Communist delegates. The United States Congress agreed to do its part, too. Congress knew that the American people would not want to turn their back on starvation and suffering.

With complete sincerity I was able to tell the General Assembly, "We usually speak here as representatives of our governments, but we are also representatives of our people. I am sure that every man and woman we represent feels as I do—that each of us who has a home and a country should bend every effort to help those who have neither."

I announced that the United States would give $23,733,000; more than all the other nations put together. It brought our total contributions to United Nations refugee programs to more than $640,000,000 as compared to the Soviet Union's zero.

No lines that I've spoken on the screen stirred me as did these. It was a wonderful thing to represent a country with a conscience.

What happened a moment later was even more stirring. As I sat down again at the United States delegation's table, a man tapped me on the back.

"Miss Dunne," he said, "may I have your autograph?"

Of all times! Of all places! I groaned. To get approached for an autograph here in the United Nations General Assembly. I cursed my movie career.

"Just put it here," the man said, and he handed me a piece of paper to write on.

Reluctantly I glanced down at it. It was a printed form stating, "On behalf of the United States of America, I pledge $23,733,000."

I signed with pleasure.

SERGEANT SCOGGINS IS HOST

WILLIAM I. NICHOLS

Editor, This Week

Pious statements are no rebuttal to Communist propaganda. Statistics on the abundance of telephones, refrigerators, and washing machines in America won't go either. It's what we do, as a nation and as individuals, that the uncommitted people of the world judge.

William I. Nichols saw one young American reply to communism in the best possible way—by his own deeds—and he has written about it here. Nichols is the editorial genius who has made the Sunday magazine, This Week, *into the most widely read publication in the United States. Distributed by thirty-eight major newspapers, it is followed by over twelve million families a week. That adds up to more than half a billion copies a year. Fifty-three now, Nichols was born in New York, graduated magna cum laude from Harvard and won a Rhodes Scholarship to Oxford. He has been Dean of Freshmen at Harvard, Director of Electrical Development for the Tennessee Valley Authority, and editor of* Sunset *magazine. He began at* This Week *in 1939 as managing editor, by 1943 was editor, and in 1955 was raised to be editor in chief and publisher. He has traveled abroad extensively as a consultant to the State Department.*

TRAVEL along the Iron Curtain can be very enlightening. Here and there it has gaps in it that let you see for yourself how criminal communism is in operation, how sinister, how false to its promises.

Not long after World War II, I took a swing around the Balkans for the State Department. In the course of it I came to the little town of Leckart at the eastern tip of Slovakia. A unique place.

In September 1945 this little Czechoslovakian town was peremptorily incorporated into the Soviet Union. However, it caused a bulge in the border, so the Russians gave the town back. That made it the only territory Soviet Russia ever relinquished voluntarily.

The eight months Leckart spent as part of the U.S.S.R. provided a vivid case history for me of conditions under the Kremlin.

There were fifteen hundred people in that town who became Russians overnight. Thereafter, every step they took, every word they uttered, was spied upon. The Kremlin had no less than eighty-four M.V.D. men and ten police dogs watching them, in addition to a network of paid informers.

The hunger and misery of those peasants! Their land was confiscated and they were compelled at bayonet point to work on collective farms. They got a wage of eight rubles a day when merely a loaf of bread cost forty rubles. They grew so desperate they used to sneak out at night, pull up wheat, and feed it raw to their families.

They were forbidden to cross the border for any reason, even to visit their relatives. Sixteen tried. They were caught and sent to slave-labor camps in Siberia. Only one of them returned alive.

"May I talk to him?" I inquired.

"You wouldn't want to," I was informed. "The poor fellow's out of his mind."

That was life in a Communist state. The tragedy is that millions of people don't realize it.

For all its viciousness, communism is a powerful, dynamic force. A kind of ecstasy goes with the idea of communism, a sort of vitality, a sense of hope and adventure, and the Communists are past masters at exploiting these emotions through their propaganda. Especially among people who've never been to the Soviet Union.

It's hard to believe how cynical and effective Soviet propaganda is. It utilizes every technique of high-pressure advertising, religious zeal, and political demagogy. Goebbels and Bilbo were pikers by comparison.

I know whereof I speak. During my trip I was subjected to some of this Soviet propaganda at an international exposition in Prague. I was stirred myself.

It was heady stuff. First the promises. Slogans like, "End All Race Discrimination," "Food for the People," "A Profession for Every Youth." Second, the shameless lies. Statements such as "The citizens of the U.S.S.R. are guaranteed freedom of speech, freedom of the press, freedom of assembly, including the holding of mass meetings, and freedom of demonstration." With photomurals of the United States nearby, showing slums, bread lines, and Negroes being lynched, as though this were the rule rather than the tragic exception. Finally the tricks to whip up excitement and a crusading fervor. Exhibits like these: A rusty typewriter used by a resistance leader. A blood-soaked coat with a card, "The jacket of our martyr, Margareta Tululane who was massacred by fascists." Plus thrilling pictures of people marching, shouting, singing. All to show that Communists were brave men, building a brave new world.

Our American exhibit was painfully drab by comparison with the Soviet. Once I'd seen them both, I could readily understand how communism managed—despite all the horrors of Soviet existence—to inspire such fanatic devotion among its adherents. I could see what lay behind the remarks of a young girl Communist from Yugoslavia.

"You people from the capitalist world," she said, "I can't figure you out. I can't respect you. We are passionate about communism, but you, you're not passionate about anything. You haven't any passion for your country, for your society, for your job, for each other."

For a long while my trip had me dejected. It seemed to me that democracy had no answer to the dynamic appeal of the Communists. Time was when our American way of life had meant clipper ships, covered wagons, the gold rush, the Yukon. It had a climate of adventure and excitement. But that was in the past. Now it seemed to me that we had little left beyond material things—refrigerators and the like—with which to offset the Communists' insidious propaganda. They weren't enough. I was sure of it.

Then, at the very end of my trip, I met Sergeant William Scoggins of the United States Army. He proved to me that I was wrong. He demonstrated that democracy had something else to offer. Something that could stand up to communism on its own terms and win the struggle for man's loyalties.

I bumped into Scoggins in Vienna—in a curious manner. Years and years before, I'd stayed at the Hotel Cobenzl, an old castle high up in the Vienna woods. It was a charming spot. The stars of the Max Reinhardt Company used to come there after the theater, and we'd all sip wine together, looking out over the shining blue Danube. Everything romantic in my youth was inextricably wrapped in this hotel, and I was anxious to go back.

I knew a lot had happened to the Cobenzl since I'd been there. The Germans had taken it over during the war as the headquarters of an antiaircraft battery. They'd painted its lovely white walls a dismal green and surrounded it with squat wooden barracks. Later,

Russian troops had attacked it, scarring it badly with mortar shells and machine-gun bullets.

After V-E Day it'd been turned into a U. S. Army displaced-persons camp for refugees from Yugoslavia, Hungary, and Rumania.

Still I wanted to see the Cobenzl again before I left Austria for home.

A jaunty young American sergeant stepped out as I drove up. "What can I do for you?" He grinned.

"I'd like to talk to the commanding officer," I said.

"You came to the right man. I'm the boss."

"Isn't there any officer around?"

"Nope. Just me. Bill Scoggins."

This twenty-four-year-old Texan was the only American soldier there. He had 1376 people in his sole care. Pathetic, homeless, countryless people, sick in body and in spirit. Old, wrinkled people with indescribably sad eyes, and young people with equally sad eyes. Ragged, rickety children, 371 of them, mostly war orphans. At least two of them war-made cripples. One, a ten-year-old girl, had had an arm shot off. Another, an eight-year-old boy, had lost a leg to a ten-ton bomb.

Scoggins had to be father, mother, and "boss" to all of these lost souls.

"Nobody wants 'em," he explained. "They're just a bunch of jokers left over from the war, but somebody's got to take care of 'em."

He'd had no training for his assignment. Until the war, he'd been an engineering student at a New Mexico mining school. For two solid years he'd fought through Italy, France, and Germany with the 45th Division. Following that, a spell as an executioner of Nazi war criminals. A dirty job, but it had to be done. Next, occupation duty in Austria, and, out of a clear sky, came this one-man detail to Cobenzl.

It was miraculous what he'd accomplished singlehanded. I'd seen other D.P. camps. Hellholes, most of them. Grim, prisonlike enclaves, teeming with surly people, and lice. Filth all over, and no one trying to do much about it. Bored, disinterested officers, so no real organization. Families separated, children untended. Food inedible. Black marketing rampant. Everywhere, cloying idleness. Men and women, by the thousands, with nothing to do save sit and stare, vacantly, despondently into space.

Not at Cobenzl. "I'm sort of fond of these people," Scoggins said to me. "I want to make 'em happy."

And you could see he meant it. He had a gay, friendly word for everyone of the refugees. "Hi, Mom," he'd say as we passed. Or, "How you doin', pal?" to a young boy. Always with a big, warm smile.

Every inch of his camp was clean and neat. The people were clean and neat, too. Scoggins insisted on it. The older, sicker residents were living in the castle, the others in the barracks. No matter where they were housed, Scoggins saw to it that each family was kept together, that it was given a little space for itself, an area it could call its own. He'd searched war-ravaged Vienna through for odds and ends to make their surroundings more comfortable. He'd scrounged extra chairs, ramshackle, perhaps, but still usable, tables, scraps of material for curtains.

He'd constructed a special nursery for the children, beautifully decorated with Mother Goose murals. He talked a couple of Red Cross girls into painting them.

Even the food was good. He'd started a garden on the castle grounds to supply fresh vegetables.

All this would not have counted a whit, of course, if the refugees had been condemned to perpetual idleness. They weren't. Scoggins had found work for them all, something, anything, to give purpose to their lives again.

He'd obtained jobs for the able-bodied on neighboring farms. The feebler ones he employed in the garden or in the camp administration.

He hadn't missed a soul. Out in front of the castle I saw an old, old man, of ninety or more, with the suffering of the ages distilled in his eyes. Scoggins told me about him—tenderly.

"That guy has really had a hard time. His wife was killed by Tito. One of his sons was killed in the resistance movement and the other was taken away by Tito and has never been heard from since. He's really alone."

Scoggins had even given this ninety-year-old man a job. He'd made him official baby sitter.

The old man loved it. "It's much better now," he said to me. "I'm doing something useful."

Then he whispered, "Isn't that sergeant a wonderful man?"

An Austrian general, a distinguished veteran of both world wars, who'd accompanied me on the trip to Cobenzl, put it differently.

"Look at that boy," he declared. "He represents the best that's in America. If the Russians were running this camp they would have sent in hundreds of troops. Everyone would have been regimented and everyone would have been miserable. But this one sergeant is doing it better, all by himself, just by using ingenuity, leadership, and human sympathy."

I felt much happier about democracy's prospects as I drove back into Vienna. Democracy had an answer to Communist propaganda. I was convinced of it.

I said then and I say now: Let the Communists have their violent, destructive passion. We Americans have the "Sergeant Scoggins spirit" on our side—a quiet, controlled kind of passion, for decency, fair play, working together, maintaining order. In the long run—if we understand this spirit, and live up to it—people will choose democracy, any time, any place, over communism's lies and the misery and cruelty which lie behind them.

IN THE JUNGLES OF INDIA

DICKEY CHAPELLE
Photographer and Foreign Correspondent

---

*From Berlin to Bombay, Dickey Chapelle has seen American
assistance programs in operation. She has seen the good our
men and our dollars have done, and she has seen how they have
done it.*

*As a foreign correspondent, Miss Chapelle is probably the
most adventurous, and the bravest, in many a decade. The
Hungarian Communists will agree with that statement. They
tried to brain-wash her, and got nowhere. Born in Milwaukee
thirty-nine years ago, she quit Massachusetts Institute of Tech-
nology to go into newspaper reporting. In 1940 she added a
camera to her typewriter. The only woman correspondent-
photographer accredited to the Pacific Fleet, she participated
in the invasions of both Iwo Jima and Okinawa. After the war
she covered relief work in fourteen European countries, including three behind the Iron Curtain. Then she spent two years
in India, Iran, and Iraq reporting on the Point 4 Program.
Late in 1956 she became the center of an international incident
when she was arrested crossing the Hungarian border to aid
refugees from the revolution to escape. For fifty-two days the
infamous Hungarian secret police kept her in a Budapest
dungeon and attempted by torture to break her spirit. They
couldn't, and the U. S. Government finally secured her release.
Nothing daunted, she was soon off to Algeria to cover the
civil war there. This is her story of the men who represent
the United States abroad.*

Lᴵᴷᴱ other Americans who gather news overseas for a living, I
know something at first hand about the "Hate America" campaign. I've been spat upon, cursed, threatened, and imprisoned on
three continents just because I am an American. But that's merely
one side of the coin. I've also seen love for America in foreign lands,
and heart-warming gratitude for our assistance.

If you ask me, the difference between the two attitudes lies mainly
in the degree of understanding which foreigners have of the United

States, and of the everyday, democratic people that most Americans are. The Communists and the other agitators whose job it is to stir up hatred of America don't make much headway when the truth about us—and our motives—is really understood.

Unquestionably we Americans are rotten propagandists. For all our slick advertising techniques, we don't know how to explain ourselves. We are very lucky, though, in the type of men we have representing us abroad. Through their own example they often clear up carloads of misconceptions.

I saw this for myself, one sultry afternoon, deep in the jungles of India.

Murmadia was the place. It was a backward little village of eighty or ninety clay huts, situated far down at the southern end of the province of Madhya Pradesh. It took me eight hundred miles of hard driving past screeching parrots and man-eating tigers to reach it.

The purpose of my trip was to watch India's new community development program in action. I had a particular interest in this project because the Ford Foundation was financing a "leadership training" school for the Indans near Murmadia, and the U. S. Government was providing an educational advisor. I wanted to see whether our American aid was doing good. Or harm.

I couldn't have gone at a better time. The village was in the throes of a raging crisis as I drove up the winding, dusty road and parked my jeep alongside a banyan tree.

Dozens of men, dressed only in loincloths, were clustered about a circle whitewashed on the heat-baked earth. They were waving their fists and jabbering angrily at each other. The headman, an erect, dignified figure draped in white, was trying to address them, but no one would listen. They were all too excited.

Two of the group, who were wearing shorts rather than loincloths, came over to me. They were students at the nearby "leadership" school. It was part of their training to serve this village, living in it, figuring out its problems, and helping the villagers to solve them.

"What's all the hassle about?" I asked them.

Before they could answer, a tall American in rumpled khaki, with hair like corn straw, stepped out from behind a hut.

"We sure been hopin' you-all would get here," he drawled. "We're mighty proud of the job these boys are doin'."

He was Paul Creech, a former Air Force officer who had been a vocational education expert in Bryan, Texas, until he came to India. Now, he was the Point 4 advisor to the leadership trainees' school.

Calmly he explained what the dispute was about.

The whitewashed circle marked the location of what was to be a well, the first source of clean water in all the hundreds of years that village had been there.

Always before, the people of Murmadia had taken their water from a contaminated pond. And washed in it, too. Year in and year out, this had caused horrible outbreaks of dysentery, typhoid, and bilharzia—a frightful parasitical disease which leaves its emaciated victims a prey to any passing germ—but none of the villagers had known any better.

After much effort the two young students had convinced the villagers of the need for pure water. Then they'd located the water table and designed a simple well with a pulley mechanism that the villagers could construct themselves.

The fight now was over when the well should be dug. For the rice was ready to be harvested in the fields, and many of the villagers thought it much more important to get in the rice crop than to guard their families against disease.

"Nothing can matter more to us than the rice," they shouted in Urdu.

"And your children?" the others were arguing. "Do not their lives matter to you?"

"Sickness has ever been with us. It always will be. It is the will of God."

I looked at Creech. I saw him nod at the two students. Quietly they stepped forward.

"We two shall begin digging the well," they said. "Anybody who wishes may dig with us."

I waited to see if anyone would join them. A few did. But no more. The others stayed where they were. Some even jeered. I could have cried.

Suddenly Paul Creech walked over and grasped a pickax. Without a word, he, too, fell to digging. The villagers near him froze with astonishment; they'd never seen a white man do manual labor. Never.

As word of this incredible happening spread through the village, women with water jugs on their heads paused in mid-stride, and farmers carrying rice on their shoulders turned toward the well. There was an excited buzz.

Only the two students were unmoved. They had heard Creech say scores of times, "In America, a leader does everything he expects others to do."

All at once the headman took up a pickax too. One by one, others followed him. Soon, there were close to one hundred men at work, almost everyone in the village. Under the trainees' direction they organized a regular basket brigade to bear off the broken earth.

Murmadia was going to have its well. And America had won some new friends.

Goma, the headman, put it into words. The night the digging was finished he stood silhouetted against a flickering background of torches and said:

"You have come a long way, Paulcreech. . . ." He spoke it as one word. "And it is good that you have come. For you have taught us something important. That Americans do not feel themselves better than other people. Someday you will go back to your country. Tell your people that you have helped us. Tell them that perhaps someday we can help them. Tell them that we would like to."

Later one of the young students confided to me the villagers' new phrase for pure water. They call it, "American water."

NIGHT OUT IN AMSTERDAM

LEONARD PARIS
St. Louis Editor

Tourists can do much harm to their country's reputation. Or great good. Leonard Paris can attest to that. As an official of Trans World Airlines, he traveled many thousands of miles and saw many thousands of our tourists on the move.

A Wisconsinite, born in 1912, Paris was educated in journalism at DePauw University, taught high school in Muncie, Indiana, for eight years, went to New York and got to be an editor for This Week, *then* Collier's *and* Look. *He also wrote for many other fine magazines. After five years with TWA he transferred himself, bag and baggage, to St. Louis, where he is now an editor of the Monsanto Chemical Company magazine. He wrote this story.*

Not long ago I had a date to take twenty-five women night-clubbing in Amsterdam. It was an exciting evening. At one point I thought it was going to end in a free-for-all.

My "dates" were part of a group of one hundred and twenty women from Fort Wayne, Indiana, who were making a grand tour of Europe. And they were doing it up brown. They'd chartered special TWA planes to fly them from country to country; they were staying at the best hotels; they were eating at the finest restaurants; and they were sight-seeing like mad. There wasn't a palace, a museum, or a good shop that they missed. Or a cabaret. Although they ranged in age from seventeen to seventy-four, late hours meant nothing to them.

"Sleeping is for when we get home," the seventy-four-year-old remarked.

This evening a number of the women had said they wished to hit the top night spots of Holland. I called for them at their hotel at nine.

They made a stunning sight. They were of all shapes and forms, true, but they had one thing in common. They were smartly dressed and perfectly groomed. They really looked like a million dollars.

First, we visited a couple of the big show places of Amsterdam. About midnight we stopped in at a small night club noted for its hot jazz. The girls wanted to see whether Dutch musicians could "swing it" as well as Americans.

They could.

During one of the intermissions a bleary-eyed drunk, unkempt in a drab, rumpled suit, started glowering at us from a nearby table.

"Typical American capitalists' wives," he babbled. "Dripping with furs and jewels. Wrung from the sweat of the workers."

The man spoke English with an accent, more middle European than Dutch. His companion, very embarrassed, tried to hush him. "Why don't you leave them alone," he said. "Americans are not so bad."

The loudmouth wouldn't be squelched. "That's the trouble with you Dutch. Always apologizing for the Americans. And why? Just because you want their filthy dollars."

He wouldn't even subside when the band began to play. "You think American aid saved you? You'd be much better off by yourselves instead of being in debt to those American leeches."

He made so much noise that everyone in the club started to stare in our direction. My happy group of American women commenced to stir uneasily, and I noticed the cigarette girl glancing nervously around for the manager.

Minute by minute the drunk grew nastier. He stumbled to his feet, a glass of beer in his hand, and shouted over the music.

"I want to drink a toast. Down with the capitalist tyrants! Long live the working classes."

Some waiters rushed over to quiet him. He was a big man and he roughly shoved them aside. Then he started toward our table. Obviously he was itching for a fight.

Before he reached us, one of my Fort Wayne lady friends got up from her seat. She was a small, round woman in her early fifties, with something of the look of Queen Victoria about her. She held up her hands and the band stopped playing.

"I'll join in the last part of that toast," she said firmly in the tense silence. "I happen to be one of the working class myself. I'm an armature winder and I earn about sixty dollars a week. My capitalist boss made it possible for me to be here tonight."

The girl next to her shot to her feet. "I'm a welder, and if this is what exploitation means, I'll buy it."

Another girl followed suit. And so it went, all around the table. Finally the last of my innocents rose. "See, we're all workers here. From the same factory. We're seeing Europe on our vacation."

By this time most of the people in the club were on their feet, cheering. The leader of the band grinned, turned to his men, and led them in a stirring version of "The Stars and Stripes Forever" while the drunk stormed out the door.

Later I asked the little woman who stood up first what had given her the courage to do it.

"I just wasn't going to let any old Communist spoil my fun," she answered. "I saved three years for this trip."

REVOLUTION IN HUNGARY

LEO CHERNE
Chairman, International Rescue Committee

In the minds of most of the world's peoples the name "America" connotes freedom. Despite Communist propaganda and lies, they still believe in the principles that underlie the American form of government. So much so that they are prepared to die to achieve them for themselves.

Leo Cherne has beheld the corpses of men, women, and children who did die for this goal. In October 1956 he was one of the few Americans to reach Budapest during the tragically short-lived Hungarian Revolution. He brought medical supplies to the freedom fighters from the International Rescue Committee, a gallant organization he heads that was founded in 1933 to aid victims of totalitarianism. New York-born in 1912, Cherne went to New York University and got a law degree at New York Law School. Instead of practicing law, though, he went in for economics. The Research Institute of America, which he directs, is one of the wisest and most successful business-counseling services in the United States. Cherne's insight into foreign affairs—and the frequency with which his predictions of coming events have proven true—have made him a favorite lecturer at such august institutions as the War College and the Industrial College of the Armed Forces. He told me this story of Budapest under fire.

SOME revolutions die at birth. Others, where the people are united in a good cause, live on indefinitely, no matter how savagely they are at first suppressed.

I know.

The night was pitch black and there was no electricity to ease the darkness. The power lines had been cut. But the suburbs of Budapest were dancing with light when I got there.

Every window of every house had a small candle burning in it.

Those candles were symbols of support for the great fight against communism that was in progress throughout the country. Although Soviet tanks were poised to crash into the city, the citizens of Budapest were saying to each other, "We will never give up our dream of freedom."

Always I will remember the sight of those hundreds of thousands of flickering candles. For me their flames epitomize the gallant, invincible spirit of the Hungarian people.

I was in Hungary on a mission of mercy. And for something even more than that—to tell the Hungarians that the people of the United States were identified with them in their struggle against Russian oppression.

I'd left New York on an hour's notice with Angier Biddle Duke, the president of the International Rescue Committee. We took with us fifteen thousand vials of terramycin and other medicines that had been generously contributed by Americans anxious to alleviate Hungarian suffering.

The plan was for Angie Duke to mobilize I.R.C. facilities in Vienna while I tried to get to Budapest with the drugs.

Marcel Faust, the manager of I.R.C.'s Vienna office, was to accompany me on the drive. He's a quiet, slender man of forty, Austrian-born but now an American citizen.

Marcel had a battered 1950 Chevrolet convertible. Quickly we loaded it with the drugs, rolls of bandages, and some bundles of old clothes. There was still a little room in the car so we pushed in thirty loaves of long Viennese bread.

It is a hundred and seventy miles from Vienna to Budapest by road. They were cold, frightening, dangerous miles. Twenty-two times we were stopped at the point of a gun.

Just to cross the frontier was a searing sensation. For the first mile into Hungary there is not a house, not a tree, not a bush. It is a no man's land punctuated only by sentry boxes.

I felt the real, nauseating kind of fear that a person who has been fighting communism for years experiences when he knows that he is in Soviet territory. Here are no telephones to the West. No one to appeal to for help. No one to protect you against the dictators if it is their will to stand you against a wall and shoot you.

It was even more scary when we got to Budapest. Although the suburbs were necklaced in candlelight, the city itself was in darkness. The shooting was too close for candles to be displayed here.

Everywhere were evidences of the fighting: Shell-shattered buildings, gutted tanks, burned-out trolleys, tilted at crazy angles, overturned cars. Hundreds of twisted corpses. Here and there, wounded men and women, lying in the streets and doorways, moaning for help.

For a while it would be eerily quiet. Then cannon would snarl and machine guns would crackle viciously.

This was the first revolution in modern annals to erupt completely spontaneously. After eleven years of Communist despotism and brutality the Hungarians could stomach no more. When the AVOs—the hated secret police—shot down a group of students staging a peaceful demonstration for freedom, the people of Budapest took to the barricades.

All Hungary soon followed suit.

The Kremlin dispatched Soviet troops and tanks to smash the uprising. Unarmed though they were, every element of the population linked hands to drive the invaders out.

The heroism of the Hungarians was incredible. One girl in her teens jumped on top of a Red Army tank and shoved a Molotov cocktail in the turret peephole.

The tank burst into flames. So did the girl.

A child with a rifle taller than he (boys of ten fought) ran in front of a tank and tried to shoot up at its peephole.

The tank rolled over him. Nothing was left but a mashed, bloody form.

His mother was nearby. "He was a good, brave boy," she sobbed.

I talked personally with the leaders of the revolution. And with dozens of the combatants. I wanted to find out where their yearning for freedom had come from. After all, the Hungarian nation had never, in all its history, known true democracy.

I learned the answer to my question. It was an inspiring one. The Hungarians had been looking to America.

Despite eleven years of violent anti-American propaganda by the Communists, and years more of Nazi lies before that, the Hungarians still regarded the United States as the main fountain of freedom.

Again and again I saw this during the twenty-four tense hours I spent in Budapest.

As we were driving into the city we were flagged down by a cluster of grim-looking civilians carrying Tommy guns.

"*Medicinen! Medicinen!*" I nervously shouted.

"Who are you?" one of them said in German.

"Americans," we answered.

"With medicine for us?"

"Yes."

He almost wept. "God bless you for coming."

Next morning we visited a command post of the Freedom Fighters, the impromptu organization of students and workers which led the fighting against the Russians.

The command post was hidden in a building within a building. We had to pass through the blackened skeleton of a tenement gutted by Russian shells, then through a large courtyard where hundreds of people were feverishly learning how to shoot a rifle. After that we came to a small shabby house. This was it.

We mounted a flight of rickety stairs and entered a tiny room with no windows. The sole illumination was from a single dim electric bulb hanging from the ceiling.

The officer in charge was seated at a narrow table in the center, signing mimeographed orders for each unit.

To my amazement, she proved to be an attractive, dark-haired girl of nineteen or twenty.

I told her that I'd come all the way from the United States to bring drugs and encouragement to the revolutionaries.

A radiant smile broke over her tired face. "I knew we could count on America," she said.

Later that day I was at the headquarters of the newly resurrected Social Democratic Party.

It was jammed to the rafters. I've never seen so many people crowded into one place. And such beaming, happy people. They were almost overwhelmed with joy at the thought of being able—for once—to organize their own free political party.

I spoke with the heads of the new party.

"We're going to build a true democracy here—like in America," they vowed, "or die in the attempt."

I gave the Social Democrats the thirty loaves of bread.

Three men could easily have carried the bread in from the car. The party heads assigned thirty—one per loaf.

Never will I forget the way those thirty men paraded through the milling crowd, one behind the other, each bearing a loaf of bread as carefully as if it had been the crown jewels.

"Look!" they said. "Gifts from America!"

Time ran out on me fast in Budapest. Before I could get to meet half the people I wanted to, word came that the Russians were close to cutting the Vienna highway. If we were to get out, we had to make a dash for it.

In leaving Budapest, I had hopes that the revolution might prevail. I'd seen such superb heroism, such ironclad determination to fight, such devotion to freedom.

Unfortunately my hopes did not survive long. Too many Russian tank columns were on the move toward Budapest. It was obvious that the ruthless men in the Kremlin were resolved to smash the Hungarian uprising regardless of the cost in innocent lives.

Yet I cannot say that I was disheartened when I departed Hungary after a wild ride over back roads. In my ears were still ringing the words of a leader of the Freedom Fighters.

"What are your chances of success?" I asked him.

"We may not win now," he said to me, "but we cannot lose. Once a nation has tasted liberty, it will not forget the flavor."

I came back to the United States filled with admiration for the Hungarians. And with admiration for America too. It was a wonderful thing for me to learn that the Hungarians thought what we have was worth fighting for.

THE MAN IN THE STREET

HENRY M. JACKSON
United States Senator from Washington

Inside the Soviet Union itself, the things America stands for are known and, by many, cherished. Senator Henry M. Jackson saw a graphic example of this during a ten-thousand-mile tour he made of the U.S.S.R. in the summer of 1956, and he told me about it.

Jackson, a Democrat, is the junior senator from Washington. Forty-six years old now, he was born in the state of Washington and worked his way through the University of Washington, college and law school. He made such a mark as prosecuting attorney of Snohomish County that he was elected to Congress in 1940. He wasn't yet twenty-nine when he took his seat. After six successive terms as a representative, Jackson ran for the Senate in 1952 and won despite the Eisenhower landslide. Throughout his eighteen years "on the hill," he has been a steady liberal, backing measures to help public power, labor, the Indians, and foreign aid. In recent years he has been rendering yeoman service as a public "watchdog" on national defense matters.

THREE Americans were out sightseeing in a Soviet city two years ago. One was Senator Henry M. Jackson. The second was a U. S. Army officer, the third a Russian-speaking official of the U. S. Embassy. It was a unique day for them. In the tour they were making of the U.S.S.R., they'd managed for once to shake off their Kremlin-appointed guide.

As they walked down the street, a young man suddenly accosted them. He was about thirty years old, quite well-dressed for a Russian, with the look of a professional person. More than this cannot be told about him. The Soviet secret police might start searching for him.

"Are you Englishmen?" the young man said in Russian.

The Embassy official replied. "No. We're Americans."

"Americans! That's even better," the young man said excitedly. "I've wanted so long to talk to an American."

"Why?" the Embassy man asked.

"Because you Americans are such lucky people. You can read what you want, hear what you want, say what you want. We can't."

The young man peered nervously over his shoulder to see if anyone were listening. He knew he was risking his life to speak like that.

"Always remember," he went on. "*They* aren't fooling us about you Americans. We Russians want this to be your kind of a world."

Then he walked away. Fast.

Senator Jackson came home from Russia with hope.